Georges Rodenbach

Georges Rodenbach

Critical Essays

Edited by
Philip Mosley

Madison • Teaneck
Fairleigh Dickinson University Press
London: Associated University Presses

© 1996 by Associated University Presses, Inc.

All rights reserved. Authorization to photocopy items for internal or personal use, or the internal or personal use of specific clients, is granted by the copyright owner, provided that a base fee of $10.00, plus eight cents per page per copy is paid directly to the Copyright Clearance Center, 222 Rosewood Drive, Danvers, Massachusetts 01923. [0-8386-3588-1/96 $10.00+8¢ pp, pc.]

Associated University Presses
440 Forsgate Drive
Cranbury, NJ 08512

Associated University Presses
25 Sicilian Avenue
London WC1A 2QH, England

Associated University Presses
P.O. Box 338, Port Credit
Mississauga, Ontario
Canada L5G 4L8

The paper used in this publication meets the requirements
of the American National Standard for Permanence of Paper
for Printed Library Materials Z39.48-1984.

Library of Congress Cataloging-in-Publication Data

Georges Rodenbach : critical essays / edited by Philip Mosley.
    p. cm.
    Includes bibliographical references and index.
    ISBN 0-8386-3588-1 (alk. paper)
    1. Rodenbach, Georges, 1855–1898—Criticism and interpretation.
I. Mosley, Philip.
PQ2388.R413Z66 1996
848'.809—dc20
                                                    95-17061
                                                        CIP

PRINTED IN THE UNITED STATES OF AMERICA

Contents

List of Illustrations   7

Contributors   9

Introduction
    PHILIP MOSLEY   11

The Soul's Interior Spectacle: Rodenbach and *Bruges-la-Morte*
    PHILIP MOSLEY   17

Ophelia Becomes Medusa: Reversals and Ambiguity in *Bruges-la-Morte*
    JOYCE O. LOWRIE   41

Temporal Aesthetics and the Euphemization of Death in *Le Carillonneur*
    ROBERT ZIEGLER   63

Le Carillonneur: Transcendence and Symbolization
    PAUL GORCEIX (translated by ELAINE L. CORTS)   82

Rodenbach, Hellens, Lemonnier: Paradisal and Infernal Modalities of Belgian Dead City Prose
    DONALD FLANELL FRIEDMAN   99

Souls under Glass: Poetry and Interiority in the Work of Rodenbach and Maeterlinck
    PATRICK LAUDE (translated by ELAINE L. CORTS)   113

With Georges Rodenbach—Bruges as State of Mind—The Symbolist Psychological Landscape
    DOROTHY M. KOSINSKI   129

Symbolization of Urban Space in *Bruges-la-Morte* and in Andrei Bely's *Petersburg*
    PETER I. BARTA   161

From Novel to Film: Cinematic Expression and Aesthetic Integrity in Roland Verhavert's *Brugge-die-Stille*
    MICHÈLE K. LANGFORD   175

Appendix A: Some Further Links between Rodenbach's Work and the Cinema
  PHILIP MOSLEY   187

Appendix B: From Rodenbach to Korngold: The Intertextual Genesis of *Die tote Stadt*
  PHILIP MOSLEY   190

Bibliography   195

Index   201

Illustrations

Fernand Khnopff, *Frontispiece for Bruges-la-Morte*	106
Fernand Khnopff, *L'Entrée du béguinage*	108
Lucien Lévy-Dhurmer, *Portrait of Georges Rodenbach*	130
Fernand Khnopff, *Secret-Reflection*	136
Fernand Khnopff, *I Lock My Door upon Myself*	137
Gustave Moreau, *Orpheus Lamenting at the Tomb of Eurydice*	138
Alphonse Osbert, *Evening Antique*	142
Odilon Redon, "Vision" from *Dans le rêve*	144
Odilon Redon, *The Dream*	145
Odilon Redon, *Closed Eyes*	147
Edvard Munch, *The Starry Night*	149
Vilhelm Hammershoi, *Open Doors*	150
Emile Gallé, Vase	152

Contributors

PETER I. BARTA is Lecturer in Russian at the University of Surrey. He is coeditor of *The Contexts of Alexander Pushkin* (1988), editor of *The European Foundations of Russian Modernism* (1991), and collaborator with the editors of *Historical Lexicography of the German Language* (1990–91).

ELAINE L. CORTS is an adjunct instructor in French at Broome Community College, SUNY. She has translated work by Colette, Philippe Sollers, and Stuart Merrill for the journals *Kalliope, Rampike,* and *Confrontations.*

DONALD FLANELL FRIEDMAN is Associate Professor in the Department of Modern Languages at Winthrop University. His work in Belgian studies includes *The Symbolist Dead City* (1991), *An Anthology of Belgian Symbolist Poets* (1992), and a translation of *She Confused Sleeping and Dying* in *Four Plays by Paul Willems* (1992).

PAUL GORCEIX was Professeur d'Université titulaire at Poitiers from 1972 to 1990 and is currently at the Université Michel de Montaigne, Bordeaux III. His many publications include *Les Affinités allemandes dans l'oeuvre de Maurice Maeterlinck* (1975), *Le Symbolisme en Belgique* (1982), and *Realités flamandes et symbolisme fantastique: "Bruges-la-Morte" [1891] et "Le Carillonneur" [1897] de Georges Rodenbach* (1992).

DOROTHY M. KOSINSKI is an art historian and Curator of the Douglas Cooper Collection, Basel. As well as contributing journal articles on nineteenth- and twentieth-century art, she is the author of *Orpheus in Nineteenth-Century Symbolism* (1989).

MICHÈLE K. LANGFORD is Professor of French Literature and Cinema at Pepperdine University. She is the author of *Les Menageries intimes* (1983), a study of animal imagery in French poetry, and editor of *Contours of the Fantastic* (1990), a collection of essays on the fantastic and science fiction.

PATRICK LAUDE is on the faculty of the Department of French at Georgetown University. His numerous articles on nineteenth-century French literature include several on Rodenbach, and he is the author of *Rodenbach: Les Décors de silence* (1990).

JOYCE O. LOWRIE is Professor of French at Wesleyan University. Several of her articles have been on Théophile Gautier, Gustave Flaubert, Jules Barbey d'Aurevilly, and Jean Lorrain, and she is the author of *The Violent Mystique* (1974).

PHILIP MOSLEY is Associate Professor of English, Communications and Comparative Literature at the Pennsylvania State University. He is the author of *Ingmar Bergman: The Cinema as Mistress* (1981), and translator of Rodenbach's *Bruges-la-Morte* (1986) and *Tea Masters, Teahouses* (1982) by the Belgian poet, Werner Lambersy.

ROBERT ZIEGLER is Professor of Humanities at Montana Tech and author of some thirty essays on the fin de siècle, including studies on J.-K. Huysmans, Jean Lorrain, Rachilde, Joséphin ("Sâr") Péladan, Marcel Schwob, Octave Mirbeau, and Georges Rodenbach.

Introduction
Philip Mosley

This collection of critical essays—the first book in English on Georges Rodenbach—seeks to better acquaint the English-language reader with the Belgian writer, whose life and literary career in many respects epitomize the Decadent Era of the late nineteenth century. Yet to consider Rodenbach as merely a typical dandified aesthete of that time would be to overlook the remarkable thematic and stylistic continuity underlying his work. Although Rodenbach's poetry may appear conventional beside that of many of his contemporaries—such as Stéphane Mallarmé, Jules Laforgue, and Paul Verlaine—most of Rodenbach's writing in both poetry and prose offers the reader an original, if romanticized, image of his native Flanders and particularly of the city of Bruges. His pervasive interest in Bruges suffuses his work with intriguing symbols and themes appropriate to an evocation of the quiet, spiritual atmosphere of the "dead" city.[1]

The renewal of critical interest in Rodenbach corresponds to a broader revival, which began about twenty-five years ago, of interest in the culture of the nineteenth-century fin de siècle. The 1960s counterculture—with its interest in esotericism, nonconformist behavior, drug use, and permissive sexuality—played a significant part in refocusing attention on the exotic aspects of the late nineteenth century, especially in the visual arts. From about 1965 to 1972, an international upsurge of books and art exhibitions sought to review and reappraise the exponents of symbolism, Art Nouveau, and aestheticism in their various styles and groupings.[2] This initial endeavor of art historians has continued apace,[3] while the literature and cultural history of the period also began to receive fresh attention in the 1970s, notably from German scholars such as Erwin Koppen and Hans Hinterhäuser. Critical interest continued into the 1980s in work by scholars such as Jean Pierrot, Anna Balakian, R. K. R. Thornton, Jennifer Birkett, Lothar Hönnighausen and, most recently, Laurence Porter.[4] The wave of enthusiasm for the period shows little sign of abating, and is now feeding into current debates on sexuality and gender in literature and art as, for instance, in recent work by Bram Dijkstra, Camille Paglia, and Elaine Showalter.[5]

At the same time Rodenbach's reputation has also benefited from recent efforts to consider Belgian literature in French as a phenomenon in its own right, independent of the dictates and constraints of the French cultural establishment. Since the late 1960s Belgian writers and critics, especially those of a younger generation, have attempted to articulate a clearer sense of Belgian identity. This process has involved the calling into question of a longstanding Belgian diffidence caused by the dominance of French literature, as well as the assertion of a more skeptical attitude toward the influence of the latter on French-language Belgian writing. This skepticism was initially boosted by a form of cultural nationalism known as *belgitude.* However, the concept of *belgitude* has largely given way to an awareness of independent cultural identities of various kinds within each region. This cultural reassessment has generated many reexaminations of both the history and ideology of francophone literary production since the inception of the Belgian state in 1830.[6] Two important areas of study in this respect are the "Young Belgium" literary movement of the fin de siècle, which included Rodenbach, and the now declining subculture of Flemish francophone writers, which included not only Rodenbach but also his more celebrated compatriots, Emile Verhaeren and Maurice Maeterlinck.

The revaluation of Belgian literature in French is contributing to a broader understanding of *francophonie* today. The francophone movement—which took shape in the 1960s, particularly through the efforts of the presidents of Senegal (the poet, Léopold Ségar Senghor) and Niger (Hamani Diori), and which led eventually to the appointment of a French government minister of *francophonie* (Alain Decaux) in 1988—continues to reorientate and reappraise the role of diasporic French language and culture throughout the world.

This collection of essays thus seeks to enter into the spirit of these various revaluations by adopting a comparative literary approach to the work of Rodenbach. In addition to my own essay, the reader will discover three essays (by Joyce Lowrie, Robert Ziegler, and Paul Gorceix) specifically on Rodenbach's two best-known novels, *Bruges-la-Morte* and *Le Carillonneur,* plus one (by Michèle Langford) on a film version of *Bruges-la-Morte;* one (by Donald Flanell Friedman) comparing Rodenbach's dead city prose with that of two other Belgian writers, Camille Lemonnier and

Franz Hellens; one (by Peter Barta) comparing Rodenbach with the Russian writer, Andrei Bely; one (by Patrick Laude) comparing aspects of Rodenbach's poetry with that of Maeterlinck; and one (by Dorothy Kosinski) placing Rodenbach in the context of symbolist art. I have also contributed two appendices, one elaborating links between Rodenbach's work and the cinema, the other describing the genesis of Erich Wolfgang Korngold's opera, *Die tote Stadt,* based on *Bruges-la-Morte.* Two of the essays (by Paul Gorceix and Patrick Laude) were originally written in French and have been translated into English.

A number of acknowledgments and sincere thanks are in order. Preparation of this collection would not have been possible without the generous support of a Fellowship from the Institute for the Arts and Humanistic Studies (George Mauner, director) at the Pennsylvania State University. K. Bruce Sherbine, director of Academic Affairs at the Worthington Scranton Campus of Penn State, kindly agreed to grant me released time from certain teaching duties for one semester. The Ministry of Culture and Social Affairs, French Community of Belgium (Jean-Luc Outers, *premier conseiller*) generously awarded me a study grant in 1991, permitting several weeks of research in Brussels. Most of this work was undertaken at the Archives et Musée de la Littérature in the Bibliothèque Royale Albert Ier. The staff of the Archives et Musée, especially Frans De Haes and Jean Danhaive, were unfailingly welcoming and helpful. With his tireless efforts on behalf of the international promotion of Belgian literature in French, Marc Quaghebeur, *commissaire au livre* at the ministry, voiced his enthusiasm for this project from its inception. Elaine L. Corts willingly and diligently undertook the task of translating the two French essays. Caroline D. Eckhardt, head of the Department of Comparative Literature at Penn State, lent her prompt and full support for my IAHS fellowship application. Last but by no means least, John Fletcher, my doctoral supervisor at the University of East Anglia in the 1970s, encouraged me to take the path of comparative literary studies and coaxed dissertation chapters from my early interest in Rodenbach and the literature of his time.

Notes

1. The silence of the dead city is one of the most distinctive themes in his work. Rodenbach is therefore as important in his own way as Mallarmé and Rimbaud, in the same period, to the development of a postromantic concept of silence. See Ihab Hassan, *The Literature of Silence* (New York: Knopf, 1967);

Susan Sontag, "The Aesthetics of Silence," in *Styles of Radical Will* (London: Secker and Warburg, 1969); George Steiner, *Language and Silence* (Harmondsworth: Penguin, 1969).

2. Examples of the exhibitions include *Autour de 1900* (1965); *Sacred and Profane in Symbolist Art* (1969); *The Symbolists* (1970); *Esthètes et magiciens* (1970–71); *La Belle Epoque* (1970–71); *Peintres de l'imaginaire: Symbolistes et surréalistes belges* (1972); *French Symbolist Painters* (1972). Examples of the books include Noel Richard, *Le Mouvement décadent: Dandys, esthètes et quintéssents* (Paris: Nizet, 1968); Philippe Jullian, *Dreamers of Decadence: Symbolist Painters of the 1890s* (New York: Praeger, 1971); John Milner, *Symbolists and Decadents* (London: Studio Vista; New York: Dutton, 1971); Francine-Claire Legrand, *Le Symbolisme en Belgique* (Brussels: Laconti, 1971); Edward Lucie-Smith, *Symbolist Art* (New York: Praeger, 1972).

3. See for example Robert Goldwater, *Symbolism* (London: Allen Lane, 1979); Robert L. Delevoy, *Symbolists and Symbolism* (New York: Rizzoli, 1982); John Robert Reed, *Decadent Style* (Athens: Ohio University Press, 1985); Michael Gibson, *The Symbolists* (New York: Abrams, 1988); Pierre-Louis Mathieu, *The Symbolist Generation, 1870-1910* (New York: Skira/Rizzoli, 1990).

4. Erwin Koppen, *Dekadenter Wagnerismus: Studien zur europäischen Literatur das Fin de Siècle* (Berlin: de Gruyter, 1973); Hans Hinterhäuser, *Fin de Siècle: Gestalten und Mythen* (Munich: Finck, 1977); Jean Pierrot, *The Decadent Imagination, 1880–1900* (Chicago: University of Chicago Press, 1981); Anna Balakian, ed., *The Symbolist Movement in the Literature of European Languages* (Budapest: Akademini Kiado, 1982), which includes Elizabeth Hess, "The Symbolist Movement in Belgium," 565–74; R. K. R. Thornton, *The Decadent Dilemma* (London: Edward Arnold, 1983); Jennifer Birkett, *The Sins of the Fathers: Decadence in France 1870-1914* (London: Quartet Books, 1986); Lothar Hönnighausen, *The Symbolist Tradition in English Literature: A Study of Pre-Raphaelitism and Fin de Siècle* (Cambridge: Cambridge University Press, 1988); Laurence M. Porter, *The Crisis of French Symbolism* (Ithaca: Cornell Unversity Press, 1990).

5. Bram Dijkstra, *Idols of Perversity: Fantasies of Feminine Evil in Fin-de-Siècle Culture* (Oxford: Oxford University Press, 1986); Camille Paglia, *Sexual Personae: Art and Decadence from Nefertiti to Emily Dickinson* (New Haven: Yale University Press, 1990); Elaine Showalter, *Sexual Anarchy: Gender and Culture at the Fin de Siècle* (New York: Viking/Penguin, 1990).

6. See, for example, "La Belgique malgré tout: Littérature 1980," *Revue de l'Université de Bruxelles* nos. 1–4 (1980); *Lettres françaises de Belgique: Mutations* (Brussels: Archives du Futur/Editions Universitaires, 1980); *Alphabet des lettres belges de langue française* (Brussels: Association pour la promotion des lettres belges de langue française, 1982); René Andrianne, *Ecrire en Belgique* (Paris: Fernand Nathan; Brussels: Editions Labor, 1983); Robert Frickx and Raymond Trousson, *Lettres françaises de Belgique: Dictionnaire des oeuvres*, 3 vols. (Paris: Editions Duculot, 1988); Marc Quaghebeur, *Lettres belges entre absence et magie* (Brussels: Editions Labor, 1990); Special topic: "Lettres belges d'expression française," *Ecriture* (Lausanne) no. 36 (autumn 1990).

Georges Rodenbach

The Soul's Interior Spectacle: Rodenbach and *Bruges-la-Morte*
Philip Mosley

GEORGES Rodenbach was born on 16 July 1855 at Tournai, Belgium. In November of that year the Rodenbach family moved to Ghent, where young Georges was brought up and educated, first at the *école moyenne,* then at the Collège Sainte-Barbe, and lastly at the University of Ghent where he studied law.

Rodenbach came from a family of writers. His grandfather, Constantin Rodenbach, published a notable medicolegal opinion in 1828; an uncle, Alexandre Rodenbach, published a well-known work on the blind and the deaf-mute in 1855; and his father wrote a tourist guide to Dinant as well as several works on weights and measures. However, the best known of his literary relatives remains his cousin, the Flemish poet Albrecht Rodenbach who, in a French sonnet addressed to Georges in return for a copy of his cousin's poems *Les Tristesses,* may have been the first Belgian to use two specific words for different and subsequently confrontational linguistic identities: "Vous, jeune fransquillon, moi, jeune flamingant."[1]

Rodenbach began his literary career in 1876 with the publication of a sonnet, "Fidelity," in a Brussels magazine. With his friend Emile Verhaeren, whom he had met at the Collège Sainte-Barbe, he frequented a Catholic literary salon in Ghent, reading his poetry there. In 1877, his first collection of poems, *Le Foyer et les champs,* was published and it drew praise from the Catholic press. Graduating as doctor of law, Rodenbach went to the bar in Ghent. In pursuit of a family tradition he was sent by his father to Paris for a probationary period, and while there, he attended the theater, contributed to such magazines as *La Plume* and *La Jeune France,* and became acquainted with Victor Hugo, François Coppée, and Théodore de Banville. Between November 1878 and June 1879, twenty-one of his "Parisian Letters" appeared in the Brussels weekly *La Paix.*

A second volume of poems, *Les Tristesses* (1879), was published in Paris, and one of the poems in it, "Le Coffret," quickly became famous. When he returned to Ghent in July 1879, Rodenbach complained about his native culture in a letter to Verhaeren, revealing both genuine frustration with his situation and a somewhat short-sighted view (given his later affiliation with it) of the potential of Belgian writing: "Quant à faire de la littérature en Belgique, m'est avis que c'est inutile et impossible" (To go in for literature in Belgium, in my opinion, is useless and impossible).[2]

In 1883 Rodenbach became a partner in the legal practice of Edmond Picard, an older writer with a strong social conscience. Settling in Brussels and continuing to publish a variety of literary works, he stepped down from the bar in 1886 and thereafter devoted himself entirely to writing. A third volume of poems, *La Mer élégante,* was published in 1881, and a fourth one, *L'Hiver mondain,* came out in 1884, as did *La Petite Veuve,* a one-act prose sketch written in collaboration with Max Waller. Of another collection of poems, *La Jeunesse blanche* (1886), Rodenbach's only biographer to date, Pierre Maes, remarked that it was "un moment d'heureux équilibre entre la rigidité parnassienne et la mollesse excessive des premiers symbolistes" (a moment of happy balance between Parnassian rigidity and the excessive looseness of the early symbolists) (*BLM,* 108). Also in 1886 his first novel, *La Vie morte* (an early version of *L'Art en exil*), was serialized in *L'Indépendance Belge.*

Within two years of his 1879 complaint about Belgian literary inactivity, Rodenbach (along with Waller, Verhaeren, Max Elskamp, Maurice Maeterlinck, and Charles van Lerberghe) became involved nonetheless in a Belgian literary revival, which demonstrated the existence of a vigorous strain of Belgian writing as well as a degree of resistance to the hegemony of Parisian culture. The most potent symbol of this revival was the review *La Jeune Belgique,* published from 1 December 1881 to 25 December 1897, and whose chief editor was Waller. The movement that coalesced around the review was not consciously nationalistic, though it had something of that effect on its observers. Organized around a quest for total artistic freedom, its ideology was primarily aesthetic, yet its aesthetics for the most part failed to transcend the dominant literary conventions of the day. Its youthful vitality notwithstanding, it still drew accusations of dilettantism and exclusivity. This climate of suspicion emerges in a statement by Picard, cofounder of the radical review *L'Art Moderne,* in the issue of 12 January 1890:

> Art has in our time assumed an aristocratic aspect. It has gradually drawn away from the masses. . . . It exists only for a few who call themselves the elite. . . . A scornful sort of shibboleth has entered into circulation, born of anger at not being understood except by the finer spirits: the artist should produce works only for the rare species of the highly cultivated.[3]

Though influenced by Picard, Rodenbach was among those writers who rejected Picard's call for a politically committed national literature. Nonetheless he made a fiery speech at a banquet in 1883 given by *La Jeune Belgique* in honor of his fellow Belgian authors Octave Pirmez (then recently deceased) and Camille Lemonnier (whose novel *Un Mâle* [1880] had been snubbed by literary officialdom), in which he declared:

> Ce banquet n'est pas seulement une fête—c'est aussi un combat. C'est en quelque sorte la veillée d'armes d'une troupe de conscrits décidés à tout et qui viennent, à cette heure solennelle, vous reconnaître et vous saluer comme leur 'Maréchal des lettres.' (*BLM*, 107)

> (This banquet is not only a celebration—it's also the launching of an offensive. In a way, it's the eve of battle for a group of fully committed conscripts who come, at this solemn hour, to greet you and salute you as their "Literary Field-Marshal.")

Uneasy with both Picard's political radicalism and the ultra-aestheticism espoused by Waller and Albert Giraud, Rodenbach (along with Verhaeren and others) broke with *La Jeune Belgique* in 1886. Yet within two years, and in spite of the progressive symbolist position of Albert Mockel's new review *La Wallonie,* Rodenbach had effectively detached himself from the whole Belgian revival by leaving the country for good. He settled permanently in Paris, having taken up an appointment as correspondent for the *Journal de Bruxelles,* in which he published his weekly "Parisian Letters" until 1895. More important, he began also to contribute to *Le Figaro.* He lived first at 27 rue Boursault, then from 1892 to 1897 at 2 rue Gounod. Finally he moved to a private hotel at 43 boulevard Berthier, where a commemorative tablet was placed in 1923 (there is also a bust of Rodenbach in the Luxembourg Gardens). In August 1888 he married Anna-Maria Urbain (1860–1945). They had one son, Constantin, who was born in 1892, the year in which *Bruges-la-Morte* was published.

Rodenbach's aestheticized vision of Bruges was much more in tune with sophisticated Parisian tastes than with those of the majority of his compatriots. Even though his native literary scene was transformed in the 1880s, it would be hard to imagine that Rodenbach unwillingly exiled himself. The wealth of activity, the network of contacts, and the chance of literary celebrity offered by Paris have all continued to lure francophone writers away from Belgium. Despite his earlier distancing from the excesses of aestheticism, Rodenbach in Paris became more concerned with a decadent sensibility and with the purity of the French language than with conscious promotion of the cause of "politically correct" young Belgian writing. He soon became part and parcel of the metropolitan literary scene, forming friendships with many leading writers of various styles and affiliations: Coppée, Villiers, Edmond de Goncourt, Alphonse Daudet, and, most important, Mallarmé, whom he first met at Théodore de Banville's salon in 1878.

More than one commentator is of the opinion that Rodenbach's decisive move to Paris also began the period in which his oeuvre solidified around certain characteristic elements.[4] A shift thus occurs, most markedly in his poetry—between *La Jeunesse blanche, Du silence* (1888), and particularly *Le Règne du silence* (1891)— but also in other works published in these several years: "L'Amour en exil" (1888), a short story; "Agonies de villes" (1889), an article dedicated to Bruges; and *L'Art en exil* (1889), a reworked version of the novel *La Vie morte*.

Bruges-la-Morte is the novel that made Rodenbach famous and established his reputation as an accomplished practitioner of the so-called symbolist novel. He became known as a major exponent of "dead city" writing and of a romanticized vision of Flanders. First published in ten installments in *Le Figaro* from 4 to 14 February 1892, the novel first appeared in book form four months later, published in Paris by Marpon and Flammarion, with a frontispiece by the Belgian artist Fernand Khnopff and thirty-five photographic illustrations. In catering to the contemporary Parisian taste for exoticism, *Bruges-la-Morte* was the most successful French literary publication of 1892, if not ultimately the most significant in critical opinion, that honor going undoubtedly to Maeterlinck's play *Pelléas et Mélisande,* a work that did not, however, have the immediate impact of his compatriot's novel. Verhaeren wrote of *Bruges-la-Morte* that "Bruges fut chantée par Rodenbach parce que, parmi toutes les villes de la terre, il la croyait le mieux d'accord avec sa mélancolie. . . . Bruges est le principal personnage du livre et rien n'explique mieux le roman et rien ne renseigne mieux sur le poète lui-même" (Rodenbach sang the praises of Bruges because of all the cities in the world he considered it most in tune with his sense of melancholy. . . . Bruges is the book's protagonist and nothing better explains the novel or tells us more about the poet himself) (*BLM*, 110).

None of the other works by Rodenbach published after *Bruges-la-Morte* enjoyed its immediate and widespread success. In spite of long fallow periods of critical interest, it has continued to be issued in French-language editions up to the present day (see the bibliography). A Brussels edition (1977), closely followed by one in Paris (1978), bears witness to the revival of interest in both author and period, culminating in a further Brussels edition of 1986. Basing itself on the original 1892 edition with variants from the 1891 manuscript, the 1986 edition seeks to rectify faulty textual detail accumulated over the years of repeated publication.[5] The novel has also been translated into several languages (see the bibliography).

From 1895 Rodenbach suffered from a serious chest complaint as well as neurasthenia, and his health deteriorated rapidly. On 24 December 1898, he died of typhlitis in Paris, aged forty-three, and was buried four days later in Père-Lachaise Cemetery.

* * *

In an essay, "La Poésie nouvelle," originally published in the *Revue Bleue* (Paris, 1891), Rodenbach declared: "Nous nous enthousiasmons de nouveau pour l'idéal! Les belles émotions nerveuses, nous les voulons. Le réel nous écoeure. . . . C'est l'impossible lui-même que nous aimons" (Once again we are fired with enthusiasm for the ideal! We are after beautiful nervous excitement. Reality sickens us. . . . We love the very impossible).[6] *Bruges-la-Morte* is about a search for the impossible and about the effects, too, of an individual's powerful and self-deceiving imagination. It tells of a widower, Hugues Viane, whose obsession with the memory of his dead wife and with the daily practice of a cult of remembrance leads him into a fatal entanglement with her apparent double, a young dancer, Jane Scott, whom he meets by chance in the streets of Bruges. This subject is reminiscent of "Véra," one of the *Contes cruels* (1883) by Villiers de l'Isle-Adam, a writer whose influence on Rodenbach's prose style is also evident in Rodenbach's own collection of stories, *Le Rouet des brumes* (1901). In "Véra," the Count of Athol similarly devotes himself (though in total solitude, unlike Hugues) to the memory of his dead wife, soon falling prey to fantasies of reunion with her spirit.

The mental world of visions and fleeting thoughts, where "tout est songe, tout est solitude et silence" (all is dream, solitude, silence),[7] is the substance of Rodenbach's writing in this novel. Following the symbolist lead, Rodenbach endeavors to give a literary form to his most abstract and extraordinary ideas. Throughout his work we find a complex but consistent intertextual relationship between certain key images and themes, as well as an underlying emotional and inspirational unity. Another reason for the success of *Bruges-la-Morte* at the time is that it was appreciated particularly by those writers and readers who were enthusiastic about the potential development of symbolist aesthetics in fictional form.

Symbolism, however, is not easy to define and, like most cultural labels, has all too easily been used as a convenient term to denote a particular aesthetic theory and an artistic practice within a certain historical period. In spite of a welter of manifestos and public statements, there never was, as earlier critics preferred to maintain, a single school or group of symbolist writers or artists. Rather, a cluster of common aesthetic values and expressive techniques, allied to a certain cultural sensibility, gave a measure of coherence to a particular type of creative activity within the period. For example, Hubert Juin prefers to call that era between the Paris Commune of 1871 and the advent of the twentieth century an instance of those periodic "mises en suspens de l'Histoire" (suspensions of history). Following Louis Forestier, Juin calls this period "l'avant-siècle," an ideological gap between the two centuries in which "tout est possible" (everything is possible).[8] During this time, he argues, there was a coexistence, whether harmonious or uneasy, between the conventional, the realistic, and the fantastic in literature and art. Although their activities were not organized according to the doctrines of a movement as such, the proponents of symbolism nonetheless shared a particular interest in the Wagnerian concept of total art, in polyvalent structures and meanings, and in a purified and intimate articulation of ideas, feelings, and dreams.

Regardless of the aesthetics of symbolism, as definitive as they might have purported to be, some naturalist writers and critics, inspired by empirical and positivist thought, claimed that *Bruges-la-Morte* barely merited the status of a novel. Even Rodenbach, in his foreword, chose to call it "cette étude passionnelle" (this study of passion) (*BLM*, 9). He was, in any case, more of a poet than a novelist, at least in the sense of his dominant creative impulse, and so the lyrical tone of his prose comes as no surprise. Yet in his preface to the penultimate Belgian edition of the novel (*BLM*, 12), Gaston Compère suggests that Rodenbach was still a better prose poet than versifier, and that the poetic quality of the novel is more seductive to the reader than any of his collections of poems. This view is questioned in different ways by two more recent commentators. While agreeing that Rodenbach was "incontestablement moins narrateur et psychologue qu'homme de contemplation et d'imagination poétique" (incontestably less of a narrator and psychologist than a man of contemplation and poetic imagination), Patrick Laude places more importance on the poetic works than on those in prose.[9] Finding Compère's assessment to be somewhat summary, Christian Berg points to the technical accomplishment of Rodenbach's other major novel, *Le Carillonneur* (1897), while also reminding us of the need to consider "des tentatives de toute une génération pour échapper aux clivages traditionnels entre les différents genres qui se partageaient, à l'époque, le champ littéraire" (efforts of an entire generation to escape the traditional split between the different genres which shared the field of literature at the time).[10] Another recent commentator, A. W. Raitt, perceives the evolution of a hybrid genre (part-story, part-prose poem) in the prose of Rodenbach, Rémy de Gourmont, Edouard Dujardin, Henri de Régnier, Camille Mauclair, and others, which he attributes to the influence of Villiers, an influence that we have already noted in connection with the subject matter of *Bruges-la-Morte*.[11] If that novel continues to exert a greater fascination on the modern reader than do any of Rodenbach's collections of poems, it is so perhaps on account of the sustained integration of its poetic language into the narrative structure of the text, allowing for a heightened, at times almost ethereal, dimension to coexist with the forward thrust of the plot. Anchored in the specifics of time and place (the religious calendar, the accurate topology of the city), the development of the plot of *Bruges-la-Morte* is wedded to Rodenbach's detailed, impressionistic observation of personal experience. Though less abstract and dematerialized than some symbolist language, this evocation is by no means limited to a set of objective correlatives. Mallarmé perhaps best described him as a "sensationist." Finding *Bruges-la-Morte* "aujourd'hui assez pénible à relire" (pretty laborious rereading today), Liliane Wouters and Alain Bosquet even doubt Rodenbach's proximity to the symbolists "proprement dits," preferring to view him as closer in outlook to Alfred de Musset (for his psychological insight), Charles Baudelaire (whom Rodenbach called a "spiritual father"), and Maurice Rollinat (author of *Les Névroses*, 1883).[12]

Further critical difficulty arises from the fact that for the symbolist writers, or at least for those opposed to the principles of naturalism, the major mode of writing was poetry, followed by drama and the short story. It is therefore highly problematic to speak of the symbolist novel as such, unless, that is, one is referring specifically to the development of the interior monologue from Dujardin to modernist writers such as James Joyce. By the same token it is equally difficult, in spite of their clear connections with its aesthetic principles and social context, to assign writers like Guy de Maupassant and Villiers de l'Isle-Adam to naturalism, given the former's occasional taste for the weird and his increasingly pessimistic tone, and the latter's consistently romantic idealism. Even the early career of Huysmans, before he developed his decadent sensibility in the mid-1880s, is firmly rooted in naturalism. It is perhaps safer to assert that the literary production of the last twenty years of the nineteenth century includes a sizable number of fictional texts, disparate in both tone and structure, but sharing a resistance to the tenets of naturalism and consequently indicating their preference for more introspective, idiosyncratic, and spiritual experiences.

Such writing was an ideal medium for the expression of hypersensitive aesthetic, psychological, and physical conditions; a discourse, moreover, that aspired "à refuser les réalités du social et à réhabiliter cette fraction de la classe dominante qui est faite d'oisifs et d'esthètes" (to refuse social realities and to rehabilitate that fraction of the dominant social class made up of men of leisure and aesthetes).[13] Broadly speaking, this describes what is generally thought of as the pervasive decadent sensibility, in which writers propagated a species of perverse, affected individuals who valued art over nature, and morbidity over vitality.

Yet, like symbolism, late nineteenth-century decadence—which might be said to have originated in Théophile Gautier's preface to the 1868 edition of Baudelaire's *Les Fleurs du mal*—is a difficult and unstable concept. In the relativistic and iconoclastic mood of poststructuralist criticism, the term has been especially subjected to careful reexamination. Though the problematic of decadence was already being addressed by literary critics in the 1960s, Richard Gilman may have been first of the new skeptics in denying any literary historical value to the term by claiming that "there never was a time when Decadence was definitive, since nobody agreed on what the definitions were. What existed were figures, works, unloosed visions."[14] More recent commentators, such as Jacques Marx and Maarten Van Buuren, turn to the renewed interest in literature and medicine, basing their arguments about decadence on the respective concepts of neurosis and hysteria, which Freud had already begun to investigate during the 1890s. Another progressive approach is that of Jean de Palacio, who both stresses the generical hybridity of decadence and goes so far as to invert conventional priorities by suggesting that "en réalité, naturalisme et symbolisme apparaissent comme des modalités de l'esprit de Décadence" (in reality, naturalism and symbolism appear as modalities of the spirit of Decadence). Then again, rejection of the romantic cults of nature and ideal love have tended to come to mind as distinctive features of the decadent imagination. However, Jean Weisgerber limits the phenomenon of decadence to three parameters—aristocratic aestheticism, scientific (or pseudoscentific) cult, and antibourgeois revolt—and concludes that it constitutes "une *tendance latente* qui concerna quantité d'individus à un certain moment, *grosso modo* entre 1880 et 1910, au-delà même parfois d'un point de vue comparatiste" (a latent tendency that concerned a certain number of individuals at a certain moment, *grosso modo* between 1880 and 1910, sometimes even beyond a comparative viewpoint).[15]

In stating that "il faut surtout croire aux individus" (one must above all believe in individuals) (*Evocations,* 240), Rodenbach showed his allegiance to a code of extreme individualism. Unfortunately a fine line seemed to exist between the positive and negative aspects of this code, with the result that its intelligent self-consciousness tended often to degenerate into narcissism, and its brave idealism into sickly introspection. Like many of his contemporaries, Rodenbach had no apparent desire to reform society, though he flirted with fashionable liberalism during his "Young Belgium" years. Such individuals were typical products and benefactors of the ascendancy of the *haute bourgeoisie,* often freed from token professional careers to become men of letters. Rodenbach's sustained and disciplined personal commitment to art did compensate somewhat for his overall lack of social conscience. He believed passionately in the supremacy of the imagination, and in the expression of his soul "comme en du verre, enclose en du silence, / Toute vouée à son spectacle intérieure" (as if enclosed in glass and in silence, given over to its own interior spectacle).[16]

Admittedly often melodramatic in tone, *Bruges-la-Morte* does succeed in presenting a powerful image of abnormal behavior in a setting at once resistant and conducive to it. For instance, one of the novel's most striking contrasts is between Hugues's usual state of grief-stricken ineffectuality and the violence of his final action, the murder of Jane Scott. Yet this semidelirious act also corresponds to the unusually fevered and ecstatic mood in the streets of Bruges on the day of the Procession of the Holy Blood. This suggestion of a strong element of psychological realism in the novel explains Rodenbach's otherwise unlikely debt to Taine and to positivism, betokened by the author's emphasis on environmental influences, recognizable urban locations, classifiable mental states, and clear cause-effect relationships. If we are now willing to accept the notion of decadent diversity, such apparent inconsistencies show instead the fertile imagination of a writer alert to the stimulating contest of ideas. Certain critics have confirmed this view. Paul Gorceix attests to the fundamentally hybrid nature of *Bruges-la-Morte* by dealing separately with its realistic and poetic aspects.[17] Similarly, Jeannine Paque follows a trajectory in Rodenbach's fiction, away from the comparative realism of *L'Art en exil* (1889) to its furthest distance in *Bruges-la-Morte,* followed in *Le Carillonneur* by a return to a more realistic vein.[18]

The plot of *Bruges-la-Morte* builds steadily to a crime of passion. Rodenbach carefully introduces the social and psychological motivation for the murder of Jane, the triggering impetus being her profanation of a sacrosanct tress of Hugues's wife's hair, with which he strangles her after a wild struggle in his house. Rodenbach presents Hugues's fatal obsession with Jane, based on her uncanny resemblance to his wife, in such a way as to seem both a disorienting nightmare of abnormal psychology and a logical cause of the ultimate tragedy on which the plausibility of the plot clearly depends.

Rodenbach also skillfully evokes the contrasts in the Flemish mentality between an outward appearance of conformity and an inner taste for the fantastic and the macabre. His distinctive depiction of conservative Flemish provincial life and its effect upon Hugues's behavior serves to bolster the psychological realism of the novel. The consequent inference that the pious environment of Bruges is dangerously repressive—"il semble que, des innombrables couvents, émane un mépris des roses secrètes de la chair" (a contempt for the secret roses of the flesh seemed to emanate from the countless convent houses) (*BLM,* 43)—might pass for a thinly veiled attack on bourgeois Catholicism, were it not for the fact that Hugues clearly enjoys an ambiguous relationship to the church, its practices, and its morality. Thus Rodenbach remains teasingly discreet in his erotic references: "les passions, les accointances des sexes hors mariage y sont toujours l'oeuvre perverse" (passions and extramarital relations are always perverse acts there) (*BLM,* 43). As Janine Dakyns says, an important aspect of the symbolist obsession with the Middle Ages was the perverse association of the sacred with the profane, of the ecclesiastical with the erotic, and the fascination, at times quite fetishistic, with religious ritual and liturgical bric-a-brac.[19] Rodenbach explores the theme of a man's relationship with the church more explicitly in another novel, *La Vocation* (1895), in which the hero, Hans Cadzand, wants to become a priest but abandons his plans when sexual pressures combine to destroy his self-confidence.

The spiritual environment of Bruges also plays a part in controlling the development of *Bruges-la-Morte,* with the city itself becoming the main "character," and Hugues to some degree a victim of circumstance. Born in Tournai and raised in Ghent, both cities that preserve elements of their medieval histories and religious institutions, Rodenbach was able to identify readily with Bruges. Though he never lived there, it was both his father's and his grandfather's home. In his essay on Bruges, Huysmans touches on Rodenbach's family attachment: "Cette ville lui appartient, est devenue en quelque sorte son douaire, et sa vue se profile, même lorsqu'il n'en parle point, derrière tous ses romans et tous ses poèmes" (That city belongs to him, has become, so to speak, his dowry, and the view of it, even when he is not speaking about it specifically, looms up behind all his novels and poems).[20] Rodenbach confirms this attachment in a letter written in 1894 to the Bruges critic, Arthur Daxhelet: "Il y a de l'atavisme dans les oeuvres et l'hérédité ici aussi explique mon amour pour cette Bruges admirable, que je serais heureux d'avoir assurée d'un peu de gloire auprès des esprits artistes de la France" (There is atavism in works of art, and heredity also explains my love for this admirable Bruges, for which I'd be happy to have assured a little glory in the French artistic mind).[21]

Rodenbach was, however, keenly aware of the contrast between Bruges and Ghent, in spite of their clear historical parallels. Ghent had also experienced a fateful decline from medieval power and grandeur, but it had never resigned itself to the slow decay that cocooned Bruges in its medieval beauty after the fifteenth century. Even the Beguinage in Bruges was already declining in Rodenbach's time. Ghent, on the contrary, had become infused with the artistic and commercial spirit of northern Flanders, best exemplified by the great port city of Antwerp. Rodenbach set *L'Art en exil* in Ghent. The novel concerns a highly refined artist, Jean Rembrandt, who desperately tries to resist the materialism and philistinism of the province. It thus anticipates *Bruges-la-Morte* both in its fatalism and in its treatment of the city as an influential force that almost assumes the status of a character, although it is less romanticized than in the later novel. However, it should be noted that the romanticized image of medieval Bruges, to which Rodenbach appears to be looking back, overshadows the actual state of the city in its prime. At the time it was by no means a quiet, picturesque haven, but a bustling, industrial city where rich and poor were equally subject to its rigorous practices of manufacturing and marketing, and the beauty of its architecture reflected the prosperity of its trade.

Rodenbach grew up in an area of Flanders that he describes as being like a "cemetery" of dead cities. In articles published between 1888 and 1894 (collected posthumously in *Evocations*) he refers to some of these other forgotten Flemish towns: Ypres, Furnes, Courtrai, and Audenaerde—"en ce silence de province si proche d'ici et qui semble si lointain" (in that provincial silence so close yet seemingly so far from here) (14). In other articles, he also discusses the "death agonies" of Damme (also in Flanders and home of Hans Cadzand, the hero of *La Vocation*), of the Dutch island of Walcheren (specifically the towns of Middelburg, Vlissingen, Veere, and Domburg); and of St.-Malo in France. As most of these examples suggest, the dead city theme in the literature of the time was frequently associated with water and with low-lying coastal cities, so also with the many legends and myths of fabulous drowned places, those lost cities, countries, and even continents beneath the sea.[22]

On account of its former supremacy the death of Bruges remains for Rodenbach "la plus taciturne et la plus émouvante" (the most taciturn and moving) (*Evocations,* 14). Yet Rodenbach considered Bruges even in his own time to be an ideal city of art, an inspiring blend of the real and the fabulous, the nodal point of West Flanders yet strangely isolated from the outside world by its archaic, monastic atmosphere. He declared that he wished to be the painter of Bruges as Turner had been of Venice, but Rodenbach's truer ancestors in this respect are the great Flemish mystical painters, Hans Memling and Jan van Eyck. The success of *Bruges-la-Morte* prompted the French neoimpressionist, Henri Le Sidaner, to turn an eight-day trip to the city in 1897 into a one-year stay that ushered in a vogue for Bruges among artists of the time.

Bruges had already inspired other nineteenth-century writers such as William Wordsworth, Henry Longfellow, and Dante Gabriel Rossetti, all of whom wrote poems evoking its peculiar atmosphere. It continued to attract poets—notably Rainer Maria Rilke, Stefan Zweig, and Ernest Dowson (who wrote a story about it)— as well as later prose writers like Henry Miller. Rodenbach went further than anyone in devoting his work almost exclusively to the city, fixing its spirit firmly in the fin de siècle consciousness as a symbol of quiet beauty, of severe Catholic practice, and of the past represented in the present.

Rodenbach was aware nonetheless of the movement in his time to bring Bruges out of its four-hundred-year decline by creating a new seaport ("Bruges-port-de-mer"), but to his mind the city was "la reine détrônée" (the dethroned queen), far more deserving to be called "Bruges-Porte de l'Art" (*Evocations,* 14, 109–10). This debate forms the backdrop to *Le Carillonneur,* in which the hero, Joris Borluut, finds peace and quiet in the Bruges belfry where in the end, having been humiliated by the successful endeavors to modernize the city, he hangs himself in one of the bells that symbolize his allegiance to the old-fashioned Bruges.[23] Though criticized for depicting Bruges so as to appeal to the exotic tastes of the Parisian reading public, Rodenbach was only expressing his greater interest in the emotional than in the purely descriptive aspects of the city. His image of Bruges falls somewhere between the regional realism of Georges Eekhoud and the visionary symbolism of Verhaeren, eschewing both the proletarianism of the former and the progressiveness of the latter's protomodernist, though somewhat ambivalent, image of "villes tentaculaires" (tentacular cities).

Michel Décaudin argues that from 1894 to 1898 symbolist literature began to place more emphasis on the beauty of nature and on positive aspects of life.[24] Corresponding to this shifting sensibility was a reaction to Rodenbach's image of Bruges as a fatal trap, notably in Camille Mauclair's *L'Ennemie des rêves* (1899), in which the hero rejects Bruges in favor of a woman's love and the sun of Marseilles. This counterimage continued into late symbolism: for instance, in a 1914 essay entitled "The Living Bruges," the Finnish poet V. A. Koskenniemi dismissed Rodenbach's image as a delusion. Thus we may see that in preferring a positive ending to *Die tote Stadt* (1920), his operatic version of Rodenbach's story, the Austrian composer Erich Wolfgang Korngold was following an established trend (see Appendix B).

The morbid-sounding title of Rodenbach's novel was not to the liking of the citizens of Bruges. In 1899 the city refused a monument to Rodenbach by the sculptor George Minne, preferring instead to honor in that manner one James Weale, an English guidebook writer! It was left to the citizens of Ghent to unveil a memorial sculpture to Rodenbach by Minne in 1903. At a time when commercial revival was a distinct possibility and was perceived as an urgent need, the sensitivity of the Bruges citizens was understandable. If today it seems that they were uncharitable in rejecting a tribute to the city's principal celebrator, it must also be remembered that in the novel Rodenbach was not trying to promote social change. On the contrary, he was seeking to establish the unique character of the city as a potent symbol of resistance to any such change.

Though the city began to "die" when the River Zwyn retreated in 1475, it survives for Hugues just as his wife lives on in his mind: "Bruges était sa morte. Et sa morte était Bruges" (Bruges was his dead wife. And his dead wife was Bruges) (*BLM,* 24). Given the inevitable and psychologically credible, if fantastic, crime with which the novel climaxes, one may say that the action also depends upon a fatalistic, alluring vision of the city itself. Striving to keep alive the memory of his wife, Hugues binds himself willingly to Bruges, which best represents in both mood and material form the experience of a living death. He goes there to be at one with himself and his preoccupations, but the city proves to be a snare and delusion. George Ross Ridge reminds us that fin de siècle literature abounds with images of Paris as the modern Babylon, from which rich, world-weary cosmopolitans seek to escape to spas or seaside resorts.[25] Sometimes too, like Hugues, they find that there is no escape in their chosen place of refuge, which becomes as evil an influence as its supposed opposite, the teeming metropolis. This dual identity of Bruges imposes its own mysterious authority on the wild fluctuations of Hugues's impressionable mind, again inviting the view that, for instance, like Paris as the real "hero" of Zola's novels, Rodenbach's conception of Bruges as a deterministic environment owes as much to the tenets of naturalism as to the idiosyncracies of the decadent mind.

We should remember, however, that the distinctive texture of Rodenbach's novel depends throughout on these realistic elements being held in thrall by intricate patterns of poetic language, which the author carefully weaves to reveal basic links between his characters, the development of the plot, and the fatal influence of the city. An accumulation of well-known symbolist techniques—such as correspondence, synesthesia, and the elaboration of refined or arcane images—serves to articulate the "démon de l'Analogie" (demon of analogy) (*BLM,* 37), a complex of unfortunate but irresistible identifications that underpin the novel. Rodenbach's prose in *Bruges-la-Morte* thus displays a tension between the exigencies of narrative structure and the value of philosophical reflection, resulting in a pseudolyrical style (owing something perhaps to Laforgue's *Moralités légendaires,* 1887) characterized by frequent exclamation, repetition, and unfinished phrases. Such rhetorical flourishes may occasionally detract from the novel's verisimilitude, but equally they contribute to the maintenance of a crucial equation between the forces of mind and matter, as well as between the abstractions of individual consciousness and the concreteness of the physical world.

Rodenbach conceived of Bruges as identical to his own temperament: "Toute cité est un état d'âme" (Every city is a state of mind) (*BLM,* 73). Defending Rodenbach's vision against local criticism, Verhaeren in 1899 had no doubt that Rodenbach chose Bruges as the subject of his novel because, of all cities, it was the one most in tune with his own sense of melancholy. A mood of pessimism pervades the novel, suggesting that Schopenhauer's philosophy (which Rodenbach learned mainly from Elme Caro's classes in Paris and from his friendship with Louise Ackermann, whom Hubert Juin describes as "la prêtresse parnassienne du pessimisme")[26] was more than a mere matter of fashionable influence, and that it most likely convinced Rodenbach of the virtue and desirability of solitude. Bruges and its Beguinage perfectly symbolized the monasticism and purity deemed so important to the spiritual artist, for whom withdrawal into isolation was a prerequisite of integrity and high-mindedness. Also, as exemplified by Joséphin ("Sâr") Péladan's Mérodack in *Le Vice suprême,* Léon Bloy's Marchenoir in *La Femme pauvre,* Huysmans's Des Esseintes in *A rebours* (of whom Hugues is a less narcissistic version), and his Durtal in *Là-bas,* "numerous heroes of novels published during the eighties and nineties lived a life dedicated to retrospection."[27]

The reclusive existence of Hugues and the mystical atmosphere of the city both suggest that Schopenhauer's advocacy of asceticism was a significant influence on the construction of *Bruges-la-Morte*. In a tendency culminating in Proust's cork-lined chamber, some writers and artists, like Xavier Mellery and Henri de Régnier, retreated into fantastic seclusion. Yet Lionel Johnson found equally perverse delight in the tension between a necessary detachment and an equally insistent desire to be part of the fashionable social round. Though Hugues represents perfectly the antisocial stance, Rodenbach was quite the opposite in his Parisian years, being on all accounts a man about town given to lively repartee and dandyish style.

Rodenbach found further inspiration in images of cold, empty interiors as symbols of the lonely soul, inducing him to poetic plethora by way of a transformation of naturalist environments as social witness boxes into something more appropriately spiritual, private, and implicit. Silence, the most characteristic of all Rodenbach's themes, marks these gloomy locations, and is central to the muffled, introspective atmosphere of *Bruges-la-Morte.* Overlooking a canal, Hugues's silent house magnifies his sense of solitude. The house is a protective haven until Jane's disrespectful visits defile its sanctity. Hugues is so highly strung that, like Des Esseintes, he cannot bear even the slightest noise: "Pourquoi les bruits, pourquoi les voix semblent-ils déranger la charpie et rouvrir la plaie?" (Why do voices and noises seem to cause disturbances and even reopen wounds?) (*BLM,* 23). Given that "aux souffrances morales, le bruit aussi fait mal" (Noise even has a bearing on the suffering of the mind) (24), Hugues even fears the volume of harmonious sound: "Depuis la mort de sa femme, il n'avait entendu aucune musique. Il avait peur du chant des instruments. Même un accordéon dans les rues, avec son petit concert asthmatique et acidulé, lui tirait des larmes" (Since the death of his wife he had listened to no music at all, fearing the sound of musical instruments. Even a street accordion with its asthmatic and slightly sharp wheeze could bring him to tears) (33). Silence is his balm, protecting him from the chafing of everyday sounds, of which one of the few he can still bear to hear is that of the organ of Notre-Dame, in whose vast aisles another reassuring gloom continues to surround him.

Rodenbach describes the silence of the Beguinage in Bruges as "quelque chose de vivant, de réel, de despotique qui vit là, seul, comme en un royaume élu pour son exil, qui veut, qui commande, qui se montre hostile à qui le dérange" (something alive, real, despotic, living there all alone, as if in a kingdom chosen for its exile, desiring, commanding, showing hostility to any disturber) (*Evocations,* 27). Likewise any external noise tends only to graze the imperious silence that reigns over the sadness of Hugues's own domestic existence. When he begins to succumb to the spirit of Bruges for the second time, he finally realizes what constitutes its peculiar influence: "leçon de silence venue des canaux immobiles, à qui leur calme vaut la présence de nobles cygnes; exemple de résignation offert par les quais taciturnes" (lesson in silence from the still canals, their calm ennobled by the presence of stately swans; example of resignation offered by the taciturn quays) (*BLM,* 71). Hugues inhabits a city where there appears to be little danger to his chosen life of silent grief. So, when his ill-fated affair with Jane reaches its climax to the vibrant sounds of the Holy Blood procession and the pealing of all the city's bells, his sense of security is shattered in more ways than one.

Hugues's greatest weakness is his idealization of the superficially attractive but ultimately ruthless Jane, as a result of which the identities of a dead and a living woman become indistinguishable to him. This situation again recalls Villiers: in *L'Eve future* (1886), the lovelorn Count Ewald fatally fails to distinguish a real woman from an android made over in her image. The morbid eroticism of Rodenbach's novel manifests itself chiefly in images of voyeurism and fetishism. Intoxicated by the resemblance between his wife and Jane, Hugues gazes longingly but uncomfortably at the young dancer, while his daily routine already includes the trembling adulation of a tress of his wife's hair. His silent devotions in front of objects associated with his wife are as blatantly erotic as they are subtly religious.

Jane Scott, a refreshingly physical woman, notices his perversity at once and cannot understand his "allures anormales" (peculiar behavior), or his "muettes contemplations" (silent raptures) (*BLM*, 41). His relationship with Jane soon reveals his sexual impotence. He is attracted to her only insofar as she represents the living image of his wife, and this attraction is powerful enough to override the prohibitive social aspect of their liaison. As their affair unfolds, Hugues's problems multiply. He desires Jane as an idealized wife-surrogate, but she refuses this role, preferring to express her own natural womanliness, although accepting some of the social privileges that arise from her association with him. His helpless indulgence of her whims only increases his difficulties. He is unable to resolve the tension between his sexual sublimation and Jane's physical attractiveness, as first the one, then the other, holds sway over him. In spite of enraptured late-night encounters, Hugues fails to elicit from Jane any kind of sympathetic response. They have opposite views of what constitutes correct behavior in their personal lives. Yet the "demon of analogy" continues to blind Hugues to their mutual incompatibility. As with Bruges itself, the surface image masks a deeper, more dangerous truth. For too long Hugues remains unaware that his blissful silence is a symptom of a chronic sickness, slowly infecting him as it has infected the city where, for all their deceptive beauty, the still waters of the canals are thoroughly stagnant and unwholesome. It is this dualism of good and evil, of pleasant and unpleasant, of sacred and profane in Bruges and Jane, that threatens to tear Hugues apart. Both city and woman are the "demons of analogy," the traps of superficial allure, the persuasive tempters who simultaneously lead Hugues in different directions, toward a terrifying and inescapable situation over which he no longer has any control.

Another element that may have a bearing on Hugues's submission to evil influence is satanism, of which medieval Bruges was known to have been a center. Huysmans believed that there was still a diabolical cult in the city, which he describes, in his essay on Bruges, as "à la fois mystique et démoniaque, puérile et grave . . . cachant sous son calme d'emprunt on ne sait quoi de félin et d'étrange" (at once mystical and demoniacal, frivolous and grave . . . hiding beneath its borrowed calmness heaven only knows what strange and feline things). He goes on to suggest that although the devil in Bruges is hidden, "on le sentait, en flânant par ses rues" (wandering the streets, you sense his presence), and he notes that incense and sulfur are the city's two typical and conflicting smells.[28]

Devilry may be on the loose in the streets of Bruges, but the city also proffers Hugues its pious side. Rodenbach's equal emphasis on this aspect reflects his belief in the practice of art as a form of religious zeal for sensitive souls. The contemplative life, for poets at least, is akin to a religion of which "ils sont les prêtres ordonnés et silencieux, transsubstantiant dans les mots tout l'infini divin" (they are its silent, ordained priests, their words transsubstantiating all of divine infinity) (*Evocations,* 277).

For Rodenbach, as for Maeterlinck and Verhaeren, the principal symbol of Flemish spiritual life is the Beguinage. Microcosm of the city in the case of Bruges, its quietistic discipline powerfully symbolizes the withdrawal that Hugues seeks so eagerly in secular life. Both Hugues and his servant Barbe attach themselves vicariously to the monastic life around them. Barbe, whose greatest wish is to end her days as a lay sister in the Beguinage, is a naturally taciturn woman, one of those who trudge around the city "âgées et se taisant, comme si elles avaient dépensé toutes leurs paroles" (aged and silent, as if all their words had been spent) (*BLM,* 68). Hugues' domestic setting makes a further connection with Huysmans, since Des Esseintes also employs silent servants and goes to great lengths to ensure total quietness in his house, imposing "un rigide silence de moines claustrés, sans communication avec le dehors, dans des pièces aux fenêtres et aux portes closes" (a strict silence of cloistered monks, without contact with the outside world, in rooms with closed doors and windows).[29] Des Esseintes installs an old couple on the first floor, decks out the woman in a nun's habit, fits deep carpets to their floor, oils and lines their doors, and obliges them to wear thick felt slippers. Compared with these drastic measures, Hugues's demands on Barbe are relatively few, and it is only the guilt she feels at condoning the presence of Jane in her master's house that ultimately breaks her long-standing loyalty to Hugues and drives her away.

Rodenbach interrelates several prominent symbols in *Bruges-la-Morte*. For instance, the sound of bells, dual symbol of joy and sorrow, reminds Hugues of the ambiguities of his environment and of his relationship with Jane. Rodenbach likens the sound of the bells to the dropping of water—"une rumeur . . . grise qui traîne, ricoche, ondule sur l'eau des canaux" (a grey distant clamor drifting along, glancing off and undulating on the water of the canals) (*BLM*, 48)—or links both bell and water to the theme of tearful penitence: "Et partout, sur sa tête, l'égouttement froid, les petites notes salées des cloches de paroisse, projetées comme d'un goupillon pour quelque absoute" (And everywhere, the small salty notes of the parish bells dripped on his head, as if flung from a brush during an absolution) (*BLM*, 24). These images also correspond to another urban backdrop, the relentless late autumn drizzle, while the swaying cloaks of the Beguines resemble the bells in both color and shape.

Rodenbach also compares the sound of the bells to the song of the swan. As in the theater of Maeterlinck, the swan in Rodenbach's novel is an occult symbol joining man, the animal world, and the invisible. It presents an alluring image of feminine grace and purity but, though beautiful, is also a harbinger of death in its song. Rodenbach compares the Beguines to swans: "elles ont moins l'air de marcher que de glisser, et ce sont encore des cygnes, les soeurs des cygnes blancs des long canaux" (they seem less to walk than glide, and furthermore they are swans, the sisters of the white swans of the long canals) (*Evocations*, 27). Floating on the Minnewater (Lake of Love) beside the Beguinage, the swans presage the death of Jane and at the same time conjure up Ophelia-like apparitions of Hugues's dead wife.

The most potent reminder of his wife is a reverently preserved tress of her hair, the main object of Hugues's obsessive cult of remembrance. Women's hair was of great symbolic importance both to the symbolists and the Pre-Raphaelites, as well as later to the practitioners of Art Nouveau, to whom it was more purely decorative than symbolic of mysterious beauty. It also forms the subject of one of Maupassant's excursions into fantastic realism in his short story, "La Chevelure," which tells of a hair fetishist who ends up in an insane asylum.[30] Like much else in *Bruges-la-Morte*, the image of hair is ambiguous, symbolizing both the benign (the enduring memory of his wife) and the malevolent (the instrument of Jane's death). In this respect it is worth noting that Rodenbach's family had for two centuries owned a casket (the subject of his poem "Le Coffret") containing the hair of deceased family members. According to Rodenbach's son, Constantin, "Mon père y a pieusement déposé 'la mèche blanche' de sa mère. Celle du poète, à sa mort, fut ajoutée par sa femme" (My father dutifully placed his mother's "white lock" in it. On his death, that of the poet was added by his wife).[31]

Water is ubiquitous in Bruges, and a symbolic association of water and death pervades the novel. An association already traced in his poems *Le Règne du silence,* published one year earlier, the canals form a perfect setting for the death of beautiful and beloved women. Death by water becomes a slow, soft, feminine drifting away, a gentle release from pain, a nonviolent renunciation, a return to a fluid, amniotic state. Hugues's wife is omnipresent, an Ophelia-figure whose spirit passes timelessly through the heart of the city: "Dans l'atmosphère muette des eaux . . . Hugues . . . l'avait mieux revue . . . retrouvant au fil des canaux son visage d'Ophélie en allée" (In the mute atmosphere of the lifeless waters . . . Hugues . . . was better able to see her again . . . to discover in the line of the canals her Ophelia-face floating along) (*BLM,* 24). In an allusion to the gravedigger's speech in *Hamlet,* Hugues too begins to succumb to the fatal invitation of the beckoning water, "s'en venant au-devant de lui, comme elle vint au-devant d'Ophélie" (coming to meet him, as it came to meet Ophelia), filling his mind with "le désir d'avoir fini sa vie et l'impatience du tombeau" (a desire to put an end to his life, an impatience for the grave) (24).

Gaston Bachelard's analysis of the Ophelia complex is entirely relevant here, and he maintains that one may fairly interpret *Bruges-la-Morte* as the "ophélisation d'une ville entière" (ophelization of an entire city).[32] Citing Huysmans's phrase, Bachelard calls water the "melancholizing element," that of total dissolution, wherein death is elementary. Moreover, Rodenbach associates water and silence, especially (like Maeterlinck, Gabriele D'Annunzio, and Poe) in the image of water's still, silent depths. Equally to the point is Jean Pierrot's discussion of "elemental reverie," an underwater theme developing in the work of Flaubert and Jules Verne to become a popular idea in the literature of the fin de siècle. Pierrot also indicates the popularity of the aquarium image in the work of Rodenbach and several of his contemporaries, among them Huysmans, Laforgue, Maeterlinck, and Verhaeren.[33] The still waters of the canals absorb the living and "sleep" like the dead, but they are also agents of reflection, like so many mirrors. "Alone and palely loitering," like the celebrated rider in Keats's "La Belle Dame sans Merci," Hugues represents a strange (in)version of a familiar symbol of romantic agony, the solitary lady gazing in her mirror as she awaits the return of her beloved. He also represents the popular decadent image of the androgyne, whereby a sexual reversal permits the male to assume the role of the abandoned innocent passing away his time in mournful solitude.

Abundant glass, window, and mirror images in the novel return us to the "soul's interior spectacle," that concern with the myth of the narcissistic individual, who seeks withdrawal from social intercourse and vests interest only in experiencing the depths of the self. Gérard Genette examines the phenomenon of narcissism in the context of baroque poetry, basing his analysis on the textual evidence of an "évanescence substantielle," manifested chiefly in the theme of flowing water. Following Jacques Lacan, he observes the establishment of a double identity in the water's reflection: "La fin qui menace le reflet dans l'eau, et qui exprime son existence paradoxale, c'est la mort par engloutissement, où l'image imprudente s'abîme dans sa propre profondeur" (The end that threatens the reflection in the water, and which expresses its paradoxical existence, is death by engulfment, wherein the imprudent image is swallowed up by its own depth).[34] The image of death by drowning relates to the postromantic resurgence of an old theme from antiquity and innumerable folk legends: the doomed city vanishing beneath the waves. Starting with Poe's poem "The City in the Sea" (first version, 1831), this theme goes on to inspire both symbolist/decadent literature and early science fiction, as well as music (most notably in Lalo's opera *Le Roi d'Ys* and Debussy's "La Cathédrale engloutie"). The theme also appears in a transposed version in Rodenbach's Bruges, a city abandoned by the sea that had originally given it life.

Lacan's theory of the construction of the subject in the pre-Oedipal "mirror" stage, whereupon the infant first fixes on the gratifying nature of an apparently integral self-image, may be usefully applied to *Bruges-la-Morte*. The infant's fixation may continue to lead the individual into a realm of misleading images, as in Hugues's inability or plain unwillingness to distinguish the image of Jane from that of his wife. In such reflections nothing is seen clearly, just as in his reveries Hugues sees the cherished face from the past appear, then disappear again, in the murky, uncertain mirrors of his house or of the water of a canal. Believing that Rodenbach's entire work is so concerned with an obsessional return to childhood that a psychoanalytical dimension to his texts becomes impossible to ignore, Christian Berg proposes a progressive identification of Hugues's dead wife with a mother figure, and a consequent identification of both these figures with Bruges. In the end

Hugues is left alone with the city, which finally combines *three* images of unattainable female bodies: wife, mother (symbolized by the stone tomb of Marie de Bourgogne, the stone buildings, and even, at one stage, by Barbe's compassionate tone), and *soror dolorosa*.[35]

Mirrors are also instruments of surveillance, epitomized in the novel by the *espion* (spyglass), which, says Bachelard, in its clear, vigilant, aggressive nature, is the exception in Rodenbach's writing, since all other mirrors are veiled, with the same grey existence as the surrounding water of the canals. One of Rodenbach's stories, "L'Ami des miroirs," tells of a man whose obsession with mirrored reflections leads him ultimately into madness.[36] This theme of mirrors and madness is also reminiscent of the climax of Poe's story "William Wilson." Much else in Rodenbach reminds us of Poe— not for nothing did Mallarmé say of *Le Règne du silence,* "C'est très beau et très Poe, cela."[37] The theme of the vengeance of the dead recalls *Ligeia,* while Hugues is also a *flâneur* like Poe's "Man of the Crowd." Although the London weather in Poe's story is every bit as grim as in Rodenbach's Bruges, and though both heroes are solitary and contemplative figures, a difference lies in the respective descriptions of city streets: quiet and deserted in Rodenbach, frantic and teeming in Poe.

Hugues's every move is under the regard of either water or glass. Each watches, accuses, condemns. Bruges is a drowning pool; it is also a maze, a hall of mirrors. Wherever Hugues turns, there follow distortion, confusion, and madness. And whatever Hugues does, there follows the abysmal, spectacular sinking of his soul.

Notes

A preliminary version of this essay appeared in *Strathclyde Modern Language Studies* 9 (1989): 25–40.

1. See Hubert Juin, *Ecrivains de l'avant-siècle* (Paris: Seghers, 1972), 50; Oscar Thiry, *La Miraculeuse Aventure des Jeunes Belgiques, 1880–1896* (Brussels: La Belgique Artistique et Littéraire, 1910), 197.

2. Cited in appendix to Georges Rodenbach, *Bruges-la-Morte* (Brussels: Editions Jacques Antoine, 1977), 107. Subsequent references in the text (*BLM*) are to this edition. Translations of both primary and secondary material are my own.

3. Cited by Robert L. Delevoy, *Symbolists and Symbolism* (New York: Rizzoli, 1982), 107.

4. See Patrick Laude's support of Anny Bodson-Thomas's view in his *Rodenbach: Les Décors de silence* (Brussels: Editions Labor, 1990), 8.

5. 1977 edition (see n. 2); *Bruges-la-Morte* (Paris: Flammarion, 1978); *Bruges-la-Morte,* ed. Christian Berg (Brussels: Editions Labor, 1986).

6. Rodenbach, *Evocations* (Brussels: La Renaissance du Livre, 1924), 242–43. Subsequent references in the text are to this edition.
7. Rodenbach, *Oeuvres* (Paris: Mercure de France, 1925), 2:8.
8. Hubert Juin, *Fernand Khnopff et la littérature de son temps* (Brussels: Editions Lebeer Hossmann, 1980), 5–10.
9. Laude, *Rodenbach,* 7.
10. Berg, *Bruges-la-Morte,* 1986 edition, 131–32.
11. A. W. Raitt, *The Life of Villiers de l'Isle-Adam* (Oxford: Clarendon Press, 1981), 156. Raitt also observes that when Rodenbach, Dujardin, and Mauclair turn to verse, the influences on them become primarily Mallarmé and Verlaine.
12. Liliane Wouters and Alain Bosquet, *La Poésie francophone de Belgique, 1804–84* (Brussels: Editions Traces, 1985), 79.
13. J. Dubois, in *Manuel d'histoire littéraire de la France,* ed. Pierre Abraham and Roland Desne (Paris: Editions Sociales, 1977), 5:454.
14. Richard Gilman, *Decadence: The Strange Life of an Epithet* (New York: Farrar, Straus and Giroux, 1979), 99.
15. Jacques Marx, "Décadence: Mal du siècle ou maladie fin de siècle?"; Maarten Van Buren, "Art, maladie et diable: Hystérie et littérature dans la fin-de-siècle"; Jean Weisgerber, "Ebauche de synthèse des communications et des débats," in *La Littérature de fin de siècle, une littérature décadente?,* Actes du Colloque International de septembre 1990, no. spécial de la *Revue Luxembourgeoise de Littérature Générale et Comparée,* 347–61, 362–68, 388–90. See also A. E. Carter, *The Idea of Decadence in French Literature, 1830–1900* (Toronto: University of Toronto Press, 1958); Entretien avec Jean de Palacio, "'Enseigner' la Décadence?" *Equinoxe* no. 6 (1991): 9–17.
16. Rodenbach, "Aquarium mental," in *Les Vies encloses* (Paris: E. Fasquelle, 1896), 7.
17. Paul Gorceix, *Le Symbolisme en Belgique* (Heidelberg: Carl Winter, 1982), 61–82.
18. Jeannine Paque, *Le Symbolisme belge* (Brussels: Editions Labor, 1989), 64.
19. Janine Dakyns, *The Middle Ages in French Literature, 1851-1900* (Oxford: Oxford University Press, 1973).
20. Joris-Karl Huysmans, *Oeuvres complètes* (Geneva: Slatkine, 1972), 16:219–20.
21. Cited by Pierre Maes, *Georges Rodenbach, 1855–1898* (Gembloux: Duculot, 1952), 209.
22. On the dead city theme, see especially Hans Hinterhaüser, "Tote Städte," in his *Fin de Siècle: Gestalten und Mythen* (Munich: Fink Verlag, 1977), and Donald Flanell Friedman, *The Symbolist Dead City: A Landscape of Poesis* (New York: Garland, 1990). Among the many other writers who have used this theme, there is a striking similarity to Rodenbach's description of the Dutch island of Walcheren in H. P. Lovecraft's "The Shadow over Innsmouth," in *The Best of H. P. Lovecraft* (New York: Ballantine, 1982), 257.
23. For analyses of *Le Carillonneur,* see the essays in this collection by Paul Gorceix and Robert Ziegler.
24. Michel Décaudin, *La Crise des valeurs symbolistes: Vingt ans de poésie française, 1895–1914* (Toulouse: Privat, 1960).
25. George Ross Ridge, *The Hero in French Literature* (Athens: University of Georgia Press, 1961). See especially chap. 4, "The Decadent: A Cosmopolitan in Babylon."

26. Juin, "Lecture de Georges Rodenbach," in his *Ecrivains de l'avant-siècle*, 49.
27. Dakyns, *Middle Ages*, 232.
28. Huysmans, *Oeuvres complètes,* 16:221, 223.
29. Huysmans, *A rebours* (Paris: Fasquelle, 1965), 46–47.
30. See Appendix A for a cinematic connection with Maupassant's story.
31. Constantin Rodenbach, Letter to Louis Pierard, 4 February 1948 (offering the casket, the original manuscript of the poem "Le Coffret," and other memorabilia, including unpublished material, to the Académie Royale de Langue et de Littérature Françaises de Belgique), Fonds Georges Rodenbach, Archives et Musée de la Littérature, Brussels.
32. Gaston Bachelard, *L'Eau et les rêves: Essai sur l'imagination de la matière* (Paris: José Corti, 1942), 121.
33. Jean Pierrot, *The Decadent Imagination, 1880–1900* (Chicago: University of Chicago Press, 1981), 235–37.
34. Gérard Genette, "Complexe de Narcisse," in *Figures* I (Paris: Editions du Seuil, 1966), 24.
35. Berg, "Lecture," in *Bruges-la-Morte* (1986), 126–29. Friedman, *The Symbolist Dead City,* also examines the imagery of submergence in water as well as the unconscious significance of the canal city.
36. For a detailed analysis of mirror imagery and the technique of *mise en abyme* in *Bruges-la-Morte,* see the essay by Joyce Lowrie in this collection. "L'Ami des miroirs" first appeared in the posthumous short story collection *Le Rouet des brumes* (Paris, P. Ollendorff, 1901).
37. Cited by François Ruchon, ed., *L'Amitié de Stéphane Mallarmé et de Georges Rodenbach* (Geneva: P. Cailler, 1949), 59. Poe's "The Tell-Tale Heart" is the probable source of the "train lantern murder" in Rodenbach's story "Suggestion." The theme of mirrors and madness finds striking visual expression in "The Haunted Mirror," an episode in the Ealing Studios compendium film, *Dead of Night* (1945).

Ophelia Becomes Medusa: Reversals and Ambiguity in *Bruges-la-Morte*
Joyce O. Lowrie

> La Femme, dans son essence première, l'être inconscient, folle de l'inconnu, du mystère, éprise du mal, sous la forme de séduction perverse et diabolique . . . Les chimères sombres, terribles, mortelles; chimères de l'espace, des eaux, du mystère, de l'ombre et du rêve. Au loin, la Ville Morte, aux passions sommeillantes: Ville du Moyen Age, âpre et silencieuse, aux passerelles nombreuses, aux ponts rudimentaires et primitifs, aux ruelles montantes et serpentantes . . .
> —Gustave Moreau[1]

> (Woman, in her primal essence, unconscious being, desperate for the unknown, for mystery, passionately fond of evil in its seductively perverse and diabolic form . . . Somber, terrible, mortal chimeras; chimeras of space, water, mystery, of shadows and of dreams. In the distance, the Dead City, with its somnolent passions: a City of the Middle Ages, silent and bitter, with numerous footbridges, with rudimentary and primitive bridges, with ascending and serpentine alleyways . . .)

REPRESENTATIONS of dead and dying women appear frequently throughout nineteenth-century literature and art. The romantics' tortuous delight in experiencing what Shelley called, in his poem on the beauty of the Medusa, "the tempestuous loveliness of terror," continued to be part of the fin de siècle's creative expression of frenzy and fetishism, anguish and ambiguity. But to the pleasurable shudder that the romantics experienced when they depicted severed heads or dying bodies, the symbolists added a treacherous type of tranquillity.

Georges Rodenbach's *Bruges-la-Morte* (1892) reveals a number of problematics relating to symbolist sensibility: narcissism in a text's meaning and structure, reversals in the portrayal of woman as Ophelia/Medusa, equivocal interpretations of sexuality, chiastic forms and rhetoric. The enigmatic significance of water and mirrors in this text adds elusive and mysterious elements to its makeup, creating a paradigmatic study of reflexivity, of *mise en abyme.*

Hugues Viane, the principal male in Rodenbach's novel, is a hair fetishist whose erotic fascination with death places him within the heart of symbolist aesthetics. In the beginning of the novel Viane had spent exactly half as long as he had been happily married, five years, as a widower living in a townhouse he had made into a shrine for his dead wife, who remains nameless except for the appellation *la morte.* He had turned two rooms, in particular, into a fin de siècle "temple" in which every bibelot, pillow, mirror, and portrait had become consummate icons to be worshiped.[2] The most precious object found in this "physiognomy of the interior"[3] is a strand of golden-amber hair that Hugues had cut from his wife's head as she lay dying. He braided it into a plait, and placed it inside a glass-covered box. It becomes a reliquary, a "boîte de cristal où reposait la tresse nue qu'il allait chaque jour honorer" (a crystal case where lay the naked tress that he would devotedly honor with his gaze every day).[4]

In his wanderings through the serpentine streets and over the gloomy bridges and canals of Bruges, Bruges-*la-Morte* (as the city becomes a double of the dead wife), Viane frequently sees her reflected in the water: "Dans l'atmosphère muette des eaux . . . il l'avait mieux revue, mieux entendue, retrouvant au fil des canaux son visage d'Ophélie en allée, écoutant sa voix dans la chanson grêle et lointaine des carillons" (In the mute atmosphere of the lifeless waters . . . he was better able to see and hear her again, to discover her Ophelia face floating along, to listen to her voice in the high-pitched distant song of the carillon) (26). An encounter with a woman who is a replica of *la morte,* an actress named Jane Scott, changes his life. As he becomes increasingly involved with Jane, Hugues's neighbors gossip, and Barbe, his housekeeper, is told by her confessor that she should leave her master were he to bring Jane to the house.

At the center of the novel, when Viane takes two of his wife's dresses to Jane because he wishes to see her in them as an *exact* copy of his wife, the resemblances between wife and actress begin to blur in the widower's eyes. Jane makes fun of the dresses, and her relationship to Viane changes; she mocks him, betrays him, even as he becomes more obsessed by her. When she comes to Hugues's house on the day of Bruges' grand Procession of the Holy Blood, Barbe, the housekeeper, leaves. Going to the second floor, Jane brashly opens the casement window, revealing her presence to the devout crowd below. Viane insists that she close it, and he watches, in mystical fervor, the procession's medieval-like pageantry from behind the curtains. The shrine with its reliquary containing the drop of holy blood goes by, and Viane is moved to kneel. Making fun of him, Jane prepares to leave, but then insists on seeing the two rooms on the ground floor that "communicate with one another" (102). She picks up and handles Hugues's sacred pictures and bibelots. Taking the hair from its box, she runs around the room, teasing the widower. Viane loses his head ("[il] perdit la tête"), and in a sudden frenzy, he strangles her with the golden braid. Jane dies, and Hugues looks on, dazed, since for him "les deux femmes s'étaient identifiées en une seule" (the two women had been identified as one alone) (105).

Structural Strictures

Bruges-la-Morte is composed of fifteen chapters, two of which, 10 and 11, were not included in the original manuscript. They were added later to describe how Hugues and Bruges "find" each other again when resemblances between wife and mistress begin to dissipate. The novel, then, was originally composed of thirteen chapters.[5]

The composition of the work takes the form of a diptych, or of a mirror that has been cut in half. Each half faces the other, reversing and reflecting its own imagery, so to speak. The center, or the "hinge" of the diptych, is located in chapters 6 and 7, in the work's very core. At the end of chapter 6 the narrator says: "Aujourd'hui ce sens de la ressemblance, par une diversion brusque et miraculeuse, avait agi encore, *mais d'une façon inverse* [ms. variant: *mais en sens inverse*]" (Today, by a sudden seemingly miraculous encounter, this sense of resemblance had acted again, but this time inversely) (51). At the conclusion of chapter 7, when the narrator describes Hugues's beginning disenchantment with his wife's double, he says: "Pour la première fois, le prestige de la conformité physique n'avait pas suffi. Il avait opéré encore, mais *à rebours*" (For the first time, the fascination of physical conformity could not suffice. It still worked but against the grain) (58).[6]

At the center of the text the words *à l'inverse* and the Huysmansian *à rebours* appear as a deixis of what occurs in the novel's second half: the sacred "virginal" wife, "Ophélie," is reflected as a reversed image, as a Medusa, as an actress who had initially hidden, by virtue of her resemblance to "Ophelia," her monstrous nature. P. Joret points out the contrasting monstrous nature of

Hugues himself by calling him a "Tristan-Barbe bleue" (Tristan-Bluebeard).[7]

Ophelia is twice referred to in chapter 2. Viane finds her reflected in the waters of Bruges, and it seems to him that "une ombre s'allongeât des tours sur son âme . . . qu'une voix chuchotante montât de l'eau—l'eau s'en venant au-devant de lui, comme elle vint au-devant d'Ophélie" (a shadow from the towers lengthened over his soul . . . as if a whispering voice rose from the waters which were coming to meet him, as they came to meet Ophelia) (26). "Medusa" is evoked through symbolic allusions, for instance, to hair as snakes, or to petrification. Ophelia and Medusa turn into each other in the alpha and the omega of the text, doubling back and becoming one.

The ourobouros-like structure of the novel is enhanced by use of intratextual repetition and contrast. The first and last chapters, 1 and 15, contain many of the same, as well as opposite semes, signifiers, and motifs. The first paragraph of the book begins with: "Le jour *déclinait,* assombrissant les corridors de la grande demeure silencieuse, mettant des écrans de crêpe aux vitres" (Day was fading, darkening the hallways of the large silent house, fitting crape screens to the window panes) (19); the last chapter does not begin with a day's darkening decline, but with the ominous beginning of a day: "Comme la journée avait *mal commencé!* On dirait que les projets de joie sont un défi" (How the day had started badly! One would think that all our joyful plans are like a challenge) (99). In the second paragraph of the first chapter, "Hugues Viane se disposa *à sortir*" (Hugues Viane was getting ready to go out); in the second paragraph of the last chapter, Viane hears "la porte de la maison battre à la *sortie* de Barbe" (the door of the house slam behind Barbe). While solitude is found in this paragraph, *solitaire* (solitary) is found in chapter 1. In paragraph 3 of chapter 1, the phrase "rêvassait . . . perdu dans ses souvenirs" (dreamed away . . . lost in his memories) describes Hugues's principal activity, while "il *songea* à la morte" (he dreamed of the dead woman) appears in paragraph 3 of chapter 15. The word Hugues repeats to himself at the beginning, "Veuf! Etre veuf! Je suis veuf!" (Widower! To be a widower! I am a widower!), signaled as a *mot impair* (an uneven word), is echoed by Hugues's repetition of another monosyllable in the end: "Morte . . . morte . . . Bruges-la-Morte . . ." Repeated twice, to the tolling rhythm of Bruges's bells, after "Medusa" has been strangled, the expression replicates the singleness of Hugues's situation at the beginning of the novel and underscores the unity of both women, of *la morte* with *la morte* in the "tale" of the ourobouros's mouth.

After Jane arrives, in the last chapter, she goes to the window, "ses cheveux *à nu,* clairs, attirant l'oeil avec leurs lueurs de cuivre" (her hair naked and bright, its copper gleam catching the eye) (100). The wife's "tresse *nue*" (naked tress) appears in chapter 1 (22). As Viane recalls his wife's long, wavy hair, he remembers that when it was unpinned, it covered her back. Her hair is compared to that of "les Vierges des Primitifs [qui] ont des toisons pareilles, qui descendent en frissons calmes" (those calm yet quivering tresses seen on the madonnas of the primitive painters) (20). The reader recalls these "frissons calmes" in the end, when there is a complete reversal in the *crispation* (clenching) resulting in death.

The same fetishistic signifiers are repeated at beginning and end. In chapter 1 we read the phrase "une seule syllabe, sans *échos*" (one single syllable, without echoes) (19); in chapter 15 "déjà on entendait des *échos* de musiques lointaines" (one could already hear echoes of distant music) (99); in chapter 1 the furniture is described as "ce mobilier intact et toujours pareil, *sofas,* divans, fauteuils où elle s'était assise" (this permanently unaltered furniture—sofas, divans, armchairs where she had sat) (21); in chapter 15 we read that Jane "se coucha sur un *sofa*" (stretched out on the sofa); in chapter 1 *la morte* is described as being "blanche comme la cire l'éclairant" (pale as the candle wax lighting her) (20), and in chapter 15 we learn that "Hugues avait allumé lui-même *les cires* sur l'appui des fenêtres" (Hugues had lit the candles on the window ledges) (99). *La morte*'s portraits are referred to in both chapters 1 and 15. In the latter, Jane picks up one of them and says: "Tiens! en voilà une qui me ressemble . . ." (Look here! one even looks like me . . .) (103). Furthermore, the words "bibelot," "rideaux," "plis," "écrin transparent, boîte de cristal" (bibelot, curtains, folds, transparent cover, crystal box) (21–22) are echoed in "bibelots," "étoffes," and "coffret de verre" (bibelots, materials, and crystal box) (103).

The narrator ends his first chapter by stating that the fine Flemish rain "transit l'âme comme un oiseau dans un filet mouillé, aux mailles interminables!" (paralyzed the soul like a bird trapped in the wet meshes of an endless net) (23): claustrophobia and imprisonment prevail. The final chapter also terminates in a melancholy way. As Viane listens to the tolling of Bruges's bells, the narrator compares them to "[de] petites vieilles exténuées qui avaient l'air—est-ce sur la ville, est-ce sur une tombe?—d'effeuiller languissamment des fleurs de fer!" (slow, small, exhausted old women who seemed languishingly—is it over the city, is it over a tomb?—to be shedding petals of flowers of iron!) (106). The alliterations used in both conclusions, the poetic employment of *f*s, *l*s, *s*s, and *m*s in the former, of *f*s, *l*s, and *m*s in the latter establish differences within sameness, repetition within the heart of alterity. The final words of the text then indicate the languor that follows frenzy: they are repeated "avec la cadence des dernières cloches, lasses, lentes" (with the cadence of the last bells, slow, exhausted), like women who languishingly "[effeuillent] . . . des fleurs de fer" (shed flowers made of iron) (106).

The frequency of repeated semes, or of what Stamos Metzidakis calls "phrasal and lexical repetitions,"[8] in the first and final chapters of *Bruges-la-Morte* reveals the deliberateness with which Rodenbach tightened the structure of his novel in a gesture mimetic of the text's diegesis. Chapters 1 and 15 mirror each other, causing the text to return into itself.

Onomastic resemblances also exist between Via*ne* and Ja*ne*, Hu*gues* and Bru*gues* (Bruges used to be pronounced "Brugues"), of *Rosa*lie, the nun at the Beguine convent who is related to Hugues's housekeeper, and the "quai du *Rosa*ire," where Hugues lives. Contrast is also at the heart of Vi/a/ne's name, which is composed of both life, "vie," and a suggested opposite in the negative "ne."

The word *stricture* means both "abnormal contraction of any passage or duct of the body" as well as the "act of enclosing or binding tightly."[9] As Rodenbach imposes structural stricture upon his work, he makes of his text a metafictional narcissistic narrative in which sexuality is present, as well as its opposite, the negation of the other, and therefore, of sexuality. It is "process made visible," in Linda Hutcheon's phrase.[10]

Ambiguity: Ophelia/Medusa

In its development of symbolic allusions, in its progression from virginity to blood, in its evolution from "frissons calmes" (calm shivers) to a "crispation frénétique" (frenetic clenching), and then back to reflective tranquillity, the reader detects, in this novel, ambiguous sexual imagery. Stricture refers not only to the structure of the text, but to the narrative's sexual subtext as well.

Women and men were frequently indistinguishable in symbolist art. The influence of the Pre-Raphaelites, of Rossetti, Burne-Jones, and Aubrey Beardsley, was of utmost significance in symbolism, while occult, erotic, satanic, and mystic motifs permeated thematics and style. Félicien Rops's *Pornocrates* and *The Sacrifice,* Maurice Denis's *Lutte de Jacob avec l'ange,* and *Saintes femmes au tombeau,* the numerous paintings of John the Baptist's and Orpheus's decapitation exhibit these tendencies. The various renderings of woman as a strong, dazzling, and dominating figure engendering temptation (Moreau's *The Sphinx, Salomé, Dalilah,* von Stuck's *Sin,* Armand Point's *Princess and the Unicorn,* and *The Siren,* Khnopff's *L'Art ou les caresses* and *The Blood of the Medusa,* to name but a few), go hand in hand with representation of effete and pallid men.

The symbolists were a tightly knit group, and Khnopff's friendship with Rodenbach, Verhaeren, Samain, and Maeterlinck was well established. Of Khnopff's women Verhaeren wrote: "With their glacial attraction and medusa-like perversity . . . mouths slit as if by a fine horizontal sword-cut, and smooth brows . . . [they] are above all the aesthetic expression of his ideas. His art is refined, complicated by mysterious and puzzling meanings elusively filtered by a multiplicity of allusions."[11] In Khnopff's *The Blood of the Medusa,* the monster's mysterious eyes reveal her as inaccessible, remote, even as she is a woman who is both enthralling and domineering in her animal nature.

The reversal of traditional sexual roles in *Bruges-la-Morte* parallels a similar reversal in symbolist art. Nineteenth-century proclivities toward dyadic contrasts (ideal/earthy, ethereal/grotesque, pure/defiled, high/low, in societal as well as in ideological terms) result in the Ophelia/Medusa, madonna/whore imbrications in women's depictions, as well as in the ambiguity present in representations of men's ethereal contemplation of the Beautiful, on the one hand, and of the Beast, on the other.

Because *Bruges-la-Morte*'s structure is mirrorlike, the reflections of women's and men's double natures appear on each side of the diptych, confounding the ethereal and base qualities mentioned already. Viane's "virginal" wife, in death, is like a recumbent stone statue, even though it is "evil" Medusa, (in this case, Jane) who traditionally turns men into stone. The wife is described as *gisant* (recumbent) (20), and her shorn *chevelure* (tress) is placed on the piano "désormais muet, simplement *gisante* . . ." (hereafter silent, simply recumbent) (22). In chapter 2 Viane visits Notre-Dame, where he likes to go "à cause de son caractère mortuaire: partout, sur les parois, sur le sol, des dalles tumulaires avec des têtes de mort, des noms ébréchés, des inscriptions rongées aussi *comme des lèvres de pierre*" (to enjoy the mortuary atmosphere. Everywhere, on the walls, on the ground, were burial slabs with death's heads, their notched and pitted inscriptions like lips of stone) (27). He admires the figure of Marie de Bourgogne over the tomb (note the appellation *Marie*), and observes her head "sur un coussin," her body "en robe de cuivre" (on a pillow, in a dress of brass). Jane's hair, in the last chapter, glimmers with "des lueurs de cuivre" (brass-like glimmers) (28). The statue is "*toute rigide* sur l'entablement du sarcophage" (completely rigid on the entablature), and Viane dreams of the time when he, too, will lie rigidly beside his wife, as does Charles le Téméraire.

Another pertinent reversal is evident when "evil" Jane, who mocks religion, dies as did innocent Ophelia: "Jane ne riait plus; elle avait poussé un petit cri, un soupir, comme le souffle d'une bulle expirée à fleur d'eau" (Jane no longer laughed; she had let out a little cry, a sigh, like the puff of a bubble expiring at water-level) (105). The identification of Ophelia-like imagery with Jane occurs as early as chapter 5: "Quand il prenait dans ses mains la tête de Jane, l'approchait de lui, c'était pour regarder ses yeux, pour y chercher quelque chose qu'il avait vu dans d'autres: une nuance, un reflet, des perles, une flore dont la racine est dans l'âme—et qui y flottaient aussi peut-être" (When he took her head in his hands and brought it close to him, it was to look in her eyes, searching them for something he had seen in others: a nuance, a reflection, pearls, even some flowers with roots in the soul—and which perhaps were also floating there) (43). The intertext could well be Millais's depiction of Ophelia, painted as dead, floating in the water, her mouth open and her hair spread about her, intertwined with flowers. As Gaston Bachelard says, "on pourrait . . . interpréter *Bruges-la-Morte* . . . comme l'*ophélisation* d'une ville entière" (one could . . . interpret *Bruges-la-Morte* as the ophelization of a whole city).[12]

While references to Ophelia and Medusa in the text refer the reader, constantly, to "the other side of the mirror" (and one must include, here, the ambiguity of *Barbe*'s name, which signifies the fourth-century martyr as well as a man's beard), it is only in the death of both women that they become united completely in Hugues's mind: "Si ressemblantes dans la vie, plus ressemblantes dans la mort qui les avait faites de la même pâleur, [Viane] ne les distingua plus l'une de l'autre—unique visage de son amour" (So similar in life, all the more so in death which had lent them a common pallor, he could no longer tell one from the other—single face of his love) (105). Thanatos and Eros are one.

When Hugues Viane sees Jane Scott for the first time, the narrator uses a Mallarméan formulation in having him think: "Le démon de l'Analogie se jouait de lui!" (The demon of analogy was playing with him). Jane has the same eyes, hair, and voice as his dead wife. In fact, he believes that "nulle différence ne s'avérait entre la femme ancienne et la nouvelle" (no difference could be ascertained between this woman and his wife) (39).

The rhetoric of "sameness," however, does not remain constant throughout. "Sameness" means static undifferentiation, or "a = a." But the rhetoric of "sameness" does not remain constant throughout. The narrator uses the conditional, the imperfect (which can indicate supposition), verb forms that are "contrary to fact," such as various tenses of the subjunctive (the pluperfect tense, for example, is frequently used in literary French). As in Todorov's definition of the fantastic, supposition, hesitation, conjecture are foregrounded by verbal (in its grammatical sense) and lexical means. These usages introduce a slit, a hairline cut into the tight structure and rhetoric of the text.

In chapter 4, at the beginning of Hugues's and Jane's liaison, desire transcends all difference: "Pendant de longues minutes, il la regardait, avec une joie douloureuse, emmagasinant ses lèvres, ses cheveux, son teint, les décalquant au fil de ses yeux stagnants. . . . Elan, extase du puits qu'on croyait mort et où s'enchâsse une présence. L'eau n'est plus nue; le miroir vit!" (He would gaze at her for minutes on end with a sorrowful joy, taking full stock of her lips, her hair, her colouring, tracing them with the flow of his weary eyes. . . . He felt a surge of ecstatic joy as if a deep well presumed to be empty now yielded a presence. The water is no longer naked; the mirror lives!). In the sentence that follows, however, the narrator returns to "objectified" discourse and tells us: "Pour s'illusionner aussi avec sa voix, il baissait parfois les paupières, il l'écoutait parler, il buvait ce son, *presque* identique *à s'y méprendre, sauf* par instant un peu de sourdine, un peu d'ouate sur les mots. C'était *comme si* l'ancienne *eût parlé* derrière une tenture" (To create a further illusion, he often lowered his eyelids while listening to her, drinking in that almost unmistakeable voice. The only difference was an occasional lowering in tone, a little wadding around her words which made them sound like his wife speaking from behind a thick curtain) (40). Free indirect discourse returns the reader to Hugues's thoughts, but even there, in the midst of illusion, the conditional, or a comparison, creates a division: "Ce qui *paraissait* fini . . . allait recommencer. Et il ne tromperait même pas l'Epouse, puisque c'est elle encore qu'il aimerait dans cette effigie et qu'il baiserait sur cette bouche *telle que* la sienne" (What seemed finished for ever was about to start all over again. And he would not even be cheating his wife, since he would still be loving her in this effigy, and would be kissing that mouth that was similar to hers) (41). A comparison indicates an ambiguous interstice in which two are one and one are two. As Michel Foucault says in his essay on Raymond Roussel, "le langage est cet interstice par lequel l'être et son double sont unis et séparés; il est parent de cette ombre cachée qui fait voir les choses en cachant leur être" (language is that interstice through which being and its double are united and separated; it is related to that hidden shadow that has us see things while hiding their being).[13]

In certain instances in the novel, Perseus-and Medusa-like allusions are displaced, relocated in other persons or objects. When he first follows Jane, Hugues barely realizes he has arrived at the Grand Place "où la Tour des Halles . . . *se défendait contre la nuit envahissante avec le bouclier d'or de son cadran*" (where the Tour des Halles . . . shielded itself from the invading night with the gold buckler of its dark clockface) (33–34). In his enthrallment at having found Jane, Hugues "ne voyait plus *la ville rigide*" (could no longer see the rigid city) (47). Even though chapter 8 is dedicated to housekeeper Barbe's visit to the Beguines' convent, Medusa's influence seems to permeate the very house of God: "Toutes les coiffes se juxtaposaient, leurs ailes de linge *immobilisées*" (All the coifs were side by side, their linen wings immobilized) (61). When his relationship to Jane deteriorates, Hugues spends hours walking between his house and hers. At one moment, "à pas rapides, il marchait *dans la direction opposée*" (with rapid steps, he moved in the opposite direction) (71). Hugues is unable to stay home, where memories multiply around him *"comme une fixité d'yeux"* (like immobile eyes) (73). When Barbe is told Jane is coming to the house, "[elle] sentit *tout son sang se figer*" (she felt her blood congeal) (95).

It is Jane Scott, however, whose descriptive semes most consistently evoke Medusa. To recall, briefly, the myth, Perseus was sent to decapitate snake-haired Medusa because of a boast to Polydectes that he could do so. Aided by Hermes and Athena, he was told not to look at Medusa directly when he tried to slay her because her eyes could turn men into stone. But by looking at her reflection in his shield, Perseus was able to decapitate her and avoid the fate of all others whom she had petrified. Perseus eventually delivered Medusa's head to Athena, who henceforth wore it on her aegis.[14]

Many of the myth's elements are evoked in *Bruges-la-Morte:* dark eyes, piercing looks, similes and metaphors of immobility, backward stances, reversed reflections, recoiling reactions, strangling as a symbol of decapitation. When Viane first sees Jane, "il s'arrêta net, *comme figé;* la personne qui venait *en sens inverse,* avait passé près de lui" (he stopped short, as if frozen to the spot; the person who was coming in the opposite direction had passed close by him) (28). The discourse, so to speak, repeats the novel's structure. He puts his hands over his eyes, "comme pour écarter un songe" (as if warding off a dream). He turns back ("il rétrograda," [29]), then follows her. He keeps staring at her with a look that would have seemed improper "si elle n'avait apparu toute hallucinée" (had she not seemed totally entranced). The young woman "voyait sans regarder, impassible" (could see without looking, impassive), much like Khnopff's Medusa. When Viane gets too close to her he recoils, "avec une apparence d'effroi" (in apparent fright). His reactions to her make of him a Perseus/Narcissus: "Il semblait attiré et effrayé à la fois, comme par un puits où l'on cherche à élucider un visage" (He seemed drawn and terrified at the same time, as if by the depth of a well in which one seeks to make out a face) (28).

In the final chapter there is a multiplication of references to serpents. As the procession approaches, "la musique *des serpents* et des ophicléides monta plus grave" (the solemn music of the serpents and ophicleides rose), and shortly after, "[Jane] tournait *les yeux sur lui, hérissée*" ([Jane] turned her eyes toward him, bristling) (73). Hugues's strangling Jane with the snakelike braid of hair is a final image of decapitation. The decapitated head, John the Baptist's, Orpheus's, Medusa's, and the heads, busts, and torsos of many others are repeated subjects in the art of the period.[15]

In *Bruges-la-Morte* it is beautiful hair that connects Jane Scott to Medusa. In Ovid's *Metamorphoses* Perseus is asked why only one of the Gorgon sisters has serpents for hair. He replies that before having been ravished by Neptune in Minerva's temple, Medusa was the loveliest of the three sisters: "She was once most beautiful in form, and the jealous hope of many suitors. Of all her beauties, her hair was the most beautiful."[16] After she was ravished by Neptune, Jove's daughter, shocked by what she had witnessed, punished Medusa for her carelessness by changing her locks into hideous snakes.[17] Viane's wife's hair was "d'un jaune ambre" (an amber yellow) (20), and Jane's "d'un or semblable, couleur d'ambre et de cocon, d'un jaune fluide et textuel" (of the same golden colour, really a silky amber, a fluid textured yellow) (29).

Fetishism

La morte's and Jane Scott's hair (which bring to mind Lucien Lévy-Dhurmer's golden haired *Eve,* Rossetti's auburn- and red-headed women, including *Lilith, Venus Verticordia,* and *La Ghirlandata,* and many other paintings of women with striking manes in late nineteenth-century painting) is clearly the stuff of symbolist fetishism. Freud says that fetishism occurs when "the normal sexual object is replaced by another which bears some relation to it, but is entirely unsuited to serve the normal sexual aim." Feet and hair are examples of this pathology, and he likens the objects "to the fetishes in which savages believe that their gods are embodied."[18] That the fetish is a substitute, the displacement of the object of worship into some thing other than itself becomes applicable to Hugues Viane's veneration of his dead wife's hair. Jane herself becomes a fetish, for she replaces *la morte*. "Silent devotions in front of objects associated with [Viane's] wife," says Philip Mosley, "are as blatantly erotic as they are subtly religious."[19] R. von Krafft-Ebbing stated, in 1886, that fetishism "is most commonly found in *religious* and *erotic* spheres."[20]

Applying Freudian terms to metaphor makes metaphor seem pathological when the signified is cut off from its signifier. Even though he thinks of it as "cette chevelure qui était encore Elle" (that head of hair that was still she), Viane's sacred object becomes a "tresse interrompue" (an interrupted tress), a "chaîne brisée" (a broken chain) (22). The fact that the wife has no name in the text means that she has been cut off from any personally identifiable syntagm. She becomes a synecdoche: she is nothing but a lock of hair.

Anthony Pym reminds us that Mallarmé chose "Hérodiade," the mother's name rather than the dancer's, "Salomé," for the title of his poem. Mallarmé's suppression of both dance and name was done in the interest of achieving a "reflective stillness" that "recalls the pallidity of Pre-Raphaelite beauty."[21] Rodenbach's well-documented friendship with Mallarmé[22] was undoubtedly an important factor in the former's depictions of *la morte* and of Jane Scott.

Hérodiade's "transcendent sphere," in Mallarmé's poem, as opposed to her participation in the domain of historicity, Pym states, caused her to remain "apart, retaining power through non-action. If she attracts, it is not through movement of the body but through manipulation of the mind."[23] Decapitation in symbolist art and literature attains a new meaning in such terms. The head, the sphere of thought and of "manipulation of and by the mind," is detached from John the Baptist's "historicized" body, and becomes "a transcendent value without correlative."[24]

While the decapitated head does not usually emit words (one must exempt Orpheus from this statement because he was, after all, the son of Calliope, the muse of epic poetry), it is the perfect symbolist object due to its stillness, its aesthetic invulnerability. It is simply *there,* emitting no sound. Silence and severance are related: a severed head is voiceless. The symbolist predilection for severed heads (Jean Lorrain, a symbolist/decadent novelist, for instance, ends his novella *Songeuse* with an act of decapitation) looms in the background of what would later become a commonplace in surrealist representation. One has only to peruse a text on surrealist art to become aware of a plethora of hands, feet, eyes, breasts, lips, and the like that are disconnected from a body proper. The surrealist passion for mutilation and dismemberment has symbolist antecedents.

That Viane tries to derive his virility, his manhood, his own selfhood from what he has cut off seems to be the case. He depends upon a circle of braided hair to feel that he is "held together." He worships that which will "petrify" him, save him from Bruges's watery realms, make him erect as a man. His admiration of the stone figures in Notre-Dame is an example of this desire. His peregrinations through the labyrinth of the city with its canals (which are feminized by being identified with his wife) cause him to think about the city's cathedrals: "Les hautes tours dans leurs frocs de pierre partout allongent leur ombre" (The high towers in their stone frocks lengthen their shadows everywhere) (45). That phallic towers should be dressed in "stone frocks" is an ambiguous intermingling of imagery that leads to the novel's final dramatic scene.

The description of Viane's "decapitation" of "Medusa" is unequivocally sexual:

Alors Hugues s'affola; une flamme lui chanta aux oreilles; du sang brûla ses yeux; un vertige lui courut dans la tête, une soudaine frénésie, une crispation du bout des doigts, une envie de saisir, d'étreindre quelque chose, de casser des fleurs, une sensation et une force d'étau aux mains—il avait saisi la chevelure que Jane tenait toujours enroulée à son cou; il voulut la reprendre! Et farouche, hagard, il tira, serra autour du cou la tresse qui, tendue, était ride comme un câble. (104-5)

(Then Hugues went crazy; a flame sang in his ears; blood stung his eyes, a dizziness swept through his head, a sudden frenzy, a tightening of the fingertips, a desire to seize, to wring something, to snap flowers, a sensation of vice-like strength in his hands—he had grabbed the tress of hair which was still wound around Jane's neck; he wanted to recapture it! And wild, savage-looking, he pulled the tress until, taut, it was tight as a rope around her neck.)

What is foregrounded in the passage cited here is not only violent male sexuality, but ambiguity. Hugues *seems* to be demonstrating virility by pursuing snake-haired "Medusa." Although he *seems* to be wishing to castrate her in order to repossess her strength, the text states, metaphorically, that it is he who "loses his head." When Jane takes the lock of hair, "l'amenant vers son [propre] visage et sa bouche comme un serpent charmé, l'enroulant à son cou, boa d'un oiseau d'or . . ." (lowering it towards her face and mouth as if it were a charmed snake, winding it round her neck, a boa fashioned from the plumes of a golden bird . . .), Hugues screams: "Rends-moi! rends-moi!" (Give it back to me! give it back to me!) (104). His choking Jane with the hair makes the stricture *his,* makes the "contraction" of sexuality *his.* It is *he* who will use the hair to "enclose tightly," to "constrict," as in female orgasm, Jane's neck. It is *he* who experiences "une envie de saisir, d'étreindre quelque chose"; it is *he* who, "farouche" (wild), "serra autour du cou la tresse." The subtext is declaring that what Viane fights for, kills for, in fact, is his own femininity, his own desire for female power. And after his frenzy, in a daze, he contemplates what he has done in reflective stillness. The reversal is complete in this example of symbolist androgyny. Narcissus, who was loved by both males and females in Ovid and in so many subsequent texts, is sexually double in Rodenbach as well.

Chiastic Rhetoric: *Dead Bruges*/*Bruges-the-Dead*

At the beginning of chapter 2, the narrator uses chiasmus to depict the identifications that exist between Viane, his wife, and the city: "Bruges était sa morte. Et sa morte était Bruges" (Bruges was his dead wife. And his dead wife was Bruges) (26). The chiastic trope is both a micro- and a macrostructure. The trope may be traced from Sumero-Akkadian, Ugaritic, and Hebrew poetry to ancient Greek and Latin literatures.[25] Its use "may be extended to encompass the rhetorical designs of entire works," says Thomas Mermall.[26] This is true of whole episodes and books of the *Iliad,* the *Odyssey,* among other ancient texts.[27] It is also true of *Bruges-la-Morte.*

Chiastic rhetoric (a-b/b-a), or Ophelia-Medusa/Medusa-Ophelia, is that which points to the comforting aspects of symmetry, on the one hand, and to the terrifying aspects of mirror imagery, on the other. Max Nänny calls attention to "non-progressive stasis" in chiasmus.[28] There is a certain assurance in the realization that time is stable, that there *is* a rhythm to the universe, be it described in terms of balance, reciprocity, or Manichaean opposition. But chiasmus also unveils a truth that is disquieting because mirrors return character and language back to themselves. Linear progression is abolished, making it seem as if one were dominated by forces that are beyond one's control. It reveals a pattern in a cycle that abolishes diachronic time: reality might be nothing other than a petrified reflection in a looking glass, revealing that the future is merely a duplication of the past. One is deluded into thinking that there is alterity when all is sameness, stillness, repetition.

In his study of the chiasmus in Unamuno's work, Thomas Mermall shows that one aspect of chiasmus is "the interpenetration of opposites."[29] This is true of one of Rodenbach's usages, since, schematically, the "Ophelia-Medusa/Medusa-Ophelia" structure reveals just that sort of interpenetration. In "Bruges était sa morte, et sa morte était Bruges," a struggle is latent in the heart of a seemingly simple reversal. Viane cannot remain still in his search for his dead wife: he must find her in Bruges because Bruges is identified with her. Viane is deluded, however, in thinking that the woman he sees and follows in the city is an exact replica of his wife. Jane will also tragically find that out. There is "instability of meaning and identity"[30] in Rodenbach's trope, as there is reciprocity in the oppositions of his text.

A paradox found in *Bruges-la-Morte*'s mirror structure is that, like John the Baptist's decapitated head, which does not utter words but signifies, nonetheless, the author-narrator has the "static" novel signify through words. As Ophelia, who talks her way into a watery grave, and whose "voix chuchotante" (whispering voice) is twice "heard" in chapter 2, the novel attains the power of Medusa's decapitated head. The reader is "petrified" by the strength of the text. Medusa the "Silent" signifies even when deprived of speech, since in the myth, her head continues to exert power even after having been severed. Perseus uses it to turn Atlas into a mountain; and when Perseus sets it down on a bed of seaweed to rescue Andromeda, it turns the sea matter into a coral reef.

Like Ophelia and Medusa, *Bruges-la-Morte* is both a void and a voice. While talking its way, ultimately, into silence, the novel "signifies" in the relationship the reader entertains with the text. Viane's liturgical repetition of "Bruges-la-morte," "Bruges-la-morte," in the end, recalls the novel's title, in remembrance of itself. (Repetition, one recalls, is one of the basic components of chiasmus.) And yet, a hairline breach is sliced between each of Viane's repetitions. As Barthes remarks, "le propre d'une Topique, c'est d'être un peu vide" (what characterizes a topic is its being somewhat empty).[31] A mouth repeating mechanically the title of the novel the reader has just read cannot but be "a bit empty." It remains eminently *scriptible* because it manifests a zero degree of writing in the symbol of a head that has been deprived of contemplative thought—and "speaks," nonetheless.

Mises en Abyme—*Bruges-la-Morte*

Lucien Dällenbach distinguishes three types of *mises en abyme.* The first he calls "*simple duplication* (a sequence which is connected by similarity to the work that encloses it)"; the second is "*infinite duplication* (a sequence which is connected by similarity to the work that encloses it and which itself includes a sequence that . . . etc.)"; and the third is "*aporetic duplication* (a sequence that is supposed to enclose the work that encloses it)."[32] In *Bruges-la-Morte,* all are present. Mirrors as objects are used as semes, similes, metonymies, and metaphors that reflect various miniatures of the novel within the novel. In chapter 1, the windows of Hugues's house "donnaient sur le quai du Rosaire, au long duquel s'alignait sa maison, *mirée* dans l'eau" (overlooked the quai du Rosaire along which, mirrored in the water, stretched the frontage of his house); Viane's relationship to his wife is compared to "[des] quais parallèles d'un canal qui mêle *leurs deux reflets*" (parallel quays unifying their reflections in a canal) (19). This phrase seems like an apt description of a chiasmus. As he thinks of polishing the mirrors in his rooms, Hugues thinks of his wife's reflection in them: "Et dans les miroirs, il semblait qu'avec prudence il fallût en frôler d'éponges et de linges la surface claire pour ne pas effacer son visage dormant au fond" (it seemed necessary also to sponge and wipe very carefully the clear surface of the mirrors so as not to erase her face sleeping deep within them) (21). As a symbolic pond of Narcissus, Hugues's mirror forever holds within it the image of a beautiful figure. The reflection of Jane Scott, who is both *la morte*'s and Bruges' double, is prepared when Hugues looks at the mirror and thinks about her image being superimposed upon his wife's. This, in fact, takes place when Jane looks at herself and powders her face while looking in that same mirror. On one of his walks around Bruges, Viane "longea le Quai Vert, *le Quai du Miroir,* s'éloigna vers le Point du Moulin, les banlieues tristes bordées de peupliers" (he skirted the Quai Vert, the Quai du Miroir, and crossed the Pont du Moulin, disappearing into the sad, poplar-fringed suburbs) (26).

A mirror, like Medusa, is a treacherous thing. On the outside of Bruges's houses, mirrors, called *espions,* are affixed to the windows. They are oblique mirrors that frame "des profils *équivoques* de rues; *pièges miroitants qui capturent,* à leur insu, tout le manège des passants, leurs gestes, leurs sourires, la pensée d'une seule minute dans *leurs yeux*—et répercute tout cela dans l'intérieur des maisons où *quelqu'un guette*" (the equivocal profiles of the street: little reflecting traps which, unbeknown to passers-by, capture all their antics, their smiles and gestures, a minute's thoughtful look in their eyes—transmitting all of it to the interiors of houses where someone lies in wait) (46). These "spies" reflect the novel as a whole: (a) they are ambiguous, "equivocal"; (b) they are Medusa-like in that they capture fleeting thoughts depicted in people's eyes; (c) they project all that goes on outside into the houses' interiors; (d) they reinforce the monster syndrome because "someone lies in wait."

Portraits and drawings of *la morte* are also *mises en abyme* in Hugues's contiguous rooms. They are on the mantle, on pedestal tables, on walls, depicting his wife at different stages of her life. In chapter 15, it is the portrait on the mantle that Jane picks up, remarking on its resemblance to herself. The "cheminée, guéridons et murs" (fireplace, pedestal tables, and walls) in chapter 1 are repeated in reversed order in chapter 15, achieving, thus, a subtle mirror imagery of the "mirror imagery" of Jane's looking at her "mirror" in the portrait. The semantic *mise en abyme* repeats the diegetic *mise en abyme,* achieving "infinite duplication."

Rodenbach creates two sequences of *mises en abyme* in the novel, one in the realm of music, and one in art. After having followed Jane through the streets, Viane loses sight of her when she enters a theater, but he soon discovers her on stage, where Meyerbeer's opera, *Robert le Diable,* is playing. She appears immediately after the ballerinas, who enact condemned nuns, are found in the graveyard. Awakened from death, they form a long procession, and Helena/Jane is raised from the dead, throwing off her shroud and gown. As an actress, she is a double personage from the start. Later on, Viane has Jane put *on* his wife's two dresses. When he sees Jane, he can only think that "c'était vraiment la morte descendue de la pierre de son sépulcre" (she was his wife, descending from the stone of her sepulcher) (19).[33] Before the opera begins, Hugues looks around, and it is no accident that the word *jumelles* (which in French means "twins" as well as "opera glasses"), is used to describe people's reactions to him: "D'autant plus qu'on avait remarqué sa présence et qu'on s'en étonna en une insistance de jumelles qu'il ne fut pas sans apercevoir" (all the more since he could sense that people were astonished to notice his presence through their opera-glasses) (35).

A microcosm within the novel's macrocosm is placed between the operatic and the ekphrastic *mises en abyme*. The Beguine convent that Barbe visits on feast days, and where she learns about her employer's affair, is called "une petite ville à part dans l'autre ville" (a small, separate city within the other city) (60).[34] Immediately after making this statement, the narrator refers to the nuns' weaving, mentioning the "fils inextricables des bobines" (inextricable threads of the bobbins) (63). Many references to weaving in literature (from Penelope on) are reflexive references to textuality. In chapter 5, when Viane undoes Jane's hair, the narrator says: "[il] en inondait ses épaules, les assortissait mentalement à un écheveau absent, comme s'il fallait les filer ensemble" (he would untie her hair and let it inundate her shoulders, matching it mentally to an absent tress as if he would spin them together) (43). The reference is polysemic: it occurs directly after Hugues takes Jane's head in his hands (Medusa), seeking in her eyes (Ophelia) "un reflet, des perles, une flore dont la racine est dans l'âme—et qui y flottaient aussi peut-être" (a reflection, pearls, even some flowers with roots in the soul—and which perhaps were also floating there); he spreads her hair out over her shoulders, separating the strands as if he were going to weave them together. This refers back to "les cheveux" of *la morte,* which "déployés, lui couvraient tout le dos" (when unpinned, flowed long and wavy down her back) (20). We seem to witness the activities of the novelist/narrator/protagonist/implied reader/readers who weave the various strands of narrative together, in myriad ways, to create the text.

The description of Memling's reliquary is another novel "en miniature." This magnificent work is located in Bruges's former hospital of Saint John (now the Memling Museum) founded in the twelfth century. Because it owes its name to its patron saint, Saint John the Evangelist (from the beginning it was called "domus beati Johannis," or the house of Saint John), the other John, namely, the Baptist, also became associated with it. As Hilde Lobelle-Caluwe says, both the lamb (for the Baptist) and the chalice (for the Evangelist), or their attributes alone, appear on many objects as well as on the hospital's coat of arms.[35]

Among the most renowned paintings in the hospital chapel is Memling's altarpiece of the Baptist and the Evangelist. The middle depicts the Evangelist holding a chalice with the poisonous snake inside (an allusion to the fact that an attempt was made to poison him). The Baptist is recognized by his camel-haired robe and the lamb at his side. The left-hand panel depicts the head of the Baptist on a plate that is held by a young woman (undoubtedly Salomé). His body is stretched out on the ground, decapitated. It is significant that this altarpiece should appear on the high altar of the chapel because the Saint Ursula Shrine that Rodenbach describes was given a place of honor in the same chapel in 1489. Both are there to this day. But neither the decapitated head of the Baptist (nor of Medusa) are mentioned in the novel, making of them intertextual references that must be "spied out," as in Bruges's *espions,* by the readers themselves. Saint Ursula's reliquary, however, is described minutely. The narrator calls the chapel a "sanctuaire d'art où rayonne la celèbre châsse de sainte Ursule, telle qu'une petite chapelle gothique en or, déroulant, de chaque côté, sur trois panneaux, l'histoire des onze mille Vierges" (sanctuary of art, the room containing the unique paintings where the famous shrine of St. Ursula shines, like a little Gothic chapel in gold, unfolding on each side, on three panels, the story of the eleven thousand virgins) (79). That the reliquary copies the chapel in which it is found makes of it a *mise en abyme* of the first order. That it is something like Viane's "reliquary" as well as the one featuring in the procession makes of it a double *mise en abyme.* The ekphrasis accentuates martyrdom, death, massacre, blood, wounds that resemble petals, blood that does not drip but is shed, "petal-like," from the virgins' breasts. And the virgins view their reflections in the soldiers' armor: "Les soldats sont sur le rivage. Ils ont déjà commencé *le massacre;* Ursule et ses compagnes ont débarqué. [The reader recalls Bruges's canals and watery realms.] Le sang coule, mais si *rose! Les blessures sont des pétales.* Le sang ne s'égoutte pas; il *s'effeuille* des poitrines. Les Vierges sont . . . tranquilles, *mirant leur courage dans les armures des soldats, qui luisent en miroirs"* (The soldiers are on the bank. They have already begun the massacre; Ursula and her companions have disembarked. The blood flows—but so pink! The wounds are petals. The blood doesn't drip; it sheds its petals on the breasts. The virgins are . . . peaceful, catching sight of their courage in the gleaming mirrors of the soldiers' armour) (80).

The mirror in the text reflects the reversed diegesis at the end of *Bruges-la-Morte* in which it is not "Perseus," the hero, who looks into the reflection in his shield, but the virgins who observe themselves in the men's armor. Viane is again reversed and feminized. And the metaphor of wounds being flowers, and of blood being shed petal-like ["*il s'effeuille*"], prepares the way for the last sentence of the novel in which the repetitive and weary cadence of Bruges's bells is said to resemble women who languidly "[effeuillent] des fleurs de fer" (106).

The reflexive reversals and ambiguities presented throughout the text, from diegetic to metaphoric, from structural to psychological, from rhetorical to narratological, lead to that final phrase in which Bruges's bells are equated with the feminine principle. Their sounds are compared to the plucking of petals from flowers made of *iron,* a "petrified" matter. Although "silent," in the end it is Medusa who, in her treacherous tranquillity, gets the last laugh.

Notes

1. Included by Robert de Montesquiou in *Altesses sérénissimes* (Paris: Librairie Félix Juven, 1907), 1–64. The essay was written by Moreau in 1897, and was included in the first chapter, "Le Lapidaire," of Montesquiou's book. It celebrates the occasion of Moreau's having given eight thousand paintings and drawings to the Ville de Paris, and is a commentary made by Moreau on his own *Chimères: Décameron satanique.* The particular imagery and tone of the essay applies to many aspects of *Bruges-la-Morte,* the author of which Montesquiou, in his typically malicious and witty way, referred to as "le Brugeois gentilhomme."

2. See Emily Apter, "Cabinet Secrets: Fetishism, Prostitution, and the Fin de Siècle Interior," *Assemblage* 9 (1989): 7–19.

3. In discussing Huysmans's Des Esseintes, Apter says: "Huysmans's neurasthenic hero is clearly inspired as a decorator by the ideal house that Poe, in his 'Philosophy of Furniture,' put forth as an antidote to the crass, nouveau-riche apartment that was encroaching, in his day, on the domain of aristocratic taste. The first 'physiognomist of the interior' according to Walter Benjamin, Poe stamped his domestic space with the inimitable stylistic flourishes of his literary haunted houses, but, more importantly for our discussion, he equipped it with the trappings of hidden surveillance" (9). The description applies to Viane's and Bruges's houses.

4. Georges Rodenbach, *Bruges-la-Morte,* ed. Christian Berg (Brussels: Editions Labor, 1986), 22. Further references will be included in the text. The translations of the French text are taken, in the main, from Philip Mosley's translation

of Rodenbach's novel (Paisley, Scotland: Wilfion Books, 1986). In some cases, for lexical reasons or for emphasis, parts of or whole translations are by the author of this essay.

5. See "Principes de la présente edition" written by Christian Berg in the Labor edition, 134–35.

6. All italics are added, unless otherwise noted.

7. P. Joret, "Au delà d'un masque: Une Lecture isotopique d'un poème de Georges Rodenbach," *Linguistica Antverpiensia* 18–19 (1984–85): 72.

8. Stamos Metzidakis, *Repetition and Semiotics: Interpreting Prose Poems* (Birmingham: Summa Publications, 1986), 72, 79.

9. *Random House Dictionary of the English Language.*

10. Linda Hutcheon, *Narcissistic Narrative: The Metafictional Paradox* (New York: Methuen, 1984), 6.

11. Quoted by Robert Goldwater, *Symbolism* (New York: Harper and Row, 1979), 209.

12. Gaston Bachelard, *L'Eau et les rêves: Essai sur l'imagination de la matière* (Paris: José Corti, 1942), 121.

13. Michel Foucault, *Raymond Roussel* (Paris: Gallimard, 1963), 154.

14. Mark P. O. Morford and Robert J. Lenardon, eds., *Classical Mythology* (New York: Longman, 1977), chap. 19: "Perseus and the Legend of Argos," 341–52.

15. See Dorothy Kosinski, *Orpheus in Nineteenth-Century Symbolism* (Ann Arbor, Mich.: UMI Research Press, 1989).

16. Ovid, *Metamorphoses* I (Cambridge: Harvard University Press, Loeb Classical Library, 1934), book 4, 794–803.

17. Ibid., 235.

18. Sigmund Freud, *Three Essays on the Theory of Sexuality,* trans. and ed. James Strachey (New York: Basic Books, 1962), 19.

19. See p. 33 of this volume.

20. R. von Kraft-Ebbing, *Psychopathia Sexualis: A Medico-Forensic Study,* trans. from the Latin by Harry E. Wedeck, introd. Ernest van den Haag (New York: G. P. Putnam's Sons, 1965), 36. Italics in original.

21. Anthony Pym, "The Importance of Salomé: Approaches to a Fin de Siècle Theme," *French Forum* 14 (September 1989): 316.

22. See François Ruchon, *L'Amitié de Stéphane Mallarmé et de Georges Rodenbach* (Geneva: Pierre Cailler, 1949). In this volume there is a reproduction of a portrait, by Vanaise, of Anna Rodenbach, Georges Rodenbach's wife. The painting depicts Anna from the back, with her head in profile. Her long golden hair cascades to midtorso.

23. Pym, "Salomé," 316.

24. Ibid., 321.

25. See *Chiasmus in Antiquity,* ed. John W. Welch (Hildensheim: Gerbenberg Verlag, 1981).

26. Thomas Mermall, "The Chiasmus: Unamuno's Master Trope," *PMLA* 105 (March 1990): 248.

27. See John W. Welch, "Chiasmus in Ancient Greek and Latin Literatures," in *Chiasmus in Antiquity,* 251–68.

28. Max Nänny, "Iconicity in Literature," *Word and Image* 2, no. 2 (1986): 199–208.

29. Mermall, "Chiasmus," 250.

30. Ibid., 251.

31. Roland Barthes, *Fragments d'un discours amoureux* (Paris: Seuil, 1977), 9.

32. Lucien Dällenbach, *The Mirror in the Text,* trans. Jeremy Whiteley with Emma Hughes (Chicago: University of Chicago Press, 1989), 35.

33. A manuscript variant states: "C'était *sainte Rosalie* descendue de la pierre de son sépulcre, c'était vraiment la morte ressuscitée" (37). Perhaps sister Rosalie of the Beguines' convent was named after saint Rosalie in Meyerbeer's opera, even though the reference is only evident in a manuscript variant.

34. The Beguine convent, in Bruges, even today, is "a small village" that is placed unto itself, apart, inside the larger city.

35. *Memling Museum: Bruges,* ed. Valentin Vermeersch and Jean-Marie Duvosquel (Brussels: Ludion S.A.—Cultura Nostra, 1987), 9.

Temporal Aesthetics and the Euphemization of Death in *Le Carillonneur*

Robert Ziegler

THE pervasive sense of pessimism which Jean Pierrot sees as contaminating the fin de siècle era often involves both a cancellation of hope in the future and an investment of aesthetic value in the past. Hereditary degeneration, entropic devolution, and genetic enfeeblement are commonly seen as affecting individuals and nations alike, causing them to follow "le même cheminement . . . de la jeunesse à la maturité puis à la vieillesse" (the same progression . . . from youth to maturity and then to old age). According to Pierrot's reasoning: "Les peuples européens, héritiers d'une longue évolution, seraient menacés par une décrépitude inévitable, et leur civilisation serait vouée à une mort prochaine" (The people of Europe, heirs to a long evolution, would be threatened by an inevitable decrepitude, their civilization fated to an impending death).[1] Coupled with the decadents' fear of impending social collapse and racial extinction is a revulsion for commercialism—"l'incommensurable goujaterie du financier et du parvenu" (the incommensurable blackguardism of the financier and the parvenu) anathemetized by Huysmans' Des Esseintes[2]—an impatience with the decay of taste manifested by the proliferation of brasseries and banks along Baron Haussmann's wide and barren boulevards. Oxymoronically described as "technological progress," the path to the future is not one taken by Huysmans' Durtal, who elects instead to repair to his Ligugé monastery, or by Lorrain's Monsieur de Bougrelon, who lives in exile in Amsterdam, far away from telephones, factories, bicycles, democracy, and motor cars, "a thousand hideous and barbaric things," he says, "that I cannot even imagine."[3] The implacable reality of a future debased by Americanism and greed is shunned by these characters in favor of the fictions of history and the illusions of childhood. That is why the little girls in Schwob's "Les Milésiennes" choose to hang themselves rather than grow up and face the banal horror of adulthood revealed to them in a mirror in the Temple of Athena. Similarly, Monelle's child disciples "souhaitaient se vouer à des jeux éternels. . . . Tout n'était que passé pour elles" (wished to devote themselves eternally to games. For them, there was nothing but the past).[4] Different from the dreary future that Durtal foresees is a past that he realizes can be rendered as a subjective narrative or be molded into a personal work of art. "L'histoire supplanta chez lui le roman," Huysmans writes of his protagonist: "les événements . . . ne sont pour un homme de talent qu'un tremplin d'idées et de style" (History for him supplanted the novel. For a man of talent, events are only a springboard for style and ideas).[5] Viewed from this perspective, time ceases to be an agent of death, which diminishes, disenchants, and impoverishes, and instead can be imagined in spatial terms, seen as leaving in its wake a repository of resources that can be drawn on, like a library or museum in which precious artifacts are housed. Turning away from the future, the decadents appoint themselves as curators or archivists, custodians of the dead products of time's passage that are entrusted to them to remember and beautify, to protect against what Gilbert Durand calls "la dissolution profanante du devenir et de la mort" (the profanatory dissolution of becoming and of death).[6]

Georges Rodenbach's novel *Le Carillonneur* is a work that perfectly typifies the decadents' temporal aesthetic and euphemization of death.[7] On the one hand, it negatively valorizes the time of action and desire, which binds one to a present constantly telescoped into a future of despair, while, on the other hand, it glorifies the artistic labor by which corrosive time can be transcended. Here again, as in other fin de siècle works, experiential space and time are related, as the novel is structured along a vertical axis figured by the tower into which the carillon player ascends and by the horizontal axis of his panoramic view of Bruges and the sea in the distance.

In her 1942 assessment of the author, A. Bodson-Thomas agrees that Rodenbach's works are a reflection on "la fragilité de la vie humaine et . . . l'oeuvre impitoyablement destructrice du temps" (the fragility of human life . . . and the pitilessly destructive work of time). While asserting that Rodenbach discusses both the effect of death on things and its presence in the lives of men, she allows her argument to become oversimplified when explaining his characters' preoccupation with mortality as "la jouissance, toute romantique, qu'ils trouvent dans la douleur" (the entirely romantic pleasure found in suffering).[8] Indeed, Rodenbach's novel does not merely exalt the sensibilities of a self-involved artist, or romanticize the unhappiness and intense feelings of one attracted to the absoluteness of death. Rather, it suggests how the artist's disappearance into his work may be a way for him to conquer death, enabling him to change the blind, obliterative force of time into one that ensures the continuity and endurance of human creations. Stressing the interconnectedness of experiential time and art as *praxis,* the present essay will show how Rodenbach's text equates the artist's anonymity with his triumph over death. Reaffirming the medieval view of art as inseparable from life, the artist loses himself in a work defined as the collective creation of a whole people, one enabling him to enter into a transpersonal time in which there is no more death.

A useful springboard for discussing Rodenbach's meditation on time is an application of the theories promulgated by Durand in his analysis of the creative imagination, *Les Structures anthropologiques de l'imaginaire.* Based on findings derived from social and cultural anthropology, Durand's study argues that the workings of the imagination are conditioned by the threat of time and death and can be organized around the oppositional schema of diurnal and nocturnal symbols. The former, as Durand maintains, embraces images of ascension, purification, and light, of mastery over all that can be embraced in an expansive visual field. "[L]e fidèle contrepoint de la chute, des ténèbres et de la compromission animale ou charnelle" (The exact counterpoint to the fall, to darkness, to animal or carnal compromise),[9] this emphasis on sublimity and verticality affords the hero a means to extricate himself from the web of killing time. Conversely, the nocturnal realm comprises images of inhumation, liquefaction, and quiescence, softening and mitigating what before was regarded as the threat of temporal dispossession. Dreams of oceanic regression, of descent and dissipation into Mother Earth give rise to what Bachelard calls "rêveries de repos" (reveries of repose) and stand in contrast to the diurnal conqueror's climb to lofty heights. Finally, by confederating affective memory and art in their common opposition to temporal disintegration, Durand asserts that the therapeutic function he ascribes to each is to rescue man from his fear of the ephemeral and aleatory, to offer him a sense of coherency and permanence in the face of existential drift, and to testify to "his will to endure."[10]

An artist-embalmer like other fin de siècle characters, Rodenbach's hero, Joris Borluut, works not to create the new, but to restore and preserve the old, making imperishable the creations into which his ancestors had projected themselves in centuries gone by. Thanks to his painstaking architectural reconstructions, the dead city of Bruges survives, identical to its past self, "belle de sa mort parée. Telle, elle serait éternelle, non moins que les momies elles-mêmes, d'une éternité funéraire qui n'a plus rien de triste, puisque la mort y est devenue oeuvre d'art" (beautifully adorned by her death. In this way, she would be eternal, no less so than mummies themselves, eternal in a funereal way that no longer has anything sad about it, since death has become a work of art).[11] A link in the unbroken chain of all those safeguarding human artifacts against temporal despoliation, Borluut accepts the anonymity of his task, defending continuity against innovation, tradition against originality, as part of an enduring collaborative work that denies him the glory of authorship coveted by his colleague Bartholomeus—"cet orgueil de durer, de vaincre la mort et le néant" (that pride of enduring, of conquering death and nothingness) (266).

To an extent, *Le Carillonneur* elaborates on themes first developed in Rodenbach's more widely read early novel *Bruges-la-Morte* (1892). Here the setting is unchanged, as Borluut is a denizen of the same crepuscular city, a place of serene canals and requiem masses, of bells tolling the death of the hours and of its citizens, where the mist-effaced silhouettes of Beguines retreat to their cloisters like regrets that are muted and diffused into a lenitive fog. As Hugues Viane had remained in perpetual mourning for his deceased wife, he had turned his home into a mausoleum where her absence was enshrined. So, too, Borluut sanctifies a city that had survived its own passing, a "veuve de l'Histoire" (widow of history) (95), awaiting only the sculpting of its tomb. An obsession with recovering the past leads both men to preserve undisturbed the places containing it, so that Hugues's wife's wardrobe, the drapes in her empty room, the undusted mirror still holding a trace of her beloved image are all kept as they had been: "Sa chambre était toujours prête, comme pour son retour possible" (Her room was always ready as if for her possible return).[12] Borluut is also committed to changing nothing, respecting the memory of "la belle morte" (the dead beauty), not tricking out her remains with cheap, cosmetic renovations, but restoring the dignity of her old age. For each man, art is a religion practiced to keep faith, securing the departed against corruption and forgetfulness.[13] And as Hugues, for a while, had withdrawn from the world the better to rejoin his wife, Borluut makes a covenant with the past, marrying the city in order to act as its protector. Doing otherwise, he believes, would be an act of apostasy or adultery: "Sans lui, la ville serait en ruine, ou répudiée pour une ville jeune" (Without him, the city would be in ruins or rejected in favor of a young city) (95).

Yet when the widower and carillon player betray their compact with the past, they are exiled from the eternity in which they were united with their loved ones. Since they reimmerse themselves in the time of desire and sexual passion, the temple of their memories is opened up and violated. In the same way that Hugues's mistress, Jane, a cheap impersonator of the dead, had swept into his house and driven out the presence of his wife, so Borluut's infidelity, his choosing a woman over Bruges, is punished when the city is replaced with a tawdry counterfeit. Instead of bringing Bruges's history into sharper focus, Borluut sees his successors substituting a vulgar copy, not respecting the subtle nuances of aged buildings and dusty stones, but polishing and scouring, constructing with bright oak and new, pink bricks. Borluut is appalled as he watches the city he loves being turned into a small, degraded Paris, its calm and dormant life exchanged for noise and lurid colors. As in the modern capital, which Huysmans would also judge unrecognizable, Bruges's noble silence is overwhelmed by a cacophony of whistles and screeching tramways, its evocative, tortuous streets ruled out into straight and sterile thoroughfares (300).

Inasmuch as Borluut's love is professed in the language of architecture, his devotions paid to an entire city's history, it is natural that Bruges should be mapped out around its temporal landmarks. By privileging certain sites as containers of time, by establishing the tower where Joris works as a vantage point from which he enjoys positional domination over the turbulent lives led below, and by describing the extra-urban space of the sea as a negation of time, a locus of tidal obliteration, receding waters and endless dunes, Borluut assigns a different temporal meaning to each of the places that he frequents. Paradoxically, he enters the competition to replace Bavon de Vos, the former carillon player, in order to ensure that a traditional art form is not debased and vulgarized, to guarantee that the music of the bells attests to the endurance of the city's past glory. Yet at the moment of his triumph, he feels no satisfaction but only a sense of claustrophobic doom. At first, his skills are used to deny the ascendancy of time so that, when he plays traditional folk songs, "[l]es cloches séculaires rajeunirent, proclamèrent la vaillance et l'immortalité de la Flandre" (bells that were centuries old became young again, proclaiming the valor and immortality of Flanders) (10). Like Durtal, who prefers the graceful severity of medieval plainchant to the trivial strains of popular music, Borluut bridles on hearing contemporary tunes (7). Yet after his victory by public acclaim and formal investiture by the governor and aldermen, when he is given the key to the tower, he feels that a death sentence has been passed on him. "Ce fut comme s'il venait de prendre en main la clé de son tombeau" (It was as if he had taken into his hand the key to his tomb) (13).

Liberation from the periodicity of carnal appetite, a subterranean descent and burial, asphyxiation inside the darkness of the earth are likened to his subsequent disembodiment and ascent into the rarefied climate of the tower. Sublimation and purification are experienced as a foreshadowing of death, as the impression of cleansing elevation, of rising "above life," becomes the same thing as an emancipatory termination of life, with its monotonous, rhythmic desires, its material fixations and attachments to other people who are all condemned to die. "*La vie,* tant de choses tristes, méchantes, impures; *au-dessus,* c'est-à-dire un envolement, . . . un reposoir magique dans l'air, où tout le mal fondrait, mourrait comme dans une atmosphère trop pure" (Life: so many sad, cruel, and impure things; above: that-is-to-say a taking flight, . . . a magic altar in the air where all evil would melt away, where it would die in an atmosphere too pure to sustain it) (25).

In Rodenbach's pages, Borluut's initial climb up into the tower is presented as a spiritual ascesis. Becoming progressively etherealized, the carillon player rises, but fears casting off the flesh, since rebirth to the light at the summit entails a preliminary death to the body of darkness. As Durand affirms: "L'ascension constitue donc bien le 'voyage en soi,' le 'voyage imaginaire le plus réel de tous'" (Indeed, ascension constitutes the "journey into the self," the "imaginary journey which is the most real of all").[14] A psychic journey fraught with self-doubt, it is one whose successful completion dispels the hallucinations that issue from the shadows, changing the darkness into a final transfigured emergence into the brightening, windlashed sanctuary in the sky. Perhaps nowhere else has Rodenbach conveyed more forcefully the experience of metamorphosis and renewal than in the description of his protagonist's initiation to the heights. At first, his climb up the dark and winding staircase is experienced as a dizzying penetration into the depths of the earth, through a petrified landscape of coal bordering on an underground lake or sea. The sense of directional inversion is registered as a confusion of high and low, anticipating the imminent sensation of ascensional vertigo, the fascinated horror of falling into the sky, of being sucked upward into *"le gouffre d'en haut"* (the abyss above) (28). Yet before he reaches the platform, Borluut pauses at the edge of the subterranean water, a reservoir of the unhappiness and strife that he is leaving behind him.

Bachelard has described Rodenbach as a poet of water, calling his characterization of Bruges an "ophélisation d'une ville entière" (the ophelization of an entire city).[15] Here the unfathomable black lake is a point of transit into another world, and signals Borluut's attainment of a new awareness of self. Even later, after he has grown accustomed to his ascent into the tower, his exposure to the wind at the top is likened to an immersion, to searing ablutions of air that leave him "rafraîchi, ventilé par cette large brise qui venait des plages du ciel" (refreshed, aerated by that ample breeze that came from the beaches of the sky) (92). Blowing over the waters of misery, the wind rises, carrying on its currents the complaints and cries of those below, sounds of suffering that are condensed, attenuated, and eased as they begin to dissolve, "à se transmuer de douleur en mélancolie et de larmes en pluie" (turning pain into melancholy and tears into rain) (29). It is this underground sea of grief that Borluut abandons as he climbs the staircase out of the world, "échelle dressée contre le temps et la mort" (a ladder leading out of the realm of time and death).[16] This is the ocean containing what Bachelard calls the water of regret, a clepsydra measuring out the inexhaustibility of lachrymal time, "le temps [qui] tombe goutte à goutte des horloges naturelles" (time that falls away drop by drop from natural clocks).[17]

Worn away by centuries of bellringers' patient footsteps, the stairs themselves have begun to turn to dust and sand, "sablier de l'Eternité" (hourglass of eternity) forever tolling the end of time (27). The higher Borluut goes, the freer he feels of the weight of everyday cares, purged of the night he has taken into himself. His disorientation inside the vertical labyrinth of the tower yields to a sense of reenergized confidence and directional certainty. Cast off are the darkness and its phantasmagoria. The obscene touch of a bat with its "ailes de velours mou" (wings of soft velvet) (27), a shadow suddenly metamorphosed into "une bête accroupie et qui va s'élancer" (an animal that is crouching and ready to spring) (26), are the theriomorphic images of viscosity and pullulating motion that had provoked Borluut's revulsion in the face of temporal instability.[18] The impression of a heavy descent through the serpentine coils of a stairwell, past walls like shrouds, down to the bottomless water at its base convey "l'attitude angoissée de l'homme devant la mort" (man's anguished attitude in the presence of death).[19] Yet this horror soon gives way to a feeling of luminous buoyancy, of an ascent into the ether, as light air fills his lungs and turns his climb into flight. Standing at the top before the keyboard, Borluut is absolved of his past and washed clean by the gusts, delivered, reborn, "libre et nu dans l'air salubre du haut lieu" (free and naked in the salubrious air of the high place) (31).

Visually dominating the city below, Borluut later observes the shrunken futility of the lives of the people to whom he feels artistically and positionally superior. Loving Bruges, but not its people, the carillon player takes in the whole of the city as if it were an unfinished canvas awaiting him to cover it with beauty. Borluut's professional grandiosity is reinforced and spatialized by his living in the sky, and leads him to despise what is small and far away. Repressed by being consigned to the forgotten plane of the quotidian, his problems seem fugitive and unimportant. "Qu'est-ce que les mécomptes d'amour, les caprices d'une femme, les chagrins que tout à l'heure encore il traînait avec lui, en montant dans la tour? 'Tout cela,' se dit-il, 'ne vaut pas la peine'" (What are the disappointments of love, the volatility of a woman, the sorrows that he was just now dragging behind him while climbing into the tower? "None of that," he said to himself, "is worth the trouble") (96). High above the city Borluut practices what Bachelard calls "la contemplation monarchique" (monarchic contemplation),[20] regarding what lies beneath him with proprietary disdain. The view from high above, writes Bachelard, "donne le sens d'une soudaine maîtrise de l'univers" (gives the sense of a sudden mastery of the universe).[21] From this perspective, everything appears inconsequential, miniaturized and petty, causing Borluut to turn into a giant, growing tall from pride, embracing everything, touched by nothing. "Il se vit grand, dominant la ville, comme si la tour était son juste socle" (He saw himself as great, dominating the city, as if the tower rightly served as his pedestal) (96). Yet this sense of elevation proves as illusory as his perceived immunity to the ravages of time. And so, when he comes down from his haven in the clouds, he is dazed at first and lost for words, no wiser from having tried to rise above death but only clumsier as a consequence of having forgotten how to live.

Before, on his way up into the tower, Borluut had passed the silent dormitories of the bells, ageless virgins robed in bronze. An artist familiarizing himself with his medium, he had visited them all, noting the date they had been cast, personalizing them by assigning each a name and history. He anatomizes the tower as if it were a vast and living organism with its muscles and nerves exposed, likening "la cloche du Triomphe" (the triumph bell) to its heart, "grand coeur rouge, marqua[nt] toutes les pulsations du temps dans les rouages de la tour" (a great, red heart marking the heartbeat of time in the wheel works of the tower) (4). It is significant that in Borluut's image of the tower, the vitality of the bells corresponds to the morbidity of time, the regular pulse of the tower expressing "la mélancolie de l'heure qui meurt" (the melancholy of the dying hour) (5). An indestructible pulse measuring out the moments that it kills, the bell is like the Heraclitean figure of the river in being a symbol of constancy amid impermanence and flux, as it tolls eternally the fragments of human days that it condemns to pass away. Unconsciously, Borluut aspires to the bellringer's immortality, hoping to master time by altering its course. In the initial competition, after the bell chimes four o'clock, he starts to play traditional Flemish carols that return the listeners to their ancestral past. Bells that normally convoke the people to the funerals of their loved ones are used here to celebrate the citizens' survival in the music of their forefathers, music that comes "du fond du ciel et du fond des temps" (from the depths of the sky and from the depths of time) (8). Yet Borluut can neither partake of the incorruptibility of metal, nor yet enter into the timelessness of the buildings he restores, nor share in the inalterability of the folk songs he evokes. In trying to rise above life, to divest himself of flesh and shame, he brings his impurity with him up into the highest recesses of the tower and there projects it onto the bell symbolizing man's temporal servitude and subjection to mortal passions. There he reads what he had first repressed and then pictorially transposed onto the phantasmatic surface of "la cloche de la Luxure" (the bell of lust).

Adjacent to another bell is one that is also dark and engulfing, recalling the somber waters that Borluut had imagined in his earlier ascent. Its oceanic vastness induces a similar sense of vertigo, tempting him to surrender to the impulse to drown himself inside: "On avait la sensation d'être au bord d'une falaise qui plonge à pic dans la mer" (One had the sensation of standing on the edge of a cliff that drops straight down to the sea) (54). Inevitably, Borluut's feeling of lofty invulnerability invites his fall and imprisonment in the time of instinctual hunger, since indulgence in the sins of the flesh entails their immediate expiation. As Durand says, "ce schème de la chute n'est rien d'autre que le thème du temps néfaste et mortel, moralisé sous forme de punition" (this schema of the fall is nothing other than the theme of baneful, mortal time, moralized in the form of punishment).[22] The soft indistinctness of the teeming animal life that he had glimpsed before at the tower's base is now brought into clearer focus, humanized as images of sexual frolic, of couples embracing, body parts foregrounded as fantastic offerings that simultaneously ensnare: breasts like clusters of fruit, mouths like cups, hair like ropes that bind. Retracing the spiral path that Borluut had followed in climbing to his station in the sky is the dizzying round of the rutting figures on the bell, the satyrs' circular pursuit of their naked prey, a vision that weds a feeling of retrogression and purpose, of advancement and futility. It is unclear whether the bell is a psychic canvas onto which Borluut projects desires as confused as the intermingled bodies of the fornicators he examines or whether it acts as a mnemonic trigger, recalling poses of women seen in similar disarray long ago. Nonetheless, it is apparent that the scene depicted on the bell is internalized, becoming a pictorial transfer that Borluut can see each time he closes his eyes and gazes into himself. "Tout ce qui était sur la cloche," writes Rodenbach, "Borluut le sentit tout à coup sur son âme" (Borluut suddenly felt that everything that was on the bell was now on his soul) (56). Undressing his friend Van Hulle's dark-haired daughter in his imagination, Borluut feels an impulse to go down and seek her out, so that, having risen into his chamber of glass, he must then redescend into the opacity of desire, forsaking what Durand calls "la verticalité spirituelle" (spiritual verticality) in favor of "la platitude charnelle" (flatness of carnality).[23]

Described in terms of the familiar decadent figure of the appetizing devourer, Borluut's future wife, Barbe, is initially an embodiment of the fatal bell's image of the coy seductress. Metonymically objectified as the red, ripe fruit of her mouth, she is also the speaking subject from whose mouth there issues a torrent of invective, as soft lips turn into hard words that strike Borluut and sting like pebbles (91). Once he comes under her spell, the carillon player loses his sense of professional vigor and enthusiasm, becoming indifferent to his project of municipal beautification, visiting the tower only as a place of asylum in which to recover from the wounds left by his wife's outbursts of scathing temper. Borluut's love stories as related in the novel show him repeatedly betraying art for love and then, having been betrayed by love, returning, chastened, to his work for consolation. Consigned to oblivion—renounced in favor of a future of disappointed hope—are Borluut's own personal past and the crumbling history of a city awaiting its mortuary preservation. For a time, Borluut's dedication to ensuring the immortality of old art is subordinated to his interest in engendering new life, and he regards Memling's tryptich of Saint Barbe as a favorable allusion to his new bride, believing, too, that the fruitfulness of the donor's wife augurs the coming of the children through whom he may live forever. Reconstruction is abandoned in favor of reproduction, as the vanity of fatherhood is preferred to the hard demands of art. It is noteworthy that in the painting, it is the woman who is magnified, while the tower, the artist's sanctuary, is the image that is reduced. A self-demeaning medium that depicts art's superfluity, the tableau thus reflects its viewer Borluut's changing values. While exalting inspiration, it seems to humble execution, as it glorifies its subject over its own aesthetic rendering: at least, these are Borluut's views when he is in the throes of love. For the artist, woman motivates a recourse to his art, but it is also she who makes his art seem empty and irrelevant. First Barbe and then her sister, with whom Borluut has an affair, are able to reorientate his temporal perspective. No longer does his role consist of euphemizing death, assuring that old edifices are kept intact eternally. Instead, the love of woman "lui rendit l'amour de la vie" (restores his love of life), annuls his love for Bruges and leads the past to disappear (200), and therefore makes the sole eternity that Borluut truly covets into one of love perpetuated in an everlasting present.

However intense are these romances, they still prove vain and disillusioning, and he "abdiqua son misérable amour pour l'amour de la ville" (abdicated his miserable love to profess again his love for the city) (94–95). The unreliability of relationships built on sexual attraction is a point the novel stresses in another Durandian constellation of images: of the sea and moon, dissolution, instability and change. The ability of love to foster a selfish form of optimism is associated in the story with an economic project promoted by various civic leaders to change Bruges from a forgotten center of primitive Flemish art and lacework into a prosperous hub for shipping, a modern, thriving seaport city. One of Borluut's erstwhile friends and guests at Van Hulle's Monday gatherings, the lawyer Farazyn, becomes the champion of this cause, advocating that the city undergo a major maritime revitalization. Unequivocally the others state their opposition to this plan, recommending that the money be used to purchase the Memlings and van Eycks needed to complete the city's collection. Respect for Bruges's character with its quiet circumspection, its people's taciturnity and mystical discretion, would militate in favor of maintaining its present status as a place of religious art and convalescent spirituality. Yet as his curiosity is piqued by Farazyn's proposal, Borluut sets out one day to learn how Bruges was abandoned by the sea (106). Whereas in Dante's time the violent sea had required that a dike be built, what Borluut finds is a mournful desert of undulating sands. The ocean's whimsicality, its changing littoral configurations are likened to the fickleness and volatility of a woman. "La mer est variable," as Borluut comes to realize. "Elle aime des villes, et puis les quitte, va en baiser d'autres, du côté opposé de l'horizon" (The sea is changeable. She loves cities, and then leaves them, going on to embrace others on the opposite side of the horizon) (111). Through his immersion in the past, his having "compris . . . vécu l'Histoire" (understood and lived history) (111), he comes to see the fruitlessness of trying to alter nature's course, of imposing man's control and will on elemental forces, of reforming an untamed, wayward sea "comme une amante trop fantasque" (like a lover who was too flighty) (111). Like Barbe's choleric nature or Godelieve's imperturbable benevolence, the unfathomability of the ocean is beyond his comprehension. Once victimized by Barbe, his wife, he is abandoned by her sister, who breaks off their relationship and then sets off for a convent. Yet Borluut sees his powerlessness to resist the women's influence and goes back to the tower in an effort to forget. Responsive to these women, whose attentions wax and wane, he is like the tide in being drawn to a bright and shining countenance yet later learns that love must yield to passion's cold eclipse. Barbe's emotional imbalance, her sister's effulgent blonde serenity show them both as being dominated by the figure of the moon. Like the sea, which forsakes cities and then bestows its favors elsewhere, the moon, "un astre capricieux . . . soumis à la temporalité et la mort" (a changeable star . . . subject to temporality and death),[24] is dependable only in its regular disappearances and evasions. At the end, the sisters who differ so in personality and appearance decide to turn their face away from the man who once had loved them. With Godelieve's withdrawal to the convent at Dixmude and the sullen Barbe's seclusion in the house's upstairs rooms, Borluut is finally left alone, becoming despondent and suicidal, aware of his subjection to "le pouvoir astral de l'amour" (the astral power of love). "L'homme est sous l'influence de la femme comme la mer sous la lune" (As the sea is under the influence of the moon, so man is under the influence of woman) (240).

Borluut's forays into politics are foredoomed like his romances, as his hope to block adoption of the plan for Bruges-Port-de-Mer aborts when he does not allow for his fellow citizens' greed and apathy. As he had failed to fire a woman's love with his passionate devotion, so he fails to ignite a crowd with his incendiary speeches. Exiled to his solitary dream-life in the tower, he reassumes the pose of an elevated hero, protected by defensive pride against assault by life's misfortunes. Thus, the sun's glint turns the clock face into a shield against the darkness, and in his lonely, self-aggrandized state, he sees the belfry as his armor. This combative stance does not help him in coping with depression and, becoming more detached, he starts resembling the city. As he is deadened and anaesthetized by successive disappointments, his feelings pale like Bruges and become discolored by the rain. As if rehearsing his own suicide, he begins to separate from everything, is enshrouded in indifference, dissolved in humid resignation. Once relieved of all his duties for historic preservation, he finds that he has lost the will to glamorize the dead, and his efforts at transforming Bruges into a dignified necropolis are abandoned as he prepares to face the need to die himself.

In his study of the novel Paul Pelckmans has contended "que les rapports entre l'art et la mort sont loin d'être univoques" (that the relationship between art and death is far from unequivocal).[25] Yet there may be no real difference between the two conflicting themes, that of denying or disguising death and sublimating it as art. In the manner of morticians who repair a corpse's face, Borluut restores old Bruges's shell as an "escamotage de la mort" (a conjuring away of death).[26] Like Bruges, Van Hulle dies beautifully when his white soul flies away, vanishing into the snowy cliché of the swan rising up on languorous wings from the waters that imprison it. Yet while the poetic mystification and medical occultation of death are likened to the hero's task of adorning a city's remains,[27] when it comes to confronting his own death, his aesthetic stratagems prove ineffectual. Admittedly, the gentle masking of death, which for a while was the novel's main focus, gives way to the kind of macabre descriptions that figure so prominently in decadent literature. Thus, Borluut's resolve is shown wavering when he contemplates his physical death, like a man in despair who recoils from the coldness of the waters which soon will engulf him, or who shrinks in horror from the larval decay accompanying "le festin du cadavre" (the feast of the cadaver) (322). Borluut's final ascent into the tower recalls his inaugural climb to the top, reiterating the temporal theme of the fall, swarming animals and vertiginous motion. Vacillating, Borluut is described as needing to support himself with a rope, prefigurative of the suicide instrument, which here serves as a handrail or banister. Spiraling upward around the shaft of the stairwell, it resembles the coils of a snake, not tempting Borluut to return to the world as had the bell of lust's circular orgy, but beckoning him to finish his journey leading "au-dessus de la vie." The "Serpent de la Tentation" (serpent of temptation) that appears at the end is invested with multiple meanings: on the one hand, recalling the erotic designs engraved on the carillon player's soul—the snake as "figure de la libido sexuelle" (a figure of sexual libido),[28] shackling man to the time of desire—and on the other, alluding to death as renewal, "grand symbole du cycle temporel" (a great symbol of the cycle of time).[29] The ourobouros, which stands for a circle's completion, for life that issues from death, may also convey the temporal relation of artists to the works that survive them. To be sure, Rodenbach reverts to "le très vieux topos de la vie qui sort de la mort" (the very old topos of life emerging from death),[30] but does so to stress how an anonymous death assures the artist that his products will endure. Not creating, Borluut is the one who restores and who hands down traditions to others, playing music of unknown and popular origin, bringing old buildings back from the dead. Having relinquished the glory that derives from the signature apposed to the work he has authored, he forfeits the fame that redounds to an artist so that others' creations may last. As his renown and identity dissolve in the fog that envelops the landmarks he works on, in death he turns into the soul of the bells, is a presence suspected by no one.

Among the participants at Van Hulle's weekly patriotic assemblies there is a shared interest in reviving a collective, national past as a means of achieving personal immortality. Whether as a dilettante, a curio collector, like the monied antiquarian, a painter or architect like Bartholomeus or Borluut, or a city planner like Farazyn, each alleges a commitment to Bruges that may mask a more selfish objective. Like his compatriots, Farazyn dreams of Bruges's resurrection and its return to a state of affluence (103), a transfiguration accomplished, not through the modest and patient work of anonymous artists, but by means of the soulless, disruptive projects of reputable engineers. Although the approach he proposes and the ends he envisages are different from those of his friends, there is among them a common desire to rescue Bruges and return it to its fourteenth-century glory. But whereas Farazyn imagines Bruges as electrified and vibrant: "vivante, frequentée, riche" (alive, bustling, and rich) (104), the others prefer to see that it remains as it always has been: wet and dim, dignified and neglected, its surfaces not sullied by the lurid colors of modernity but covered with the respectfully drab patina of tradition. Bartholomeus, too, insists on replacing Bruges with a subjective vision of its past, completing the fresco commissioned to decorate the Hotel de Ville, not with a representational image of a scene from the city's history, but with a symbolic rendering of its eternal character, a four-panel chiaroscuro depicting swanlike nuns against a watery background, night-colored bells dissolving into the black mantles worn over the shoulders of the city's elderly women, "grandes cloches de drap balancées dans les rues" (great bells of cloth swinging in the streets) (173). Like Farazyn, Bartholomeus is concerned less with ensuring that his monument endures than he is with seeing to it that its creator's name lives in people's memories. As they attempt to deny death by contributing to the city's resurrection, it is not the past of Bruges that matters but the illustriousness of their own futures. For Borluut and Van Hulle, however, there is no desire to impose a personal vision on the city or to appropriate Bruges as the medium embodying their project to transcend time. Rather than dictating to later generations his strident and arrogant message, Borluut acts as a conduit through which the city's identity may be more faithfully relayed. He, in particular, is interested less in enforcing his dream's realization than in passing along architectural history, relating "*le rêve que les pierres font*" (the dream that is dreamed by stones) (262).

Conspicuously thematized in *Le Carillonneur* is the tendency of the characters to coalesce with their environment, a variation on the theme of resemblance in Rodenbach, which here expresses the hero's efforts at transcending identity. Thus, the narrator often describes Borluut's evaporation into his murky and opaque surroundings, at one point mentioning his combustion and dissipation into the acrid residue of his own inflammatory rhetoric, "une fumée de plus dans des fumées!" (another plume of smoke among others) (260). Similarly, as suicide requires acclimatization, Borluut turns into a precipitate of his despair, a bleached and dispirited dampness soon to be dispelled as chimes on the wind. Since identity itself is an illusory narrative construct meant to protect against time, "a facade . . . expressing a desire for unity in the face of dissolution and death,"[31] the effacement of the self may in effect mark the character's triumph over the forces of transitoriness and exhaustion. Thus, Borluut's surrender of the idea of authorship as a defense against the threat of oblivion, his acceptance of death as a dispersal into ambient namelessness, allows him to attain the immortality of works that are never signed by anyone. Indeed, with the exception of Van Hulle's antique clocks, the art encountered in the novel is itself environmental, identified with the medieval buildings inhabited by the people and the painted images with which Bartholomeus hopes to cover the city's surfaces. As aesthetic vision is universalized, its products become so widely disseminated that the artist can no longer lay claim to exclusive authorship or stand in a relationship of ownership to what he has produced. Borluut comes to understand that art produced on a grand scale is a collective creation and that, in passing into the public domain, it is consumed by all and authored by all. "C'est la foule qui construit les monuments," as he remarks, ". . . les cathédrales, les beffrois, les palais, ont été construits par la foule. Ils sont à son image et à sa ressemblance" (It is the crowd that builds monuments, . . . cathedrals, belfries, palaces have been constructed by the crowd. They are in its image and likeness) (48). For a truly national artwork to emerge, it is necessary that the people's soul "vibre tout à coup à l'unisson" (vibrate all at once in unison) (48), and that the architect consent to act as the conductor of a creative impulse that issues from everyone but himself. It is the artist's suppression of his identity, his professional self-effacement that enables him to sound at the same frequency as his public, so that death turns him into his work, as the carillon player becomes "une Ame dans les cloches" (a soul in the bells) (325).

When he enters into the bell that has measured out centuries by the hour, Borluut is killed by time so that he finally may transcend it. Similarly, the decentering of his temporal point of reference permits the accomplishment of Van Hulle's dream of synchroneity. By becoming more detached from the world of phenomena and people, he is able to move inside the timeless realm of his chronometric mania. Collecting clocks, he dismantles them to study their intricate internal mechanisms, yet becomes obsessed with the idea of their all striking the hour together. Then the bells and clocks that before had privatized experiential time, that had served to structure days around each person's unique schedule, begin to signal happenings that are meaningful for all. It is only by renouncing his temporal perspective that Van Hulle can fulfill his ideal "d'avoir *unifié l'heure*" (of having unified time) (88). What the narrator attributes to Barbe's superstitious nature, her viewing the adventitious as a magical causality, may instead indicate the start of time that is collectively significant. In a world in which coincidence has given way to simultaneity, a knell that sounds, a coffin spotted passing in the street, announcements for the celebration of masses for the dead, may mark the actual onset of the clock collector's stroke. So, too, Van Hulle's intuition of the striking of the clocks suggests the dissolution of the personal in the universal. Confirming the equation of the extinguishing of consciousness with the dying solipsist's belief in the destruction of the world, the bells toll an experience that must be undergone by everyone before their sound is muted as the chiming of eternity.

Thus, Pelckmans may be right in interpreting the novel as the morbid being sanitized into the comfortingly artistic. Still, this view is valid only if the death that has been euphemized is presented as an instance of artistic dispossession. In Rodenbach, the pessimism imputed to the decadents arises from a past profaned by the ambitions of a prideful few. Yet when vibrating "in unison" with the collective soul of Bruges, the artist lives in a time in which the clocks strike all at once. Only then the creative act becomes a noble form of suicide, the suppression of a nameless self survived by unsigned works. At the end, Borluut is scattered in the music of the bells, which ring out the same tidings as they had for countless years. No longer need he stand by as the city that he loves is thrust into a future of venality and noise. Instead, he is immortalized, diffused into ubiquity since the artist's time of death implies as well the death of time.

Notes

1. Jean Pierrot, *L'Imaginaire décadent* (Paris: Presses Universitaires de France, 1977), 63. All translations from the French taken from this and subsequent texts are by the author.
2. J.-K. Huysmans, *A rebours* (Paris: Gallimard, 1977), 360.
3. Jean Lorrain, *Monsieur de Bougrelon* (Paris: Union Générale d'Editions, 1974), 426.
4. Marcel Schwob, *Le Livre de Monelle,* Oeuvres complètes (Paris: François Bernouard, 1928), 4:69–70.
5. J.-K. Huysmans, *Là-bas,* Oeuvres complètes (Geneva: Slatkine, 1972), 12:30.
6. Gilbert Durand, *Les Structures anthropologiques de l'imaginaire* (Paris: Bordas, 1969), 470.
7. A separate study of time as it is figured in the symbolists might be suggested by a comparison of Rodenbach's text and Camille Lemonnier's last novel, *La Chanson du carillon* (1911), in which the city's history is again what assures its atemporal glory. Despite the more positive mood characterizing Lemonnier's book, both works describe what Donald Friedman calls "the fusion of late nineteenth century Bruges and an artistic vision which survives from its ancestral past" (*The Symbolist Dead City: A Landscape of Poesis* [New York: Garland, 1990], 76). Similar themes connect the two novels, as does their floral and lapidary imagery, which, in Lemonnier, indicates permanence rather than the dispossession accompanying time's passage. As Friedman writes: "the carillon is the reliquary of time in which hours are frozen in a cascade of molten gold and precious stones." As a result, the bells belong to "a realm of artifice in which all is fixed in beauty, ideal and static, its perfection superior to contingency" (Friedman, 77).
8. Anny Bodson-Thomas, *L'Esthétique de Georges Rodenbach* (Liège: H. Vaillant-Carmanne, 1942), 129, 131.
9. Durand, *Structures,* 136.
10. Ibid., 471.

11. Georges Rodenbach, *Le Carillonneur* (Bruxelles: Les Eperonniers, 1987), 96. All further references are to this edition and appear parenthetically in the text. In *Bruges-la-Morte*, the city is similarly preserved from the destructive effects of time, not because of the efforts of an artist like Joris Borluut, but because of the fact that it is immune to change—because, as Claude De Grève says, it has been fixed in "un temps resté hors de l'Histoire, où du moins l'Histoire s'est arrêtée, momifiée" (a time that has remained outside of history, where at least history has been arrested, mummified) (*Georges Rodenbach* [Brussels: Editions Labor, 1987], 57).

12. Georges Rodenbach, *Bruges-la-Morte* (Paris: Flammarion, 1978), 51.

13. Thus, Rodenbach writes of the departure of the guests at Van Hulle's gatherings: "Chacun regagna pensif sa demeure, heureux de la soirée où il communièrent ensemble, en un même amour de Bruges. Ils avaient parlé de la ville comme d'une religion" (Each returned pensively to his lodgings, happy for the evening which they had shared together in an identical love for Bruges. They had spoken of the city as of a religion) (23).

14. Durand, *Structures*, 141.

15. Gaston Bachelard, *L'Eau et les rêves: Essai sur l'imagination de la matière* (Paris: José Corti, 1942), 121. Expanding on Bachelard's remarks about *Bruges-la-Morte*, Paul Gorceix writes: "Quelle autre image que celle d'Ophélie pouvait cristalliser de manière plus suggestive la complexité des motifs, dont la substance du roman est littéralement tissée? L'eau et la mort, la sensualité et le mysticisme, la rêverie, toutes ces associations, Rodenbach les montre qui se superposent et se prolongent dans le psychisme de Hugues à travers l'image d'Ophélie" (What other image than that of Ophelia could more suggestively crystallize the complexity of themes from which the novel's substance is literally woven? Water and death, sensuality and mysticism, reverie: Rodenbach shows all these associations being superimposed and extended in Hugues's psyche through the image of Ophelia) ("*Bruges-la-Morte:* Un Roman symboliste," *L'Information Littéraire* 37 [November–December 1985]: 207–8).

16. Durand, *Structures*, 140.

17. Bachelard, *L'Eau et les rêves*, 78.

18. See Durand's first chapter on "les visages du temps" (*Structures*, 71–96).

19. Ibid., 133.

20. Gaston Bachelard, *La Terre et les rêveries de la volonté* (Paris: José Corti, 1948), 385.

21. Ibid., 380.

22. Durand, *Structures*, 125.

23. Ibid., 141.

24. Ibid., 111.

25. Paul Pelckmans, "Les Jeux du temps et de la mort: L'Episode de la mort de Van Hulle dans *Le Carillonneur* de Georges Rodenbach," *Revue des Sciences Humaines* 42, no. 165 (1977): 144–45.

26. Ibid., 144.

27. As Pelckmans notes, in the scenes describing Van Hulle's death, the character excluded from consideration is, precisely, the patient himself. "Pour l'idéologie bourgeoise, la mort est ainsi une scène vide où l'acteur principal n'a aucun rôle à jouer. Si l'on admet que toute idéologie sert, en dernière instance, à prévenir l'imprévisible, rien ne paraît plus sûr que cette suppression pure et simple de tout événement possible. Le vidage est d'ailleurs lié à une récuperation: la médicalisation qui, apportant à la lutte pour la survie l'appoint d'une technique toujours

plus complexe, la réinscrit dans le réseau production-consommation" (From the perspective of bourgeois ideology, death is an empty scene where the principal actor has no role to play. If one concedes that any ideology ultimately serves to forestall the unforeseeable, then nothing appears more certain than the pure and simple suppression of any possible event. This emptying is further linked to a recuperation, to the medicalizing process that, in bringing to the struggle for survival the contribution of increasingly complex techniques, reinscribes the process in the network of production and consumption) (136).

28. Durand, *Structures,* 74.
29. Ibid., 364.
30. Pelckmans, "Jeux du temps," 144.
31. Polly Young-Eisendrath and James A. Hall, eds., *The Book of the Self* (New York: New York University Press, 1987), 6.

Le Carillonneur: Transcendence and Symbolization

Paul Gorceix

(Translated from the French by Elaine L. Corts)
In tribute to Ida-Marie Frandon

> La Grande Place de Bruges, ordinairement déserte, traversée par de rares passants, des enfants pauvres à la dérive, un peu de prêtres ou de béguines, s'imagea soudain de groupes indécis, d'îlots noirs tachant l'étendue grise. Des rassemblements se formaient.[1]

> (The Grande Place of Bruges, usually deserted, crossed by rare passersby, some poor wandering children, a few priests or Beguines, suddenly was filled by indistinct groups, black islets spotting the gray expanse. Some were gathering together.)

THESE first portentous lines from *Le Carillonneur* do not miss their mark. From the outset, the novel falls within the realm of the elevated, since it is indeed the tableau of the Grande Place of the city that the narrator invites us to contemplate from the belfry, mirrored in the expression of the carillon player. The motif is introduced in a perspective that plunges downward, a distinctive characteristic of Flemish painting. An image of the city, seen from above, globally, indistinctly, where the contours of things and people are blurred and diluted. An unhinged vision of reality that leads into the themes at the heart of the novel: the dream of ascent into space, and a nostalgia for transcendence, represented by the experience of the carillon player Joris Borluut.

The novel appeared in February 1897—five years after *Bruges-la-Morte*. It is the story of a Bruges architect, elected carillon player of the Flemish city, which he would like to make the artistic capital and the destination of pilgrimages for all mankind. Fascinated by the sensual beauty of Barbe, the daughter of his friend, Van Hulle, an antiques dealer, but disillusioned as soon as he is married, by her violent nature, Joris has an affair with his sister-in-law, the gentle Godelieve. When their adultery is discovered, Godelieve takes refuge in the Beguine convent of Dixmude. Joris, despondent, devotes himself entirely to his ideal of restoring the city. However, Joris, the idealistic artist, champion of aesthetic values, soon comes into conflict with the Farazyn party, militant activists for the Flemish cause, who are working relentlessly to return the city to the economic prosperity it had known in the Middle Ages by reopening Bruges's access to the sea—this to the detriment of its glory as a dead city of the past. Joris, relieved of his post, misunderstood by the public, hangs himself from the huge bell of the belfry.

For Mallarmé, who was bound by a solid friendship to Rodenbach, *Le Carillonneur* is a "livre de maturité" (book of maturity), which possesses "cette grandeur définitive d'oeuvre maîtresse" (that definitive grandeur of a major work).[2] Hubert Juin, without hesitation, viewed it as Rodenbach's best book.[3] Werner Lambersy stated that the book was conceived as a kind of sequel to *Bruges-la-Morte* in his judicious formulation: "*Le Carillonneur* sort en chef-d'oeuvre abouti de la matrice de *Bruges-la-Morte*" (*Le Carillonneur* emerges as a successful masterpiece from the womb of *Bruges-la-Morte*).[4] Moreover, there is every reason to think that Rodenbach, in writing *Le Carillonneur,* wanted to answer the keen protest of the *brugeois,* shocked by the epithet of "dead" associated with their city.

Judging from the text itself, it seems to reveal nothing more than a human document that served as the material for a new psychology, set at the borderline of the peculiar, if not the pathological.

There is actually more similarity between the obsessions of Joris and those "neurotics," as Rodenbach defined the characters that emerged from the workshop of the Goncourts, "frères en Notre Mère la Névrose qui est la Madone de ce siècle" (brothers in Our Mother the Neurotic who is the Madonna of this century)[5] or with the depressive characters of the first novels of Maurice Barrès and Paul Bourget. Torn between two women, like Hugues in *Bruges-la-Morte,* Joris clearly appears to be the victim of the obsession that the city exerts over him: he is the strange prisoner of the belfry, the slave of "la cloche de Luxure" (the bell of lust) which he identifies with Barbe, when he yields to erotic visions, alone, in his "chambre de verre" (glass room).[6] As for Barbe, it is clear that Rodenbach wanted to represent in her a clinical case of neurosis—hereditary and exacerbated by the soul-searching that the reclusive life of the North favors. "Anémie et Névrose, déclin d'un sang vieux, mal du siècle, qui sévit jusqu'en ces villes reculées" (Anemia and neurosis, a deterioration of the old blood, the world weariness which held sway even in these out-of-the-way cities) (181). He could not be more explicit!

It is highly plausible that the novelist, merging the positivist premises associated with the pessimism of Schopenhauer, whose ardent disseminator he had become, wanted to suggest in *Le Carillonneur,* as he had in *Bruges-la-Morte,* the influence of a decadent city and its vistas on the condition of the soul of the individual.[7]

The repeated choice of Bruges as the setting of his novels suits a tactical procedure in regard to the reader. In effect, a broad portion of the thematic structure brought into play and skillfully integrated in *Le Carillonneur,* after the success of *Bruges-la-Morte,* was conceived according to "l'horizon d'attente" (the horizon of expectation) of the public. There was the Parisian public, fascinated by the exoticism of the North, mingled with the powerful traces of a decadence that was fashionable at the time: the ennui of the cities of the North, the mysticism of Flemish Beguinages, the grandeur and poverty of medieval architecture, "ville belle d'être morte" (a city, beautiful in its death), a refusal of life. Then, there was the local public in particular, who found its Flanders again in the name of the characters; thus the name of the hero Joris Borluut, chosen in all likelihood to recall that of Josse Vijd's wife, Elisabeth Borluut, donors of the famous painting, *L'Agneau mystique* by van Eyck, where, by the way, the couple was represented—an analogy with a finely calculated effect! It is certainly not by chance if a native reader recognizes the topography of Bruges, its monuments and high spots, its guilds, so important to Flemish art, its brotherhoods of painters and sculptors, its works of art (Memling), its habits and customs as well—such as the Procession of the Penitents of Furnes—"où la vieille Flandre s'atteste toute intacte et se continue" (where old Flanders is revealed entirely intact and continuing) (271). He finds himself confronted by the actuality of the times, concerning the two types of problems introduced into the account: one essentially local, the access to the sea at Bruges by the construction of the port of Zeebrugge, demanded by the supporters of the economic renaissance of the coast, but rejected by the defenders of complete authenticity for the city; the other, national, of a social and political nature: the full recognition of Flemish as the national language. The place reserved for the question of Flemish speaks volumes about the deep-felt reality of the problem at the end of the nineteenth century and even well beyond:

Il faut qu'en Flandre on parle flamand, non seulement parmi le peuple, mais dans les assemblées, en justice; que tous les actes, pièces officielles, jugements, noms de rue, monnaies, timbres, que tout soit flamand, puisque nous sommes en Flandre, puisque le français est le parler de France, et que la domination a cessé. (18)

(It is necessary that in Flanders we speak Flemish, not only among the people, but in the assemblies, in law; in all proceedings, official documents, names of streets, currency, stamps, so that everything might be Flemish, since we are in Flanders, since French is the speech of France, and that domination has ceased.)

Saying that, Rodenbach contrived *Le Carillonneur* so that his contemporaries could have the possibility of reading it as the story of a passion, a novel with three characters constructed according to a rigorously logical sketch. At the center, the life of Joris, followed by the narrator, with his comings and goings around two axes: the burning passion felt in turn for two women of a basically paradoxical nature, the other, his almost religious love-obsession for Bruges—the city representing the anchoring point to which Joris in turn comes back with each disappointment in his love life.

From beginning to end, the novel is structured around this alternating movement: a burning passion is followed each time by the return to his love for the city. Each stage is punctuated by the clarification of the narrator always present in the story. After Joris has discovered his passion for Barbe, the narrator states: "Ainsi l'amour l'avait restitué à la vie. D'aimer Barbe, il aima moins la ville, et sa désuétude et son silence" (Thus love had restored him to life. In loving Barbe, he loved the obsolete and silent city less) (77). Then, while Joris, realizing the illusion to which he has yielded, returns to his dream, the narrator points out: "Il abdiqua son misérable amour pour l'amour de la ville. Celui-ci l'envahit de nouveau, le ressaisit tout entier . . ." (He gave up his wretched love for his love of the city. This city invaded him again, entirely took possession of him . . .) (95). The movement is diametrically opposite when Joris realizes that it is Godelieve that he loves: "Qu'est-ce que cet amour pour la Ville, sinon une passion factice et glacée, dont il leurra sa solitude?" (What is this love for the city, other than an artificial and icy passion, to delude his solitude?) (195), and he sees that by turning his back on life "toute simple et si belle" (so simple and so beautiful), he is turning to death. In the last movement, after Godelieve has taken refuge in the Beguinage, Joris "s'en retourna à l'amour de la ville. Cet amour-ci, du moins, ne trompait point et ne faisait pas souffrir" (returned to his love of the city. This love, at least, did not deceive and did not cause pain) (241).

Thus the novel can be read as the diagram of the passion of Joris, insofar as the psychological evolution of the hero is retraced in these oscillations, which follow one upon the other around two poles: love for the woman—Barbe, embodying the physical and sensual side of passion; Godelieve, its more spiritualized side—and love of the city. The latter represents, strictly speaking, the fourth character in the novel, the realm of art and aesthetics, his last refuge, at least until the time when it ceases to be faithful to him by becoming the victim of the new builders. This is the last phase, the isolation of Joris in "l'inaliénable asile" (the inalienable sanctuary) (303) of the belfry where:

> Borluut la voyait tout à fait morte. Il ne voulut plus redescendre. Il l'aima davantage et sans fin. Ce fut désormais pour lui comme une frénésie, comme une dernière volupté. De monter sans cesse au-dessus de la vie, il se mit à jouir de la mort. (306)

> (Borluut saw it [the city] as being quite dead. He no longer wanted to descend again. He loved it more and forever. From then on, it was like a frenzy for him, like the last sensual delight. To climb continually above life, he started to enjoy death.)

As obvious as it is, this first reading does not completely satisfy us, since it is difficult not to notice that a "courant souterrain" (underground current) runs beneath the structure of this plot. In the eyes of Rodenbach, it is characteristic of all great works, "celles qui captivent à la fois le public ignorant et les artistes" (those which captivate simultaneously the ignorant public and the artists).[8] Actually *Le Carillonneur* possesses, well beyond its anecdotal nature, an invisible side that Mallarmé notes about *Bruges-la-Morte* where: "l'histoire humaine . . . s'évapore" (human history . . . evaporates into thin air), and where the novel, which was considered at that time to be an inferior artistic form, becomes a poem.[9] There is hardly any doubt that Rodenbach wanted to repeat in *Le Carillonneur* his performance in *Bruges-la-Morte* to "faire aboutir . . . le roman au poème" (have the novel, in the end, . . . become a poem).[10] On taking a closer look, the aesthetic design set up in this novel by the author does not deal exclusively with the study of a psyche, or even the neurosis of an individual, however apparent might be the influence of the ideology of an era marked by the themes of Schopenhauer, Taine, and Eduard von Hartmann, at that time very much in vogue. The evocation of the "états d'âme" (states of mind) of Joris, within the background of the city of Bruges, does not constitute the fundamental center of interest of the novel. To the external coherence of the story, the novelist substituted another, entirely interior, which rests on the weaving of a sort of web, composed of impressions, signs, correspondences, and analogies, so dense that it structures the story, and is barely concealed in the plot. The objective is to represent through the psychological situation of Joris a nostalgia for elevation and a leap beyond self, a desire for transcendence. In *Le Carillonneur,* we are faced with the symbolization of the existential theme of height, whose essential importance to the psyche of the individual Gaston Bachelard has shown.[11]

The repetition of the tiny phrase, in italics, which returns no less than fifteen times in the course of the story, "*au-dessus de la vie*" (above life), provides the proof that the real semantic level of the story lies here. A leitmotif that the narrator has literally made into an incantation that articulates the novel like a poem. Its subject: man's ascent, his nostalgia for infinite space—and the inevitable failure.

Thus, Rodenbach's discovery, his brilliant find, is to have combined the image-symbol of the carillon player, inseparable from his belfry, emblematic monument of Flanders, with the simultaneously existential and poetic theme of the dream of elevation above material life. This theme is indissolubly bound to a mystical experience that represents one of the fundamental components of the speculative and pictorial Flemish identity.

Moreover, in reading the beginning of the novel, we see that the narrator makes a point of defining very explicitly his subject, the axis around which the entire story revolves:

Tout en approchant de la tour, il songeait: s'en aller *au-dessus de la vie!* N'était-ce pas ce qu'il pourrait faire à présent, ce qu'il ferait dès aujourd'hui en montant là-haut? Confusément, il avait rêvé depuis longtemps cette vie de vigie, cette solitaire ivresse de gardien de phare, depuis le temps où il allait voir dans la tour le vieux Bavon De Vos. Aussi est-ce pour cela, au fond, qu'il eut tant de hâte à se présenter au concours de carillonneurs. Il se l'avouait maintenant à lui-même: ce ne fût pas uniquement par délicatesse d'art, par tendresse pour la ville et afin d'empêcher que sa beauté de silence et de déréliction fût contaminée par une musique sacrilège. *Il avait entrevu aussi, et tout de suite, l'enchantement de posséder, pour ainsi dire à soi, le haut beffroi, d'y pouvoir ascensionner à sa guise, dominer la vie et les hommes, vivre comme au seuil de l'Infini.* (24–25)[12]

(In approaching the tower, he mused: to go *above life!* Wasn't it what he could do now, what he would do from today on, when he climbed up there? In a confused way, he had dreamed for a long time of this life as a lookout, this solitary intoxication of the lighthouse keeper, ever since the time when he had gone to see the old Bavon de Vos in the tower. Also, wasn't it why, basically, he was so eager to enter the competition of the carillon players. He admitted to himself: it was not solely from artistic sensitivity, from affection for the city, and in order to prevent the beauty of its silence and its renunciation from being contaminated by a musical sacrilege. He had also glimpsed, and right away, the enchantment of possessing, so to speak, for oneself, the high belfry, to be able to ascend it as he wished, to dominate life and mankind, to live as if at the threshold of infinity.)

In this excerpt, the dream of height is represented by images, allegorical insofar as they translate, in an immediate way and without any ambiguity, the state of elevation distinctive to the life of the carillon player: "vie de vigie," "ivresse solitaire du gardien de phare." Thus, this height, initially simply physical and material, before long becomes the metaphor for moral elevation, the sign of a surpassing of the things in life that are "tristes, méchantes, impures" (sad, malicious, impure) (25)—a sublimation become allegorical in its turn, with images no less explicit, such as "envolement" (spiritual flight), "trépied" (tripod), "reposoir magique" (magical altar of repose), and the like. Furthermore, the dream of ascent ends quite naturally in a description of a flight of birds in the clouds:

> il allait vivre comme les oiseaux, si loin de la ville et des hommes, de plain-pied avec les nuées . . . (25)
>
> (he was going to live like the birds, so far from the city of men, on the same plain as the dense clouds . . .)

Nonetheless, the meaning of the allegory, initially clear and univocal, becomes complicated and cloudy when the carillon player climbs to the belfry for the first time: "tout redevint ténébreux, muet" (everything became dark and silent again) (25). The ascent, then, proves to be a dive submerging him at the bottom of a "puits" (well) (26). The metaphorical use of stagnant water is substituted for that of air, the obscurity for brilliant light, the depth for the height:

> Il lui sembla plutôt qu'il descendait, qu'il cheminait au long d'un escalier souterrain, dans une mine profonde, très loin du jour, parmi des

paysages immobiles de houille et qu'il allait aboutir à une eau . . . (26–27)

(Instead, he imagined that he descended, that he made his way along an underground stairway in a deep mine, very far from daylight, amid motionless landscapes of coal and that he was going to end up in water . . .)

The climb toward the top of the belfry, implicit ascent toward the sky and the light, turns into its opposite, becoming an underground journey through the darkness—a lengthy and arduous descent, "l'escalier de pierre tournait en courbes brèves, tortueux" (the stone stairway turned in short, winding curves)—interspersed with standstills in the darkness that suggest the crossing of "salles secrètes" (secret rooms) and the evocation of "cachots" (dungeons), of "limbes" (limbos). Much later, moreover, when Joris would embark on the same ascent with Godelieve, the journey would be long, across "salles vides" (empty rooms), and "greniers du silence" (silent attics) (203), interrupted by halts in the gloomy darkness, resembling a dive more than a climb. Joris no longer knew in which direction he was walking, "si c'était en avant ou à reculons, s'il montait ou s'il descendait" (if he was going forward or going backward, if he was going up or if he was going down) (26). The climb and the descent, the summit and the abyss, the top and the bottom, blend together:

Une fièvre de monter l'avait saisi. . . . On parle souvent de l'attirance du gouffre. Il y a aussi *le gouffre d'en haut* . . . (28)[13]

(A feverish urge to climb had seized him. . . . We often speak of the attraction of the abyss. There is also the abyss above . . .)

It is more than a little significant that Rodenbach portrayed the first ascent of Joris to the belfry by a descent into the abyss and its ending in water—since this water which he conjures, seeping through the entrails of the earth, through the geological formations from time immemorial, is no other than womb water, out of which all life comes and to which it returns, according to the neptunist theory. Actually, this ascent-descent into the darkness plays a portentous role: it anticipates the death of Joris—the indications of it are obvious: "suaires" (shrouds), "enfoncement dans d'opaques ténèbres" (a sinking into the opaque gloom), "éboulement d'on ne sait quoi dans le sablier de l'Eternité" (crumbling of who knows what into the hourglass of eternity), and so on. A death that will be evoked in an explicit manner at the time of the climb of Joris and Godelieve to the belfry:

> Ce fut tout de suite un grand émoi pour Godelieve, dans ces opaques ténèbres, cette fraîcheur de crypte. *Il lui sembla qu'ils partaient mourir à deux.* (203)[14]

> (Right away, Godelieve was quite disturbed by these opaque shadows, this cryptlike chilliness. It appeared to her that they both had set off to die.)

It certainly seems that Rodenbach wanted to suggest to the reader that he is describing a genuine initiatory journey for Joris. It is a journey strewn with traps, an analogy with the temptations and trials that this man will have to undergo during his earthly existence—the failure of his unfortunate marriage, the ruin of his ephemeral happiness with Godelieve, and the failure of his undertaking to rehabilitate medieval Bruges.

His itinerary through the gloomy labyrinth of the tower seems like the symbol of his life, the analogy of his quest for the heights, inseparable from his final submergence. The thoughts that the narrator attributes to him at the time of the climb with Godelieve provide the formal proof:

> Ma vie a été comme l'ascension noire que nous venons de faire; mais qui toujours s'acheva dans de la lumière. C'est la tour qui m'a sauvé. (205)

> (My life [confides Joris to Godelieve] has been like the gloomy ascent that we have just made; yet which has always ended in the light. It is the tower that has saved me.)

Indeed, this is about the access of Joris to the light, the light of ultimate revelation. The ascent of the tower is the symbol of this long initiation, subordinated to the renunciation of earthly things. Significant in this sense is this passage:

> Borluut avançait, joyeux de la lutte, comme si le vent . . . défaisant ses vêtements, voulait le déshabiller de la vie et le porter libre et nu dans l'air salubre du haut lieu . . . (31)

> (Borluut advanced, delighted with the struggle, as if the wind . . . undoing his clothes, wanted to undress him of life and bear him free and naked into the salubrious air of this high spot . . .)

Based on a detachment from matter and a renunciation of earthly goods, the eminently mystical character of this initiation cannot be put in more explicit terms. As Borluut moves further and further away from Barbe, he meditates:

> *Au-dessus* de la vie! Oui, vraiment! Quelle importance avait à présent sa maison. . . . Tout cela était mesquin et vain. *Il se vida peu à peu de ses souvenirs. Tout le bagage humain qui entravait son ascension.* (92)[15]

(Above life! Yes, truly! What did his home matter now? All that was odious and futile. Little by little, he emptied himself of his memories, all the human baggage that hindered his ascent.)

It cannot be ruled out that Rodenbach drew many of his metaphors from occult sources. Swept along by the revival of interest in esoteric speculation, which had emerged in the last third of the nineteenth century, the occult opened a veritable mine of poetic images to the imagination. Baudelaire, Nerval, and Villiers de L'Isle-Adam had shown the way. Actually, however, the novelist read Novalis, in particular *Die Lehrlinge zu Sais* in the very suggestive translation by his compatriot from Ghent, Maeterlinck, published in 1895. The author of *Heinrich von Ofterdingen* is definitely the poet who best forecast the use of esoteric symbolism by the representatives of the generation of 1880.

The myth of the universal "analogy," whereby the different signs of nature are linked together in a "magnetic chain," from the animate to the inanimate, furnished the ideological basis for the exuberant system of metaphors that unfolds in *Le Carillonneur*.

Once nature is no more than a vast symbol, all exchanges and all transfers, all "correspondences" become possible, a principle that Rodenbach states quite a few times in the course of the story:

> . . . est-ce que les choses ne s'appellent pas? Il y a des analogies mystérieuses. Un rythme conduit l'Univers. (127)

(. . . don't things beckon each other? There are mysterious analogies. A rhythm drives the universe.)

Or else, speaking of the pictorial genius of Bartholomeus, the fervent painter of Flemish art, he gives this explanation:

> Son génie paraissait compliqué. C'est qu'il était près de l'Infini. Il trouvait naturellement les analogies mystiques, les rapports éternels des choses. (173)

(If his genius seemed complicated, it was because he was close to infinity. He naturally found mystical analogies, the eternal relationships of things.)

With this, Rodenbach gives us the key that opens the metaphorical system very characteristic of his writing—a reservoir of analogical images that he intertwines into the account, taking care to anchor them in the psyche of his hero, whom he portrays as a man prone to duplicate each impression perceived with an inner image. Isn't this the very principle of Rodenbach's poetic writing—to go beyond thought? Within the framework of the novel, it was a true discovery. The story of the carillon player, with a quite ordinary beginning—a man, when all is said and done, divided between his love and his professional passion—takes a frankly uncanny turn, which comes close in form to a kind of internalized fantasy.

We will only take one example of this exuberant system of metaphors, that of the bell, which becomes the object of a genuine process of symbolization. Initially a simple instrument which is specific to a carillon player, the bell becomes the direct and active agent of his ruin within a subtle interplay of poetic equations. These are based in the imagination of Joris, whose disturbed state the narrator makes a point of stressing by his stay in the belfry, "*au-dessus de la vie*"—"Joris Borluut commençait à ne plus voir clair en lui-même. . . . Il se sentait à la dérive. Sa tête charriait des nuages" (Joris Borluut began no longer to know his inner self. . . . He felt he was adrift. His head was full of clouds) (58). The bell ceased to be simply an object to use in conjuring, by association, different realities. A curious phenomenon of reverberation generates analogies very remote in appearance, but which resonate more or less directly with the states of his mind.

In this inner confusion, the bell initially evokes the abyss for him:

On en regardait l'intérieur comme un abîme. On avait la sensation d'être au bord d'une falaise qui plonge à pic dans la mer. . . . Le regard n'en apercevait pas le fond. (54)

(He looked into its interior as if it were an abyss. He had the sensation of being on the edge of a cliff that plummeted straight down into the sea. . . . He could not glimpse the bottom.)

Already at work at the beginning of the story, the imagination of the neurotic subject will create, in the end, more than a simple vertigo, the idea of a fall and, by association, that of suicide:

La cloche auguste qui sonne l'heure, s'offrait . . . immense, ténébreuse, muet abîme qui l'absorberait tout. (324)

(The majestic bell which sounded the hour, offered itself, . . . immense, gloomy, a silent abyss that entirely absorbed him.)

The sensation of vertigo, purely physical to begin with, transforms into a psychological vertigo, highly erotic, after the discovery by Joris of the bell that he would call "la cloche de Luxure." We have to cite the passage almost in its entirety. A turning point in the novel, insofar as the orgiastic scenes that Joris sees on the "robe de bronze" (bronze dress) of the bell are going to play a decisive role in his choice and in his life:

Le bronze était une folle orgie, une kermesse ivre et luxurieuse, des satyres et des femmes nues tournoyant autour de la cloche qui, ronde, activait leur mouvement de sarabande . . .
Par intervalles, des couples avaient culbuté; ils s'entassaient, corps contre corps, bouche à bouche, toute la chair mêlée, dans la fureur du désir. Le bronze creusait, accusait les détails. . . . Vigne du péché, aux fougueux caprices, qui se nouait, s'élançait, retombait aux parois—et les seins pillés comme des grappes!
. . . le Sexe partout triomphait, hurlant et cynique. (55)

(The bronze was a wild orgy, a drunken and lascivious festival, satyrs and naked women twirled around the bell, which, circular, put their sarabande into motion . . .
At intervals, the couples had turned head over heels; they were piled up, bodies hugging bodies, lips pressed to lips, all their flesh intertwined in the fury of desire. The bronze accentuated the details. A vineyard of sin, where ardent fancies, once formed, soared upward, fell again onto the surface—and the breasts ravaged like clusters of grapes!
. . . Howling, cynical sex triumphed everywhere.)

For Joris, who was under the influence of these fascinating and erotic visions to the point of becoming their slave, the image of these naked women was substituted for the image of Barbe. A transference that the narrator has taken pains to prepare in presenting Barbe as the picture of the classic Spanish woman, sensual and lascivious, all the more desirable for Joris since he is a man of the North.

Barbe semblait l'étrangère; oui! mais quel arome et quelle promesse de voluptés montait d'elle! . . . Il ne savait plus maintenant où son coeur en était. . . . C'est depuis le jour où il avait vu la cloche de

Luxure . . . il s'était mis à évoquer Barbe, il avait regardé sous la cloche comme s'il regardait sous sa robe. (61)

(Barbe appeared to be a foreigner; yes! what a fragrance and what promise of voluptuous desire drifted from her! . . . Now, he no longer knew where his heart was. . . . Ever since the day he had seen the bell of lust . . . he had begun to evoke Barbe, he had looked up under the bell as if he had looked up her dress.)

The fantasy would not cease to obsess the carillon player. It would prove to be the agent of his ruin, whose premises are set down from the start of the story by the narrator, who from the beginning to the end retains a steadfastly authorial position.

From then on, the obscene bell is the object of a systematically orchestrated process of moralization, elaborating on the foundation of Catholic ethics, which Rodenbach exploits in this novel. It was very timely as a motif, since it met the expectations of a readership that he knew to be receptive to this vision of the world:

Barbe . . . était la cloche de Luxure; tous les péchés couvraient sa robe; et, en dessous, il voyait son corps nu; il imaginait cette peau de soleil qu'elle devait avoir, elle aussi comme étrangère avec son hérédité de l'Espagne . . . (57)

(Barbe . . . was the bell of lust; every sin covered her dress; and underneath, he saw her naked body; he imagined this bronzed skin that she must also have had, since she was a foreigner, with her Spanish heritage . . .)

The carnal attraction which Barbe exerts over Joris, associated with the Christian dogma of sin, is all the more potent since it is superimposed on the chastity of Godelieve in the imagination of Joris—"ce nom dont *God,* c'est-à-dire Dieu, est la racine" (this name, whose root is God, that is to say Dieu) (275):

C'était le type primitif et intact de la Flandre. Puberté blonde comme les Vierges qu'on voit dans les Van Eycks et les Memlings. Des cheveux de miel; et qui, déroulés, ondulent en frissons calmes. Le front est ogival, monte en arc cintré, paroi d'église, muraille lisse et nue, où les yeux plaquent leur deux vitraux monochromes. (60)

(She was the primitive and flawless example, typical of Flanders. Blond puberty like the virgins we see in the van Eycks and the Memlings. Honey-colored hair; and, when unwound, it undulated, rippling softly. The ogival forehead rose into a vaulted arch, the side of a church, a smooth and bare wall, where the eyes set their two monochrome stained-glass windows.)

This evocation of Godelieve by way of a mirror image of the painted virgins of Flemish primitives is the source for a type of metaphor connotative of the Christian ethic.[16]

The counterpoint to Barbe, Godelieve is associated by Joris with "la cloche noire d'une robe de béguine, qui a fait ses voeux" (the black bell of the dress of a Beguine, who has taken her vows) (57). Or else, she embodies "une clochette" (a little bell) with its "chanson blanche . . . musique d'éclaircie et d'embellie" (virgin-white song . . . the music of a brightening sky and a change in the weather) (165). When Joris plays the carillon, the image of Godelieve becomes essential to him just like "le vol blanc d'une clochette frêle" (the pure-white flight of a fragile little bell) or like the "palpitation argentine d'une venue de colombe qui annonce le salut et l'arc-en-ciel" (silvery quivering of the coming of a dove who heralds salvation and the rainbow) (163). Rodenbach employs many images commonly linked to notions of lightness, immateriality, weightlessness—and thus of spiritual elevation. He is not afraid to exploit clichés: that of whiteness—emblematic color of virginity in Christian symbolism, opposed to red, associated with erotic drives: "Sa bouche [Barbe's] trop rouge lui faisait trouver fades, par moments, les lèvres roses de Godelieve" (Her overly red lips at times made him find the pink lips of Godelieve dull) (60). Barbe's mouth "rouge comme un piment" (red like a pimento) literally becomes an obsession for Joris. It truly fulfills the function of a leitmotif in the story.

With this, we are faced with one of those antitheses which is part of the system of oppositions that compose the novel. Rodenbach has constructed an equation of elementary simplicity, all the more credible for the reader since he bases it on the troubled psyche of Joris. Barbe is the obscene bell "en bronze, l'idéal de Rubens, l'idéal de Jordaens" (in bronze, the ideal of Rubens, the ideal of Jordaens) (56). Barbe, the incarnation of Antwerp, is then the foreigner, the Spanish woman, sin, evil. As for Godelieve, she is the little bell that symbolizes "les virginales imaginations mystiques des artistes de Bruges" (the virginal and mystical imagination of the artists of Bruges) (56). Godelieve, associated with the familiar, mystical, and chaste Flanders, is the emblem of purity and innocence, that is to say, of goodness.

Analogy of the breathtaking abyss, incarnation of sensual passion and transgression, the bell, initially emblematic of the sacred, becomes the active instrument of death. It will be the tomb of Joris. Thus, a remarkable symmetry is arranged between two episodes, with the bell as the focal point where they interpenetrate, so that love and death are but one. At the beginning of the story:

> . . . il n'aimait que Barbe, tourmenté de désirs, d'une curiosité d'elle et de son amour, sans doute à cause de la cloche obscène, noire alcôve où il s'engouffrait avec elle, la possédait déjà, participait de tous les péchés représentés dans le bronze . . . (61)

> (. . . he loved only Barbe, tormented by desire, curious about her and her love, without a doubt because of the obscene bell, the dark alcove where he would be swallowed up along with her. He possessed her already, participating in all the sins portrayed on the bronze . . .)

In the end:

> . . . il choisirait une des vastes cloches. . . . C'est là qu'il fixerait la corde, très courte; ainsi il disparaîtrait tout entier dans le gouffre obscur, où personne ne le découvrirait durant longtemps, ni jamais peut-être. Joie de finir au fond d'une de ces cloches qu'il aima tant! (323)

> (. . . he would choose one of the huge bells. . . . There, he would attach the rope, very short, so he would disappear completely into the dark abyss, where no one would discover him for a long time, maybe never. The joy of dying at the bottom of one of these bells, which he once loved so much!)

From an object, an instrument, a material specific for the post of a carillon player, the bell metamorphosed into a bicephalous symbol. On the one hand, generating sexual fantasies and immorality, on the other, a genuine mark of purity and moral elevation. From the simple emblem that it was at the outset, the bell has become a participant that plays a decisive role in Joris's experience. The story, realistic at the beginning, is little by little transformed into a fantastic short story, a kind of tale that progresses on the dual fronts of reality and dream, where Eros and Thanatos, as Georges Bataille would say, vie with each other in a merciless struggle in which Joris will succumb.

In order to realize this mutation, it was necessary that an unrestrained process of symbolization be brought into play. It was as if Rodenbach had remembered the cardinal exhortation that Novalis, a symbolist before his time, had addressed to poets: "Apprenez à manier la baguette magique de l'analogie!" (Learn to manipulate the magic wand of analogy!).[17] In this passage, taken from an essay on Rodin, Rodenbach has analogy serve as one of the axes around which the problem of poetic writing revolves:

> Le poète, lui, découvre les rapports mystérieux des idées, les analogies dans les images et il les exprime par le rythme. Ce rythme est le même dans tout l'Univers.[18]

(It is the poet who discovers the mysterious relationships in ideas, the analogies in images, and he expresses them by rhythm. This rhythm is the same in the entire universe.)

The myth or rather the magic of analogy represents quite well the focus of numerous exchanges, correspondences, and reflections, nearly inexhaustible for analysis, which form the very substance of *Le Carillonneur*. From the beginning to the end, we have an endless play of reflections and echoes of "la morte" in the imagery of Bruges. It is a gold mine of reflections "à ciel ouvert" (in the open air), as Bosquet de Thoran has so skillfully described it.[19] After Novalis in Germany, after Nerval, after the evocative sorcery of Baudelaire and the alchemy of the word of Rimbaud, after the *Serres chaudes* of Maeterlinck, we should certainly recognize, sooner or later, the authenticity of the symbolism that nourishes the work of Georges Rodenbach. Having said this, it would not be an exaggeration to propose that the novelist wanted to set down in *Le Carillonneur* the account of a kind of *mal du siècle,* bordering on the mystical, and the documentation of a certain need for elevation, driven to a crisis by an invasive materialism, proceeding from the beginning of the nineteenth century to its end. In the character of Joris, his mouthpiece, hasn't he sketched out, in the final analysis, the destiny of the artist who translates in a symbolic and esoteric way the ideal of the poet, which may be but immaterial?

Notes

1. For all quotations, we refer to Georges Rodenbach, *Le Carillonneur* (Brussels: Les Eperonniers, 1987). Preface by Werner Lambersy.
2. Letter from Mallarmé to Rodenbach, not dated in the original (February–March 1897), in François Ruchon, *L'Amitié de Stéphane Mallarmé et de Georges Rodenbach,* Lettres et textes inédits 1887–98 (Geneva: Pierre Cailler, 1949), 104.
3. Hubert Juin, "Lecture de Georges Rodenbach," in *Écrivains de l'avant-siècle* (Paris: Editions Seghers, 1972).
4. Werner Lambersy, preface to *Le Carillonneur.*
5. Georges Rodenbach, *L'Elite* (Paris: E. Fasquelle, 1899), 35–36.
6. The eroticism, quite evident in the work, would alone be worth special study.

7. Concerning the influence of Schopenhauer on the generation of Belgian symbolists, see especially Christian Berg, "Le Lorgnon de Schopenhauer: Les Symbolistes belges et les imposteurs du réel," *Cahiers de l'Association Internationale des Etudes Françaises* no. 34 (May 1982): 119–35.

8. This is what Rodenbach stresses about Ibsen in *L'Elite*, "Stéphane Mallarmé," 48.

9. J. Dubois, "Le Roman symboliste," in *Histoire littéraire de la France, 1848-1913* (Paris: Editions Sociales, 1977), 5:452–58.

10. Letter from Mallarmé to Rodenbach, June 28, 1892, *L'Amitié de Stéphane Mallarmé et de Georges Rodenbach,* 6. I have indicated the passage from prose to the poetic form for the novel *Bruges-la-Morte* in my study, "*Bruges-la-Morte:* Un Roman symboliste," *L'Information Littéraire* no. 5 (November–December 1985). In this article, I insisted as well on the importance of the analogy that literally structures the novel.

11. Gaston Bachelard, *L'Air et les songes* (Paris: Corti, 1944).

12. The second emphasis is mine.

13. Rodenbach would take up again in the course of the story the ambiguity of the image, which is simultaneously one of ascent and one of fall: "Oui! un vertige chaque fois le prenait, un désir de perdre pied, de s'élancer, mais pas vers la terre, vers le gouffre, aux spirales de clochers et de toitures, que la ville approfondissait en dessous. C'est *le gouffre d'en haut* dont il se sentait l'attirance" (Yes! He became dizzy every time, a desire to lose his footing, to soar, but not toward the earth, toward the abyss with the spirals of its steeples and its roofs. He wished that the city become a deep chasm below. He was drawn to the abyss above) (93).

14. The emphasis is mine.

15. The emphasis is mine.

16. Regarding the images and symbols that Rodenbach borrows from Catholicism, see Ulrich Prill and Reinhard Kiefer, "Georges Rodenbach: *Bruges-la-Morte.* Die Moralisierte Décadence?" in *Literatur im französischsprachigen Belgien,* ed. Hans Felten and Hans-Joachim Lope (Frankfurt: Peter Lang, 1990), 11–17. In my opinion, Rodenbach's borrowing from Catholicism goes far beyond the level of images. It appears clear that Rodenbach constructed the story of Joris to a great extent on Christian morality, which forms part of the narrative structure. If Joris collapses, it is because he has committed the sin of adultery and has to be punished. It is quite clear that Rodenbach only plays upon Christian ideology, using it to compose his novel. It is part of the "horizon of expectation" of the reader—and Rodenbach knew it.

17. "Lernt den Zauberstab der Analogie gebrauchen," in Novalis, *Die Christenheit oder Europa* (1799), cited from the translation of this essay by Geneviève Bianquis: Novalis, *Petits écrits* (Aubier: Editions Montaigne, 1947).

18. *L'Elite,* 118.

19. Bosquet de Thoran, *Traité du reflet* (Brussels: Jacques Antoine, 1986), 83.

Rodenbach, Hellens, Lemonnier: Paradisal and Infernal Modalities of Belgian Dead City Prose

Donald Flanell Friedman

THE comparatist must not only demonstrate the vast scaffolding, the internationalism and subtle dynamics of literary themes and movements, but must also signal, within more limited contexts, certain national thematics and preoccupations that may underly the work of diverse authors sharing by chance a geographical determinism and by choice a stylistic. Such a concentrated focus may ultimately reveal the true richness, the metamorphosic unfolding of a movement across national borders. This approach is particularly necessitated in the case of the francophone literature of the Belgian turn of the century, a literature still in the process of being differentiated from the falsely encompassing linguistic matrix of France.

The last turn of the century produced the most death-haunted of literary movements, symbolism, in which a sense of modernity and artistic renewal paradoxically coexists with the lassitude of late epochs and disdainful repudiation of the banality of the modern world, with fear of the unknown, and a twilit nostalgia for the legendary, the passing, and the irrevocable past. From the distance of a century, the enduring fascination of symbolism is its morbidity and thanatopsis, its preference for states of imagined nonbeing, for states of suspension rather than motion, its emphasis of the nebulous rather than the definite and solidly permanent. Belgian symbolism clearly participates in the essence of the international movement that swept Europe at the turn of the century. In its broadest definition, symbolism is an *écriture* and a mystique unconcerned with mimetic representation of objects and events in their historical reality, but concerned with evocation of mood. Within this aura, Belgian symbolism has its own particular nuance, which infuses the individualistic creation of many writers who gave enigmatic expression to the mysterious depths of inner experience.

The key to this exploration was vouchsafed the Belgian symbolists by means of highly concrete imagery, culled from the exterior world, which becomes a transparent screen allowing access to inner states. In his well-known response to an inquiry by Jules Huret, Mallarmé had distinguished two types of symbolic usage, either to evoke an object gradually to demonstrate a mood or, conversely, to start with an object and, through deciphering, to disengage a mood from it. The second usage typifies Belgian symbolism. Emile Verhaeren summarized this essential mode of Belgian symbolism in an 1887 article: "On part de la chose vue, ouïe, tâtée, goûtée, pour en faire naître l'évocation . . ." (One begins with things seen, heard, felt, tasted in order to give rise to evocation . . .).[1] Symbolist creation is conceived as an absence, a severance from the world and its activities, yet the artist is reliant upon the world in order to discover what lies within him. Exterior landscape serves as the designation of the interior; the lineaments of the known may suggest the artist's hidden response to it; subjective deformation of a familiar environment may transform it into a private realm of literary experience.

Belgian symbolism comprises a poetics of strangeness and hallucination precisely because of being rooted, much more so than the symbolism of France, in a poetics of geographical place. Though sharing a common language with France and a common impetus to deny the contingencies of the mundane world in their art, the Belgian writers could mitigate cultural imperialism and establish a distinct presence in the literary world through cultivation of image repertoires of cities, objects, Flemish experiences, by entering into accord with their own northern environment and rendering it oneiric. The Belgian symbolists applied a life-subtractive hallucination to the sites of their homeland, evoking places in a manner that suggests the ambiguity rather than the definitude of the world. Rooted in the prevailing fin de siècle reception of Schopenhauer's philosophy, with its desire for the extinction of the ego, the peace of nonconsciousness as a release from life's vain struggle, the symbolists conceived of the world as an illusory fabric woven from myriad subjective perceptions, a weightless phantasmagoria doomed to vanish with the disappearance of its percipient from the theater of the world.

These twin modalities, annihilation of the self and concomitant effacement of the phenomenal, were given expression by the Belgian symbolists in the dead city thematic, obsessively recurrent in poetry, prose, and the visual arts, and rapidly internationalized.[2] Expressive of an impetus to transmute the tangible into the spectral and to effect literary imbrications of psychic states and exterior environment, the Belgian symbolist "dead" cities were actual urban loci of desuetude—Bruges, Ghent, Furnes, Malines, among others. These sites, prized for their remoteness from the rapid shift and flow of the metropolis, were most often canal cities of mirage, which call the fixity of being into question, ambiguous Atlantides, hovering in a half-state both aqueous and terrestrial. In the canal city, the Belgian symbolists found a landscape quintessentially suggestive of visionary experience. The watery depths and blindly meandering passageways of the canal city provide a structural paradigm both for the unconscious mind and a stygian zone. In Belgian symbolism, parallels may be clearly drawn between an initiatory voyage in the canal city as a severance from the world, a symbolic disincarnation and descent into the underworld, and an exploration of the tenebrous depths of the unconscious. The geographical cities were transformed into literary cities of the soul and other worlds, psychic terrain, by means of imagery of "estompe," atmospheric conditions such as incessant rain and mist that blur and enshroud the real, negate its substantial qualities, and, encompassingly, by imagery of "attente," arrest time. Lethargic cities of still water served the symbolists as ideations of an interior space of stillness in which futurity halts. Progress, obsession of the modern age, is countered by the suspended animation of a city museum in which the present is forever fused with a legendary past or devolves in a state of lingering decline.

A pivotal figure in Belgian letters, Georges Rodenbach was the first to adapt symbolist poetics of inwardness and indeterminacy to this theme firmly rooted in experience of his native Flanders. The writer did not turn to Bruges because he wished to revive the pageantry, energy, and purposefulness of the city during the days of its hegemony. For the symbolist writer, the dead city exists outside time; it belongs to neither the past, present, nor future. This temporal ambiguity is incorporated as a structural element in the experimental fin de siècle prose devoted to the dead city theme. The *récit, conte,* and brief novel are the favored forms, approaching with their minimal conversational interchange, minimal or absent description of character, the condition of an extended prose poem. Chronological passage of time is annulled or weakened by cyclical, often interchangeable walks through the substitute underworld of the canal city, by plot and narrative progression subordinate to setting, and superseded by an outpouring of imagery expressive of the moods of the lone protagonist, for whom the city serves as the speculum of his psyche. In *Bruges-la-Morte,* the 1892 novel that established the Flemish canal city as an ineluctable presence in symbolist literature, Georges Rodenbach defined the mutual penetration of place and percipient:

> Toute cité est un état d'âme, et d'y séjourner à peine, cet âme se communique, se propage à nous en un fluide qui s'inocule et qu'on incorpore avec la nuance de l'air.[3]

> (Every city is a mood and, even with the briefest stay, its soul is communicated, spreads toward us in a fluid that is inoculated and incorporated in our being with the nuance of the air.)

Rodenbach here propounds an environmental determinism that, though equally as fatalistic, opposes that of the naturalist novel. Rather than emphasizing the demonstrable effects of economic or social milieu upon character, the symbolist investigates the subtle persuasion of atmosphere upon those who succumb to it. The observations of the percipient, the projection of his interiority, constructs the literary city, but, at the same time, his mood is shaped by an incalculable nuance, the spirit of place that exerts its whispered influence.

According to symbolist convention, the atmosphere of the canal city is lethal, leading protagonist and reader to the breathless realms of Thanatos. The moods concretized by the dead city may be broadly categorized into two types, expressive of dichotomous attitudes toward inertia and solitude and related to experience traditionally associated with an afterlife. In its inertia, the canal city may suggest a necropolis and inferno, a spleenscape of transfixed pain, rife with awareness of petrification, dull incarceration, and the futility of living. Ghent, in Georges Rodenbach's 1889 novella, *L'Art en exil,* is such a linguistic construction of pain. The following passage illustrates Rodenbach's ability to attribute sentience to the inanimate cityscape and establish concordance between it and his fearful mood:

> Dans leurs cages de verre, les becs de gaz, dont la flamme se tordait au vent, avaient l'air de quelque chose qui souffre, qui a peur, qui est écrasé, qui risque à tout moment de mourir et renaître sans cesse de son éternelle agonie.[4]

> (In their glass cages, the gas jets with flames, twisting in the wind, seemed to be something suffering, terrified, overwhelmed, risking death at every moment and ceaselessly reborn from endless death-struggle.)

Typifying symbolist indirect discourse, the protagonist's emotive response is unstated, transposed and implicit in the admonitory object contemplated. Instead of offering the luminescence of hope, a lighted and certain pathway, the flickering street lamps assailed by wind bespeak threatened extinction, ever-renewed and unredemptive suffering, an emblem of the powerless human condition.

In *En ville morte,* Franz Hellens follows the model of the infernal canal city established by Rodenbach, transforming the physical aspect of his literary Ghent into the measure of an isolated protagonist's spiritual malaise.

> Le soir fonçait sur les toits. Peu à peu il les enserrait comme une proie. Le brouillard coulait entre les murs, inondait les creux et montait lentement, comme une mer où sombrait une infinité de barques immobiles. . . . A cet arrêt, tout parut s'effondrer sans bruits. Les cheminées, cependant, luttaient encore; elles se brandissaient, tordues comme des bras de noyés . . .[5]

> (The evening weighed upon the roofs. Gradually, it squeezed them like a prey. The fog streamed between the walls, flooded the hollows and rose slowly, as if a sea in which countless, motionless boats would go down. . . . By decree, all seemed to cave in soundlessly. The chimney stacks, however, struggled on; they brandished themselves, twisted, like the arms of the drowning . . .)

The buildings of Hellens's Ghent-Atlantide are anthropomorphized and struggle in vain contortion against the "estompe" of fog and livid twilight, figured as the rising and punitive water of the sunken city. The awareness of the void that haunts the mind of the protagonist is thus projected in a sinister drama of engulfment. Inextricability is inherent in Hellens's Ghent, its reptilian streets strangled in shadow, folding upon themselves and leading nowhere, figuring the solipsistic inner geography of the protagonist, regressively withdrawn and imprisoned by his mental projections. The infernal dead city expresses a tortured aspect of idealism and subsumes the literary function of the ruin in signaling universal morbidity and devastation.[6]

> Dans tous les murs percés de cavités noires pour des fonctions inconnues, une purulence s'incrustait, rongeant les contours avec l'annihilante ténacité de monstrueux cancers, épanchant de sanies, se déplaçant comme de serpigineux sarcomes, des apostèmes béantes.[7]

> (In all the walls pierced with black cavities for unknown functions, a purulence became incrusted, eating away at contours with the annihi-

lating tenacity of monstrous cancers, discharging sanies, shifting like serpiginous sarcomas, gaping abscesses.)

The houses, which should form the protective carapace of man's body, instead reveal its debility. The deterioration of this literary Ghent, expressed in virulent disease metaphors, conveys obsession with the tenuousness of life and dread of man's abject and vulnerable physical condition. In the traditional hells of Dante and Bosch, violent expiation of sin is exacted in a landscape that allegorically communicates the nature of the sin. In Hellens's ambiguous symbolist hell, this causal relationship between crime, punishment, and setting is denied. The only crime committed is the act of being. An undefined existential torment controls subjective deformation of Ghent into a place of menace and a paradigm of fall without regeneration.

Conversely, the inertia of the canal city may suggest the suavity of the faded and superannuated. Solitude in this paradisal context of the dead city is not fearsome but lenitive, associated with creative inwardness and a mood of narcoticized disincarnation. In Rodenbach's Bruges, pleasure is not derived from existence, but from imagined absolution from existence, a convalescent repose in which harsh brightness and wounding noise are banished:

> Ici la sourdine des sons s'apparie à la sourdine des couleurs, car toutes les façades s'effaçent en des nuances de jaunes pâles, de verts éteints, de roses surannés qui chantent doucement la silencieuse mélodie de teintes fanées.[8]

> (Here the muting of sound is married to the muting of colors, for all the facades are worn away into nuances of pale yellow, faint green, attar of rose which sweetly sing the silent melody of fading shades.)

In the paradisal context, the dead city is haunted by the feminine presence of nuns, beings of silence lost in contemplation, and the city, itself, becomes a maternal entity, in which the labyrinthine form and the ubiquitous presence of water suggest a uterine structure, a place of protective withdrawal and gestation of new or more profound being.[9] The Beguinage, the walled community of convents, a replica city enclosed within the remote city, itself enclosed within a network of canals, is the ultimate space of purity and silence.

> Ainsi, á travers tout ce paysage de banlieue lamentable, Jean Rembrandt arriva aux portes du grand Béguinage. Bien qu'il y fût venu

fort souvent, c'était chaque fois une surprise pour lui que cette vision archaïque évoquant tout d'un coup une ville ancienne, un enclos du moyen âge, un suave triptyque de quelque primitif. N'est-ce pas l'Agneau pascal de Memling lui-même qui paît là-bas dans cette prairie d'herbe drue? Et n'est-ce pas la colombe du Saint-Esprit envolée d'un Jean Van Eyck qui frissonne derrière cette vitre miroitante? Non! ce sont des ailes de linge, et partout ainsi, à chaque fenêtre, une furtive religieuse passe, comme en route pour le ciel. . . . Une paix mortuaire, une volonté de silence, un renoncement à la vie s'exhalaient de ces toits léthargiques et s'exprimaient dans l'agonie tintante d'une petite cloche qui, du haut de la tour, déroulait au vent comme une fumée de sons.[10]

(Jean Rembrandt arrived at the entranceway to the great Beguinage. Although he had frequently come here, each time he was surprised by the archaic vision that suddenly evoked an ancient city, a medieval close, a suave triptych by some primitive. Isn't that Memling's paschal lamb pasturing there in the thick grass? And isn't that the dove of the Holy Spirit flown from a Jan van Eyck that trembles behind that reflecting glass? No! Those are wings of linen and everywhere, at each window, a furtive nun passes by, as if on the way to heaven. . . . A deathly peace, a desire for silence, a renunciation of life breathed forth from the lethargic roofs and was expressed in the tinkling agony of a little bell which, from the top of the tower, unfurled in the wind something like a smoke of sound.)

Within the infernal Ghent in Rodenbach's *L'Art en exil,* the Beguinage offers a sacrosanct space of severance, in which all signs of human activity have been effaced. The Beguinage offers the percipient a return to the visionary realms of Memling and van Eyck, an alternative and anterior paradise, a gentle, narcoleptic realm of pacification. The modality of Rodenbach's nun is the veiled and hidden, referring to the concealment and partial revelation that is the essence of symbolist creation. Disengaged from worldly activity that imposes identity, Rodenbach's nuns are quasi presences glimpsed behind a window, icons of quiescence, of absence from the known and openness to the ineffable.

Visual artists were also drawn to the metaphorical possibilities inherent in the Beguinage. The entranceway to the Béguinage Sainte Elisabeth in Bruges figures prominently in Fernand Khnopff's 1892 frontispiece for Rodenbach's *Bruges-la-Morte,* in which the widower, Hugues Viane, wanders the underworld of the canal city in quest of memories of his dead wife. A failed Orpheus, he worships her in the guise of a double, whom he finally murders. Khnopff ignores the events of the novel as well as Rodenbach's

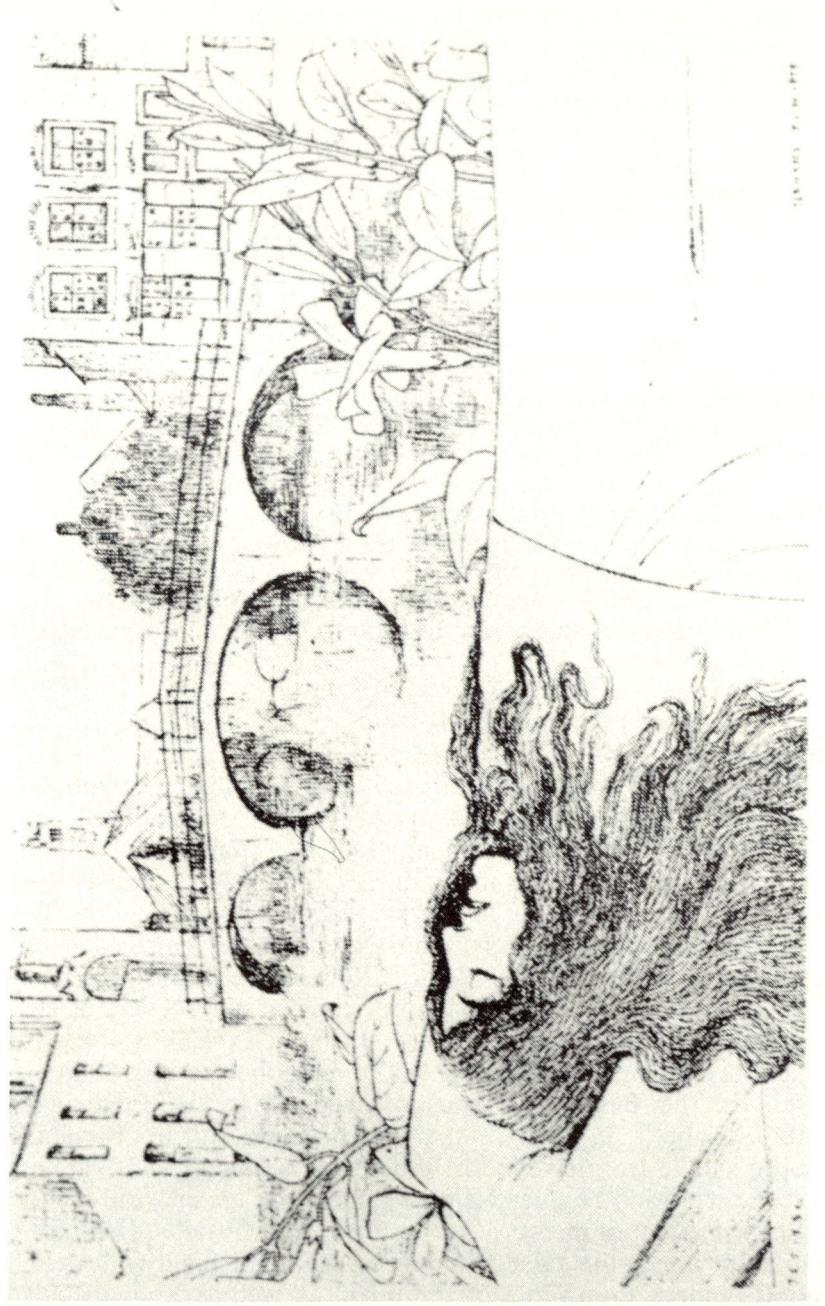

Fernand Khnopff. *Frontispiece for Bruges-la-Morte.* 1892, drawing. Whereabouts unknown (cat. rais. no. 200).

descriptions of blonde wife and mistress. Khnopff instead presents a pristine image of a dead woman, outstretched parallel to the Beguinage. Her pallor defined by her dark hair, her mouth parted and downturned, she is as if a breathing funerary sculpture. She is caught in a state between sleep and death, suggestive of absolute self-communion and exclusion of the exterior world. The stasis of Khnopff's figure has to do with introversion and trance, an abandonment of consciousness that may be the source of significant dreams. The presence of the convent entranceway in Khnopff's depiction of a woman lost in everlasting sleep underscores the desire to attain access to the closed, hidden recesses of being. The convent signals the reclusion necessary in the quest for inner beauty. In his 1904 pastel, *L'Entrée du béguinage*, Khnopff has created a Schopenhauerian landscape, emphasizing the lethargy and quiescence of the Béguinage Sainte Elisabeth in Bruges, an "extinguished atmosphere" conducive to experience of the ineffable. The arched bridge of the entranceway to the convent is a focal point of the drawing, leading inevitably to the unknown. Khnopff has reversed the romantic "Fernweh" of Caspar David Friedrich's drawings in which figures in protected interiors gaze from open windows toward vast landscapes, awakening longing for flight and absorption in the overwhelming force of nature. In Khnopff's *L'Entrée,* an absent viewer gazes toward the convent portal, ingress to unseen sacral space, and toward a facade of impenetrable, muslin-veiled windows, lured by the mystery of the hidden space of the interior. Khnopff has truncated the buildings and eliminated the sky in order to emphasize its reflection in the Minnewater. The seas, torrents, and mountain ranges of the romantic are replaced by an intimate space of depth. The stillness and concentration of the mirroring water, the diffusely radiant crepuscular lighting, convey a mood of tranquil detachment, the repletion of self-communion, the peace of self-forgetfulness.

A consummate example of the canal city as a space of imagined nirvana is found in Camille Lemonnier's *La Chanson du carillon*. Inspired by Rodenbach's evocation of Hans Memling's *Reliquary Shrine of Saint Ursula* in *Bruges-la-Morte,* Lemonnier uses this artwork both as a global metaphor for the dead city, architectural reliquary of its past greatness, and as a controlling source of imagery expressive of the beatitude of nonbeing.[11] Ursula's calm acceptance of the arrows of her aggressors leads us to a yielding, feminine space evoked in imagery of softness, melting, and drifting. Lemonnier evokes the Flemish master's vision of martyrdom

Fernand Khnopff. *L'Entrée du béguinage*. 1904, pastel. Photo: The Hearn Family Trust, courtesy Barry Friedman Ltd., New York.

in words as an edenic and sensuous garden of death in which Ursula and her entourage are the pristine flowers:

> Paradis de couleurs émaillés et tendres. Vision d'une contrée qui ne serait plus la terre. . . . Même il semble que le massacre des onze mille vierges, cette boucherie de chairs roses et neigeuses, soit ici comme une apothéose de fleurs.[12]

> (Paradise of enameled and tender colors. Vision of a realm that can no longer be the earth. . . . It even appears that the massacre of the eleven thousand virgins, slaughter of pink and snowy flesh, has transformed into an apotheosis of flowers.)

Filtered through the anterior vision of Memling, Lemonnier transforms his Bruges into a delicate "hortus conclusus," a perfumed realm of gentle death suffused with a floreated light. Pronounced delectation of nonbeing is conveyed in "estompe" imagery of weather, derived not from the penetrating mists of November, the season of spleen, but from the caressing haze of balmy summer:

> Douceur des après-midis fluides, irisés, tièdes, où même le lourd chevet de briques des églises se diaphanéise, où il pleut des duvets de cygnes et des étamines de fleurs, où la rue s'indécise d'irréel. . . . Douceur aussi de ne pas se sentir trop vivant.[13]

> (The sweetness of fluid, mild, iridescent afternoons when even the heavy, brick apses of the churches grow diaphanous, as swan's down and flower stamens rain in the air, as the street grows vague and unreal. . . . Sweetness as well of not feeling too much alive.)

Lemonnier's Bruges is diaphanous and insubstantial, enfolded in dream in a dual movement of dematerialization and aestheticization, resulting from the fusion of late nineteenth-century Bruges and an artistic vision that survives from the late fifteenth century. The confounding of present and visionary past results in the hypnogogic mood of indeterminacy, always linked to the pleasure of not being fully alive. Both the dead city and the persona who observes and hallucinates it are lightened of the weight of being.

Befitting this paradisal release, the passage of time is slowed and aestheticized, measured by the ethereal music of the carillon and evoked in imagery of sumptuousness. In keeping with the Memling motif, the carillon is the reliquary of time in which the hours are frozen in a cascade of molten gold and precious stones:

> Soudain, comme une pluie d'étoiles, comme une cascade de cristaux et de pierreries, l'averse de trilles du carillon s'écroulait, plongeait aux eaux du canal . . .[14]
>
> (Suddenly, like a rain of starlight, like a cascade of crystal and precious stones, the downpour of trills from the carillon fell, immersed in the water of the canal . . .)
>
> Une pluie d'or et de cristal, le tintement d'une pluie d'étoiles de quart d'heure en quart d'heure tombait du ciel, plongeait dans l'eau du canal.[15]
>
> (A rain of gold and crystal, the singing of a rain of stars from quarter hour to quarter hour fell from the sky, plunged into the water of the canal.)

Time falls and disappears, lost hours joyfully annihilated in a sudden shower of music. Lemonnier's timeless Bruges is a paradise of artifice, a Byzantium in which impermanence is denied and life transmuted into form. The chimes *plunge* into the canal, becoming sunken treasure, inner riches, and a reminiscence of the bells of the sunken cathedral, which lure us to our original amniotic paradise of preconsciousness, the private realm where we float in latency.

> Tout se fond; une fumée danse au bout des canaux, le paysage se dissout aux obscurités laiteuses d'une nuit d'enchantement.[16]
>
> (Everything melts; a light mist dances at the tip of the canals; the landscape dissolves in the milky dimness of an enchanted night.)

Certainly, the paradisal dead city is a realm of speculative suicide, conducive to reveries of drowning and dissolution not as absolute death, but as an equivocal immortality, a sleep with open eyes, lost in the unconscious processes of creativity. Ophelia drifting in dream is the persona of this algae-strewn elysium, which offers us a floating abandonment and entranced acceptance of the passing vision.

Georges Rodenbach established sites of his Flemish homeland as cities of the imagination, which counter the disruptive motion of the modern world. The Belgian dead city prose inspired by Rodenbach's example is an experiment in imagined suppression of purposeful, waking consciousness and an examination of the oneiric landscape that results from that suppression.[17] Both in literature and the visual arts, aspects of actual cities are emphasized, manipulated, infused with subjective mood in order to convey an enigmatic vision that is specifically symbolist in the combination of immobility and the effacement of life, whether by fog, lighting, or liquefaction. It is by no means to be construed that Flemish cities were the only urban loci that served this function. These water cities were chosen to demonstrate, within a limited context and through examples from infrequently discussed works, specific modalities of hallucination which may be operative in other provincial cities or even metropoles. No matter which urbanscape is chosen as the artist's domain of subjectivity, symbiosis between the exterior world and the inner world of its observer must be pronounced. Any city could become a symbolist "ville morte" if made to convey the poet's inner world in a manner that is life-subtractive and mysterious in its emphasized absence, isolation, fading of the present, and suspended animation. In its stasis, the symbolist dead city is, moreover, not simply a limbo but, as is evident in the works of Lemonnier and Hellens, may express decidedly paradisal or infernal experience. Whether figuring a chrysalis, a protective space where one enjoys reposeful sensations of disembodiment, or the airless closure of the tomb, the Belgian dead city is a subjective landscape of metaphoric construction. All landscape art is necessarily subjective, infused with and revealing the mood of its creator. The uniqueness of the fin de siècle canal city as a literary landscape is its thanatopsis, its negation of time and etherealization of space in order to express states of symbolic nonexistence. Geographical sites, the most noble and prestigious cities of the Flemish past, are transformed into numinous zones of solitude, an interfusion of exteriority and interiority, a multifaceted literary space of creation and nonbeing. This spatial paradigm is a prevailing convention of symbolist writing, crystallizing poesis, the process by which objective reality is transformed into an artifact.

Notes

1. Emile Verhaeren, "Le Symbolisme," *L'Art Moderne* (1887): 115–18.
2. For sustained discussion of the Schopenhauerian background of the dead city theme and examination of its international repercussions, see the author's *Symbolist Dead City: A Landscape of Poesis* (New York: Garland, 1990).
3. Georges Rodenbach, *Bruges-la-Morte,* ed. Christian Berg (Brussels: Editions Labor, 1986), 75.
4. Rodenbach, *En exil* (Paris: La Renaissance du Livre, 1910), 50. This is the title of a popular reedition of *L'Art en exil.*
5. Franz Hellens, *En ville morte* (Brussels: Van Oest, 1906), 11.
6. For discussion of the literary ruin, see Roland Mortier, *La Poétique des ruines en France* (Geneva: Droz, 1974).

7. Hellens, *En ville morte*, 13.
8. Rodenbach, *Evocations* (Brussels: La Renaissance du Livre, 1924), 17.
9. In the *Symbolist Dead City*, I discuss the nun in the work of the Belgians, Italian crepuscolari, and Rilke as a figurative substitution for the poet, withdrawn from the world in order to reach immanent divinity in the creative act.
10. *En exil*, 6–7.
11. Rodenbach's evocation of the Ursula reliquary serves as an "art poétique" on the modality of subjective landscape. The martyrs' calm acceptance of death spills over into the vernal landscape, formed by their inner joy. "Voilà pourquoi la paix, qui régnait déjà en elles, se propageait jusqu'au paysage, l'emplissait de leur âme comme projeté" (That is why the peace, which already held sway within them, spread to the landscape, filling it with their soul, as if projected) (80).
12. Camille Lemonnier, *La Chanson du carillon* (Paris: Lafitte, 1911), 151.
13. Ibid., 263.
14. Ibid., 277.
15. Ibid., 309.
16. Ibid., 73.
17. James Hillman discusses the synchronicity of the underworld and the daily world in traditional mythology. The underworld is a "psychic perspective where being has been desubstantialized, killed of natural life, and yet is in every shape and sense and size the exact replica of natural life." James Hillman, *The Dream and the Underworld* (New York: Harper and Row, 1975), 46.

Souls under Glass: Poetry and Interiority in the Works of Rodenbach and Maeterlinck

Patrick Laude

(Translated from the French by Elaine L. Corts)

> Mon âme!
> O mon âme vraiment trop à l'abri!
> Et ces troupeaux de mes désirs dans une serre
> Attendant une tempête sur les prairies![1]

> (My soul!
> Oh my soul truly too sheltered!
> And these herds of my desire in a hothouse
> Waiting for a storm in the meadows!)

> Ah! mon âme sous verre, et si bien à l'abri!
> Toute elle s'appartient dans l'atmosphère enclose;
> Ce qu'elle avait de lie ou de vase déposé;
> Le cristal contigu n'en est plus assombri.[2]

> (Ah! my soul under glass, and so well sheltered!
> In this enclosed atmosphere, all belongs to my soul;
> It deposits what it once had of the dregs or sludge;
> The adjacent crystal is no cloudier for it.)

In comparing these two passages, my intention is not to venture into the territory of a critique of influences that is the concern of a strictly historical perspective. I will be content to recall, in this respect, that the collection *Serres chaudes* (of which six poems were published in *La Pléiade* as early as 1886 and twelve others in 1887 in *Le Parnasse de la Jeune Belgique*) preceded the publication of *Les Vies encloses* (1896) and that Rodenbach was one of the first to recommend the author of *Pelléas et Mélisande* to the attention of the public in an article in *La Jeune Belgique,* dated 5 July 1886.[3] It is striking that the respective titles of the two collections evoke, as if in unison, a twofold imaginary orientation: "closure" on the one hand, conforming to the climate of interiority that characterizes the symbolist generation, and a "vital" profusion on the other, evoking the wealth of this interiority and, in particular, its subconscious dimension. The first of these orientations most often reveals a vague philosophical idealism that tends to reduce being to a simple projection, or else to a subjective perception. Undoubtedly, it is Rémy de Gourmont who deserves the credit for having expressed most directly this general attitude of the symbolist psyche, when he stated: "par rapport à l'homme, sujet pensant, le monde, tout ce qui est extérieur au moi, n'existe que selon l'idée qu'il s'en fait" (that in relationship to man as a thinking subject, the world, everything that is exterior to the self, exists only according to the way one conceives it).[4] Closure can be revealed, in this sense, to be bound up with a culture of illusion as illustrated in the "littérature en trompe-l'oeil" analyzed by Christian Berg.[5] As to the complement of this idealistic closure, it is clearly expressed in the recurrent desire to probe the elemental and unconscious depths of subjectivity, "l'Afrique intérieure de notre domaine inconscient" (the inner Africa of our unconscious domain), as expressed by Laforgue in *Entretiens politiques et littéraires* (1892).

It is from such an intellectual and aesthetic setting that I would like to read some texts of Rodenbach and Maeterlinck as divergent testimony to the thematics of contemplative closure, and to the inner life that is perhaps the essential "message" of symbolism in its poetic striving to answer these "impostures du réel" (impostures of reality), which were discussed by Christian Berg.

What strikes us from the outset is this distance between the two adverbs qualifying the protective shelter where the soul is gathered into itself and insulated from the rest of the world: "O mon âme *vraiment trop* à l'abri," "Ah! mon âme sous verre, et *si bien* à l'abri." The *si bien* of Rodenbach clearly contrasts with the *vraiment trop* of Maeterlinck. On one side, we find an address to a "woman companion" as if withdrawn in a too "fragile" retreat; on the other, the rapture of the contemplative poet in total ecstasy within his inner realm. For Maeterlinck, the principally negative character of this closure is in close solidarity with a feeling of incompleteness and consequently of expectation. In the poem "Ame" already cited, the introductory lines clearly mark, in the same manner, the desire and expectation of liberation and renewal:

> Mon âme!
> O mon âme vraiment trop à l'abri!

Et ces troupeaux de mes désirs dans une serre!
Attendant une tempête sur les prairies!

The conclusion of the poem "Serre chaude" moves in the same direction:

> Mon Dieu! mon Dieu! quand aurons-nous la pluie,
> Et la neige et le vent dans la serre![6]

(My God! my God! when will we have rain,
And snow and wind in this hothouse!)

The harsh weather represents quite a violent change in an atmosphere vitiated by the enclosed space. The "serre" is thus associated figuratively with the connotation of the verb "serrer" (to tighten) in that it suggests a contraction, an absence of existential vastness, a progressive loss of consciousness, a slow death. It is the "souffle" (breath of air) coming from the outside (the recurrent appeals to God) that will unlock the space of the hothouse. The future becomes an object of anticipation.

Far from this climate of anticipation, of revelation, or of liberation to come, the verse of Rodenbach lets fall one by one expressions of a satisfaction that revels in its present by contrast with a bygone past marked by a negative coefficient: "Le cristal contigu n'en est *plus* assombri." Moreover, in his poem, "La Vie des chambres," which forms the first part of *Le Règne du silence,* Rodenbach takes a diametrically opposite standpoint to that of Maeterlinck in rejecting the temptation of the "vents migrateurs" (migratory winds) and the convulsive jolts of his soul:

> Oui! C'est doux! C'est la chambre, un doux port relégué
> Où mon rêve, lassé de tendre au vent ses voiles,
> Dans le miroir tranquille et pâle s'est cargué.
> Las! Sans plus espérer des sillages d'étoiles,
> Et des départs vers des îles, mon rêve dort
> Dans le profond miroir, comme en un canal mort;
> Et faut-il désirer un coup de vent qui chasse
> En pleine mer, cette âme à l'ancre dans la glace?[7]

(Yes! It is cozy! This room, a gentle port of exile
Where my dream, weary of plying its sails in the wind,
In the calm and pale mirror is furled.
Weary! No longer hoping for the trail of the stars,
And departures for the islands, my dream sleeps
In the profound mirror, as if in a dead canal;

>And should I wish for a gust of wind to chase
>Into the open sea, this soul anchored in ice?)

The status of desire is directly bound to this contrast between the respective position of subjectivity in the two poets. The "troupeaux de mes désirs" in the poem of Maeterlinck evokes the passive multiplicity of inner tensions. The herd, in Maeterlinck, evokes passive suffering—submission to a fatal destiny.[8] It is in this way that desire becomes an allegorical character under the glass of deranged subjectivity. Here, it is divided into three paralyzed groups: "les plus faibles" (the weakest), "les plus malades" (the gravely ill), and "les plus tristes" (the saddest)—a triplet of sorrow and misfortune. Thus the hothouse appears to be symbol of the soul populated by a devastated and dying people, in such a way that Suzanne Nalbatian is entirely justified in placing Maeterlinck within the symbolist context of the "failing soul": "The soul is 'sick of absence,' and has the 'sickness of silence.' Both these expressions point once again to the incapacity of the soul to either nurture itself or to express itself. Indeed the soul is characterized as impotent."[9]

Michael Riffaterre, however unwilling to interpret *Serres chaudes* as "l'histoire d'une âme" (the story of a soul),[10] cannot bring himself to deny that the hothouse can be interpreted (if not always, at least frequently) as the "metaphor" for the decadent subject.[11] It is this decadent subject inhabited by deteriorating drives buried in the inmost depths of his subconscious that the mind's gusty wind will be able or would be able to infuse with the breath of life. The poem is presented at the imaginary level as a kind of pilgrimage to the drained sources of desire, and basically only probes the painful entrails of an inner world on its way to extinction. The imperative of exhortation, "allons vers les plus malades" (let us go toward the gravely ill), "allons vers les plus faibles" (let us go toward the weakest), "allons enfin vers les plus tristes" (finally let us go toward the saddest), thus suggests a plan of aid, of rescue that the poem, "Cloche à plongeur," connotes in the title and develops even more clearly. The hothouse, usually shielding a plant world threatened by the harshness of the exterior, consequently reveals its inverse imaginary value, much closer to the wall-obstacle than to the protective womb. Analogous to the glass of the hothouse, the eyes of the poem "Aquarium" form at the same time the medium of a possible contact with the exterior and the boundary rendering this contact impossible:

SOULS UNDER GLASS 117

> Hélas! mes yeux n'amènent plus
> Mon âme aux rives des paupières,
> Elle est descendue au reflux
> De ses prières
> Elle est au fond de mes yeux clos,
> Et seule son haleine lasse
> Elève encor à fleur des eaux
> Ses lys de glace.[12]

> (Alas! my eyes no longer lead
> My soul to my eyelids' shore,
> It has flowed back into the ebbing tide
> Of its prayers
> It is deep within my closed eyes,
> And only its weary breath
> Still raises just above the water
> Its frosty lilies.)

Here is nostalgia for contact with the exterior and a curse on the radical split between the inside and the outside, desire and its object. Riffaterre comments on the "tantalizing" nature of this imaginary structure in the following:

> Ce contact limité à un sens sur cinq définit une structure fondamentale de tout symbole de désir impuissant (le mythe de Tantale) ou de nostalgie: voir sans pouvoir toucher, connaître sans pouvoir posséder.[13]

> (This limited contact to one sense out of five defines a fundamental structure of every symbol of impotent desire [the myth of Tantalus] or of nostalgia: to see unable to touch, to know unable to possess.)

Yet, this paradigm of frustration is even superseded by the inability of desire to rise above the level of surface-obstacle and by its internment deep within the eyes. Notice that in this poem the "prayer," the return of the religious motif whose importance was questioned by Riffaterre, is closely related to the effort to reach the surface, and to free oneself from the prison of glass. The "reflux" toward the interior is definitely the mark of a spiritual failure.

This tension toward the outside is not the only direction of the poem by Maeterlinck: actually, whole portions of *Serres chaudes* are devoted to the exploration of the depths of the "hothouse." Now I would like to examine the forms of this exploration. Maeterlinck presents us with a great diversity of scenes or visions that are a combination of series, on the one hand, recurrent and limited in their register, and, on the other hand, contradictory. First of all, we notice among the elements of this great inner disorder, the nearly obsessional blending of one term connoting the vital energy of happiness and a second term evoking the affliction of death. For example, below is a list of eighteen words or parts of a clause, which match term for term (in the poem "Ame") by way of a related oxymoron:

mère	champ de bataille
frère	enterre
repas	sentinelle
fiancée	malade
dimanche	trahison
petits enfants	prison
cuisine	mourante
soeur épluchant des légumes	lit d'un incurable
baisers	blessés
(mother	battlefield
brother	bury
meal	sentry
fiancée	invalid
Sunday	treachery
small children	prison
kitchen	dying
sister peeling vegetables	bed of one hopelessly ill
kisses	the wounded)

Thus, we find one series associated with family warmth confronting a second series whose common denominator is adversity, in the form of suffering, of sickness, or of war. We find verses like: "je traverse un champ de bataille avec ma mère" (I cross a battlefield with my mother).[14] Each expression or each noun forms the subject, first, of paradigmatic permutations in which one or more terms with a closely related meaning are substituted and, second, of syntagmatic variations placing it in different sequential contexts. We find paradigmatic doublets like: princesse/fille de roi (princess/daughter of the king), vert/bleu (green/blue), cloche/serre (bell/hothouse), or brebis/agneau (lamb/sheep). We also find terms like "lys" (lily) situated in contexts as varied as: "Des oiseaux de nuit sur des lys" (Night birds on lilies), "Les lys jaunis des lendemains" (The yellowed lilies of tomorrow), "Des lys au fond des eaux lointaines" (Lilies at the bottom of distant waters), "Au milieu des lys que j'attouche" (Amid the lilies that I caress), "Et une ménagerie au milieu des lys" (And a menagerie amid the lilies), "Et jettent à pleines mains les lys verts dans les flammes" (With a firm grip, fling the green lilies into the flames), "Elève encore à fleur des eaux / Ses lys de glace" (Raise again just above the water / Its frosty lilies), "En suivant la trace incolore / De ses lys à jamais épars" (Following the trace / Of its lilies forever scattered), "Les lys contre les verres clos" (Lilies against the enclosed glass), "Et lys mobiles sous leurs flots" (And lilies moving beneath their waves). The tension among contradictory images, the multiple permutations, the sudden changes in imaginary associations would be, at first glance, the sign of a disorder of the symbolist psyche. This is the case for André Barre: "*Serres chaudes* colligent ces impressions hétéroclites, ces bouleversements et ces affaissements de l'âme, en proie à la fièvre d'une inquiète curiosité"[15] (*Serres chaudes* collects together these assorted impressions, and this distress and collapse of the soul, racked by the fever of an anxious curiosity).

We are quite far from the egotistic "ataraxia" characteristic of the work of Rodenbach. Thus, the "Aquarium mental" presents closure as the quasi-alchemical "leavening" in a process of modification, clarification, and purification. Desire is not a lulled and submerged power, sick or dying, where the subject focuses his eyes, fraught with the hope of awakening and elan. On the contrary, it is really the contaminating principle of impurity. The cathartic immobility of the aquarium is untouched by all movement which "déplace les lignes" (disturbs the ripples) to use Baudelaire's expression:

> Transparence de l'âme et du verre complice,
> Que nul désir n'atteint, qu'aucun émoi ne plisse.[16]

> (Transparency of the soul and its glass accomplice,
> That no desire touches, no emotion creases.)

The reference to the "lie" (dregs) and to the "vase" (sludge) expresses the necessity to shield the soul from all movement, a principle of combination and impurity that is likely to arouse buried drives. Far from suggesting the inability to establish a direct contact with the object of desire, the glass here indicates the protective frontier, which gathers the self together and "improves" it, in refusing alienation by the exterior. The outside, par excellence, is the realm of ambiguity, of difference, of multiplicity, and of movement, all representations of illusion participating in "la tentation des nuages" (the temptation of the clouds).

Certainly it is revealing that in the poem "Cloche à plongeur" Maeterlinck suggests a situation exactly the opposite to that which prevails in the "Aquarium mental," by making the aquatic element no longer the lunar and pure "dedans" (inside) that it is in Rodenbach, but the "dehors" (outside) with the diversity and inexhaustible riches of the ocean:

> O plongeur à jamais sous sa cloche!
> Toute une mer de verre éternellement chaude!
> Toute une vie immobile aux lents pendules verts!
> Et tant d'êtres étranges à travers les parois!
> Et tout attouchement à jamais interdit!
> Lorsqu'il y a tant de vie en l'eau claire au dehors![17]

> (Oh diver forever in his bell!
> An entire sea of glass perpetually warm!
> An entire life motionless within slow-paced green pendulums!
> And so many strange creatures across the surface!
> And every caress forever forbidden!
> When there is so much life in the clear waters outside!)

Fraught with desire, the feverish passion of the ocean clearly contrasts with the pure and immobile glow of the inner aquarium of Rodenbach. Nothing is stranger to the concentrated meditation of Rodenbach than this melancholy wonder—since it is impotent—before the wealth of the limitless exterior. As for the impossibility of physical contact, "et tout attouchement à jamais interdit," it appears in Maeterlinck to be one of the expressions of the malaise or "maladie" (illness) of the poetic consciousness.[18] Consciousness (the "je" hastily betrayed in the eighth line: "Et je suis un moment à l'ombre des baleines qui s'en vont vers le pôle!" [And I am for a moment in the shadow of whales who leave for the pole]) is perceived as if exterior to reality, deprived of abundance and life, condemned to a kind of impotent silence. The "plongeur sous cloche" is then, at the same time, fascinated by the fluid spectacle that files past on the other side of the glass and is engulfed by his impotence. Likewise, in "Ame de serre," the wall of glass, in the end, reveals the spectacular but illusory appearance of the objects of his desire:

> O les serres de l'âme tiède
> Les lys contre les verres clos,
> Les roseaux éclos sous les eaux,
> Et tous mes désirs sans remède.[19]

> (Oh the hothouses of the tepid soul
> Lilies pressed against the enclosed glass,
> Reeds spreading beneath the water,
> And all my desires without remedy.)

Nonetheless, in "Cloche à plongeur," the repeated exhortations articulate an effort to revive what, in the depths, vanishes and fails:

> Essuyez vos désirs affaiblis de sueurs;
> Allez d'abord à ceux qui vont s'évanouir:
> . . . .
> Allez ensuite à ceux qui vont mourir.[20]
>
> (Wipe away the sweat of your weakened desires;
> Go first to those about to swoon:
> . . . .
> Go next to those about to die.)

A major ambiguity weighs on the referent of "ceux": does it actually refer to the *autres,* to the unspecified *ils* designated in the preceding stanzas of the poem; or else, does it designate the "désirs affaiblis" themselves? This second interpretation can rely on the precedent of the poem "Ame" where the line: "Allons vers les plus malades" follows the periphrasis "et ces troupeaux de mes *désirs* dans une serre." Be that as it may, this ambiguity is evidently not quite without intention, insofar as it allows a purely allegorical, unilateral understanding of the poem to dissipate, one that would join together, term for term, inner realities and images. This referential vagueness tends to confuse levels and realms, fully utilizing what Riffaterre designates as the formal "mechanics" of decadent artificiality.

The fact remains, nonetheless, that an entire section of the work eludes to a great extent these "mechanics" each time the poet expresses a desire to break the circle of closure, of these bells, these hothouses, even these very eyes where the outside is reflected.[21] In this lies a nostalgia for knowledge or contact beyond any medium:

> Je voudrais atteindre, à travers
> L'oubli de mes pupilles closes,
> Les ombelles autrefois roses
> De tous mes songes entr'ouverts . . .
> J'attends pour voir leurs feuilles mortes
> Reverdir un peu dans mes yeux,

J'attends que la lune aux doigts bleus
Entr'ouvre en silence les portes.²²

(I would like to touch, across
The oblivion of my closed eyes,
The once pink-flowering parasols
Of all my half-opened dreams . . .
I wait to see their dying petals
Become slightly green in my eyes,
I wait for the blue-fingered moon
In silence, to open the doors halfway.)

Maeterlinck seems to us then, in *Serres chaudes,* to be a poet of nostalgia or a poet of hope for contact with being that would go beyond the kaleidoscopic reflections projected on the windows of the soul. This desire to "go out" of the stifling and decadent atmosphere of the hothouse seems likely to have been connected to the influence of Christian spirituality and in particular of Ruysbroeck on the thought of Maeterlinck. However much Riffaterre has scoffed at the restorative concern of the "rêveries des critiques catholiques belges" (the daydreams of Belgian Catholic critics)²³ of the beginning of the century, it is worth noting that the spirituality of Ruysbroeck is characterized, a fact particularly notable for a mystic, by the insistence on the spiritual theme of a "going out" of the self. From chapter 36 to chapter 45 of *L'Ornement des noces spirituelles* (The Ornamentation of the Spiritual Nuptials)—in the translation by Maeterlinck, who discovered the Flemish mystic as early as 1885—we find nearly ten instances of the terms "sortir" and "sortie" to designate the movement of the sanctified soul. Chapters 41, 42, 43, and 44 are thus devoted to four "sorties" of the soul toward God and the saints, the sinners, the souls of purgatory, and the souls of the virtuous. Moreover, the movement, the spiritual elan implied by these various "sorties" does not fail to remind us of the exhortations of *Serres chaudes,* which invite us to make our way toward the various categories of the sick and the dying.²⁴ The union with God is therefore essentially conceived in an "ex-static" and not in an "internalized" form. It is a question of drawing oneself toward the exterior, as it is in this passage of Ruysbroeck translated by Maeterlinck:

> . . . Dieu est un *océan* fluant et refluant, qui s'écoule sans interruption en tous ses amants, selon les besoins et les mérites de chacun, et il résorbe tous ceux qui sont doués, au ciel et sur terre, avec tout ce qu'ils ont et tout ce qu'ils peuvent.²⁵

(. . . God is an ocean flowing and ebbing, which seeps continuously into all who love it, according to the needs and merits of each, and it absorbs again all those who are endowed, in heaven and on earth, with all that they have and all that they can.)

Responding to a spiritual movement, diametrically opposite, the odyssey of the soul in Rodenbach illustrates a descent into a zone where diversity and movement dissolve and where the self is entirely self-sufficient, free from all external determination. The opening of "Aquarium mental" attests to this reflexivity and this self-centeredness, at the same time simple and as if infinite:

> L'eau sage s'est enclose en des cloisons de verre
> D'où le monde lui soit plus vague et plus lointain;
> Elle est tiède, et nul vent glacial ne l'aère;
> Rien d'autre ne se mire en ces miroirs sans tain
> Où, seule, elle se fait l'effet d'être plus vaste
> Et de se prolonger soi-même à l'infini.[26]

> (The calm water is enclosed in partitions of glass
> Where, for it, the world seems nebulous and faraway;
> The tepid water has no icy wind at all to air it;
> Nothing else is reflected in these two-way mirrors
> Where, alone, it appears more extensive than it is
> And seems to persist on into infinity.)

Consider the paronomasias and multiple alliterations: enclose/cloison, mire/miroir, fait/effet (enclose/partition, reflect/mirror, fact/effect), as well as the expressions at the limit of redundancy such as: "Elle est *tiède*" (the tepid water), and "*nul vent glacial* ne l'aère" (has no icy wind at all to air it), "*Rien d'autre*" (Nothing else), "*Où, seule*" (Where, alone), "*se* prolonger *soi-même*" (seems to persist). Their rhetorical function is to enhance these two aspects of reflexive self-sufficiency (redundancy) and indefinite elongation (paronomasia), or of absoluteness and infinitude, if you prefer. At a formal imaginary level, the spherical reflexivity of the aquarium provides no hold whatsoever on the exterior that would change it into the instrument, the "écran docile" (docile screen) of its forms. That way, even the aquarium-soul eludes all alienation, every exit as well as every integration.

At the textual level Rodenbach's poem joins, in this way, very different modalities from those of the syntagmatic clashes Maeterlinck enjoyed. Here the poetic enterprise is actually characterized rather as a deepening of the symbolic and allegorical potentialities of the "contemplated" object. Thus we are faced with a network of often complex and skillfully interwoven analogies, which explores or develops the vertical link between the symbol and an immanent subjectivity. The impression and the poetic significance do not spring so much from a dialectical relationship between syntagms, as they do from progressive assimilation, branching out almost indefinitely from the symbolic and analogical content of the object.[27] Mallarmé had already pointed this out quite well when he acclaimed Rodenbach's work in these terms:

> Les parties d'un poème, le même, ces *Vies encloses* pour la première fois ainsi, répercutent, avec une exactitude magique, les cas divers d'une analogie.[28]

> (The parts of a poem, the same, these *Vies encloses* for the first time, in this way, reverberate, with a magical exactitude, the various cases of an analogy.)

Mallarmé's use of the grammatical term "cas" suggests perfectly the aspect of "déclinaison" (declension) appropriate to Rodenbach's style. It is a question of declining reality in all its various relationships. It is in this declension that the same and the other "s'apparient" (make a matching pair), that the plural of *Vies* becomes "le même," the unique poem, that the imaginary vibrations of the object "répercutent" like an echo. The explicit analogical relationship constitutes the first stage of this identification:

> *Ainsi* mon âme, seule, et que rien n'influence!
> Elle est, comme en du verre, enclose en du silence.[29]

> (So, my soul, alone, affected by nothing!
> Is, as if in glass, enclosed by the silence.)

Yet this first stage opens further, onto a monism that, no longer content to scan its "ainsi," and its "comme," expresses reality in the poetic split of its unity. The soul is no longer simply signified poetically by the aquarium: the aquarium is the very manifestation of the soul. Here again we encounter a monistic practice of poetic contemplation, which comes close to the terms and the thoughts on the symbol proposed by Michel Deguy in his texts on the poetic uses of the symbol:

> Le même se dédouble en lui-même, et ainsi redouble, et ainsi apparaît comme le plus énigmatiquement proche de soi: étrange scissiparité où

chaque moitié se donne comme *dédoublement* de l'autre, ou plutôt de l'unique; ne se manifeste qu'en renvoyant à l'autre dans une circularité qui n'est pas vicieuse, vaine, mais *vie de l'unité* en elle-même—à la place de cette morne homogénéité vide du platement identique où le bon sens s'épuise à répéter qu'une pomme est une pomme.[30]

(The same is divided within itself, and in this way duplicates itself, and in this way appears as the most enigmatically close to itself: a curious scissiparity where each half is given as the double of the other, or rather of the unique; is only manifested in referring to the other in a circularity that is not depraved or vain, but the life of unity in itself—in place of this mournful homogeneity devoid of the unimaginatively identical, where common sense is exhausted in repeating that an apple is an apple.)

In this Deguy takes up a model considerably permeated by Hegelianism, which contrasts the vacuity of the immediate substance, of the A is A, with the dialectical life of the content. The two terms of the "doublet" cannot be isolated in an abstract fashion, since they are not identities related together but far more the determinations of the same content, of the same profundity. Therefore it is not that the aquarium puts subjectivity "en image" (into images) or that subjectivity "personnalise" (personalizes) the aquarium, but that the same reality, to which the aquarium and the soul attest, is shown in the relationships of the two terms. Such a poetic practice supposes a conception of the sign as a manifestion of the "profondeur de la vie" (profundity of life) or, to refer again to Deguy, "alerte" (alert) with this profundity in mind. It is important to point out that such a conception of poetry—whose fundamental axis we encounter, for example, in the work of Octavio Paz—rests at quite a distance from a purely formal structuralism. It might be appropriate to recall in this instance, as a characteristic of this last approach, the insistence of Roland Barthes on the "imagination syntagmatique du signe" (syntagmatic imagination of the sign), which we could relate to the poetic model. For Barthes, the sequential or syntagmatic imagination (in this case concerning the sign in its imaginary apprehension, not in its "scientific" reckoning) defines the very practice of the poetic genre, just as he remembers it moreover, in regard to Michel Butor, when he designates poetry as the "art-modèle de la bricole littéraire" (artistic model of literary bricolage), that is to say, the ordering of autonomous and mobile parts. It seems to me that it is precisely at this level that we can read two antagonistic conceptions of poetry that find two paradigmatic illustrations in the models proposed by Maeterlinck and Rodenbach.

Nonetheless my intention here is not to suggest a reductive typology which would mark a radical exclusiveness of one of these models in relation to the other, but to set out a general model and direction. The mystic vein that traverses the work of Maeterlinck (which finds one of its expressions in the translation of *L'Ornement des noces spirituelles* of Ruysbroeck) is enough by itself to nuance the impression of Maeterlinck the "semiotician," for whom the syntagmatic arrangement would constitute the alpha and omega of poetic expression.

In conclusion, how shall we summarize the bond that unites the poetic practice of these two poets to the concepts of interiority that their respective works involve? It would be necessary for this project to stress a semiotic conception (in contrast to a semantics based on a symbolic system) of poetry that can be drawn from the structure of *Serres chaudes,* at the same time noting its surprising and problematic association with a perception of interiority as subconscious and "sterile" multiplicity; a problematic combination insofar as we are accustomed to associate the poetics of semiotic inspiration with the dissolution of the subject and the zerological emptiness as set forth by Mallarmé, Barthes, or Julia Kristeva.

Actually such a practice places meaning outside any content, which would put stress on a "subject" to "express" and to be as if transcendent (and immanent) to the syntagms. The poetry of Maeterlinck might appear to us to be much closer to the experimental developments of surrealism, where there is an explosion of form supported by the thought of the subject in the tradition of Freudian psychoanalysis.

In the work of Rodenbach, on the contrary, and in spite of the undeniable rhetorical techniques of a typically decadent character,[31] the accent is perhaps less on language than on being or on the palpable apperception of being, the "vision"—in accordance with the general principles of symbolist theorists such as Jean Moréas or Charles Morice—and on reality in its symbolic potentialities. Interiority seems then to be a wealth of inexhaustible content called upon to unfold in the rhythm of poetic contemplation.

Notes

A French version of this essay appeared in *Les Lettres Romanes* 46, no. 3 (1992): 201–11.

1. Maurice Maeterlinck, *Serres chaudes* (Paris: Librairie Les Lettres, 1955), 33.
2. Georges Rodenbach, *Les Vies encloses* (Paris: E. Fasquelle, 1906), 12.
3. Pierre Maes, *Georges Rodenbach* (Gembloux: Duculot, 1952), 151.
4. On this point, refer to Henri Peyre, *Qu'est-ce que le symbolisme* (Paris: PUF, 1974), 135.
5. "[Literary wagers] are expressed most often from the fragments of positivist certainties and the requisites of the idealistic point of view. . . . The most celebrated among them was, of course, that of Villiers de l'Isle-Adam, as he had formulated it on several occasions during the preceding decade and notably in *Axël:* 'the world will never have, for you, another meaning than the one that you attribute to it. . . . Since you will not go outside the illusion that you make of the universe, choose the most divine!'" Christian Berg, "La Littérature en trompe-l'oeil," in *Le Mouvement symboliste en Belqique* (Bologna: CLUEB, 1990), 39. This is also in a way the sphere of "artificiality" described by Riffaterre as the fundamental category of the decadent aesthetic in his chapter from *La Production du texte* devoted to Maeterlinck. Nonetheless, we should take into account that the artificiality described by Riffaterre is of a formal and textual nature and not of a philosophical and representative character.
6. *Serres chaudes,* 16.
7. Georges Rodenbach, *Le Règne du silence* (Paris: Charpentier, 1891), 8.
8. For this we refer, for example, to the end of scene 4 of the third act of *Pelléas et Mélisande* where the appearance of a herd, which has nothing to do with the dramatic context, nevertheless fosters a symbolic relationship with the situation of the characters (their submission to fate): "*Pelléas*: They are herds that one leads to the city. . . . *Golaud*: They cry like lost children; it would seem they already sense the butcher." *Pelléas et Mélisande* (Brussels: Editions Labor, 1983), 41–42.
9. Suzanne Nalbatian, *The Symbol of the Soul from Hölderlin to Yeats* (New York: Columbia University Press, 1977), 83.
10. For example, we can consider this to be the case from the ironic parenthesis that follows his reference to one of the commentators on Maeterlinck: "R. Vivier, *Histoire d'une âme* [sic], p. 130," in *La Production du texte* (Paris: Le Seuil, 1979), 200, n. 1.
11. "Many poems in the collection go no further (than 'representing the conflict between the self and the exterior world'): they pose the comparability of the hothouse as a metaphorical vehicle and mankind as the tenor." *La Production du texte,* 204.
12. *Serres chaudes,* 63.
13. *La Production du texte,* 203.
14. *Serres chaudes,* 33.
15. André Barre, *Le Symbolisme: Essai historique sur le mouvement poétique en France de 1885 à 1900* (Geneva: Slatkine, 1970), 264.
16. *Les Vies encloses,* 12.
17. *Serres chaudes,* 59.
18. "In Maeterlinck . . . illness is conceived as the necessary condition of literary creation, thus becoming the metaphor for Poetry. From this viewpoint, the poet can only be profoundly ill, overwhelmed, not by material and physical pain, but 'spiritual' pain, thus undefined, elusive . . . by a pain that—like all poetry—has its source in fiction." Graziano Benelli, "*Serres chaudes:* Présence/absence de Verlaine," in *Le Mouvement symboliste en Belgique,* 99.

19. *Serres chaudes,* 81.
20. Ibid., 61.
21. This pertains to the poems with a religious tone, which, quite significantly, are composed in a far more regular way, from the standpoint of prosody, than the kaleidoscopic stanzas most characteristic of the "artificial mechanics" that Riffaterre esteems. These "orations" appear, in this way, as interludes to restore the unity of the composition within the "logic" of the subject's thought or the soul's story.
22. *Serres chaudes,* 82.
23. *La Production du texte,* 199, n. 2.
24. And this even if the elan in question is in this case directed toward inner realms.
25. *L'Ornement des noces spirituelles de Ruysbroeck L'Admirable,* translated from the Flemish and accompanied with an introduction by Maurice Maeterlinck (Brussels: Les Eperonniers, 1990), 233.
26. *Les Vies encloses,* 3.
27. Van Lerberghe sides with Rodenbach on this point. The aesthetic of van Lerberghe is actually an aesthetic of the "deepening" of the image: "For me, you know, a poem is above all a drawing, a plastic composition that I see. Since that is the case, an essential condition of beauty is the unity of composition, absolutely as it is for a painter. A poem, according to this process, is no more than the development of one sole image. There can be many images, but all of them should be subordinated, linked together by transitions and gradations of nuance. In short, it is *the opposite of the system of Kahn, whose poems are kaleidoscopes.*" *Lettres à Fernand Sévérin* (Paris: La Renaissance du Livre, 1924), 177.
28. Cited by Henri Mondor, *Autres précisions sur Mallarmé et inédits* (Paris: Gallimard, 1961), 161.
29. *Les Vies encloses,* 7.
30. Michel Deguy, "Usages poétiques du symbole," *Cahiers Internationaux de Symbolisme* 13 (1967): 5.
31. These techniques are particularly evident in the collections of his youth such as *La Mer élégante* (1881). On this point, see Christian Berg, "La Littérature en trompe-l'oeil."

With Georges Rodenbach—Bruges as State of Mind—The Symbolist Psychological Landscape

Dorothy M. Kosinski

In his brief foreword to *Bruges-la-Morte* Rodenbach declares that the city will function as an active and determining character in the book, that the city is almost human and associated with states of mind. This remarkable statement is elaborated in chapter 10:

> Les villes surtout ont ainsi une personnalité, un esprit autonome, un caractère presque extériorisé qui correspond à la joie, à l'amour nouveau, au renoncement, au veuvage. Tout cité est un état d'âme, et d'y séjourner à peine, cet état d'âme se communique, se propage à nous en un fluide qui s'inocule et qu'on incorpore avec la nuance de l'air.[1]

(Thus cities especially have a personality, an autonomous spirit, an almost externalized character corresponding to joy, to new love, to renunciation, to widowhood. Every city is a state of mind, and one hardly needs to stay there for this state of mind to communicate itself, to spread to us in a fluid that inoculates and that one incorporates with the nuance of the air.)

This concept of the psychological landscape or soulscape, so much at the heart of the symbolist aesthetic and which was a major theme in literature and in the visual arts, is the focus of this essay. A number of interdisciplinary but limited approaches suggest themselves most immediately—explorations of Rodenbach's milieu in Belgium; an analysis of the illustrations that accompanied many of his works; or an iconographic study of Bruges. Lucien Lévy-Dhurmer's well known portrait of the poet posed before a backdrop of Bruges or his rather romantic (but surely not symbolist) illustrations for the 1930 edition of *Bruges-la-Morte* come to mind. An exploration of the symbolist psychological landscape—not only as theme but as aesthetic goal and linked to crucial aspects of symbolist idealism (suggestion, objectifying the sub-

Lucien Lévy-Dhurmer. *Portrait of Georges Rodenbach.* 1895, pastel. Musée d'Orsay, Paris. (photo: Musées Nationaux).

jective, correspondences and synesthesia) and as manifested internationally in the works of Khnopff, Moreau, Redon, Munch, Hammershoi, Van de Velde, to name only a few, as well as articulated in a broad range of critical and theoretical literature—provides the appropriate perspective for Rodenbach's Bruges.

Rodenbach creates an atmosphere of intense emotional claustrophobia. The reader is totally enveloped by the obsessive, pathological inner world of the widower Hugues Viane, and thus is not merely an observer outside of it. As set forward by Rodenbach, Bruges emerges as a powerful psychological being, and not just a projection of Hugues's morbid imagination. Distinctions between character, action, setting, and theme are manipulated and obfuscated. Traditional symbolic or metaphoric structures are eschewed in favor of a symbolist synonymy. Mirror reflections and insistent symmetrical structure give form to this city-as-state-of-mind. Synesthesia gives it voice.

The cityscape is transformed not only through the projection of the widower's inner trauma but moreover through the total identification of the dead wife, *la morte,* with the city of Bruges. The gently undulating, glistening arteries of Bruges are a mirror, multiplying and amplifying the defunct and depressing medieval environment. It is precisely the poetic, mythic, and psychological richness of water that allows for the transformation of cityscape into psyche-scape. Gaston Bachelard grasped not only the correct allusion but the scope and tenor of Rodenbach's poetry in his identification of the "ophélisation" of an entire city.[2]

There exists simultaneously the similarity between or mirror confrontation of *la morte* and her double, Jane Scott. The destruction at the heart of the "plot" is determined by this all important (non)resemblance. This reflection of *la morte* and her double determines the very structure of the book, and has been likened very convincingly to a great diptych, its (metaphorical and literal) hinge located at the center of the text.[3] Though the resemblance of the dead woman and the actress has reality only in the widower's imagination, this mirror reflection of the dead wife and Jane establishes a spatial dimension, an imaginary or nonexistent space that accommodates the mirror confrontation of the two women, and which is perpendicular to the horizontal, watery Ophelia plane of Bruges and its canals. The resemblance becomes perfect only with Jane's murder, her violent removal from the vertical or perpendicular space to the horizontal plane of the watery surface, her transformation into another Ophelia: "Les deux femmes s'étaient identifiées en une seule. Si ressemblantes dans la vie, plus ressemblantes dans la mort qui les avait faites de la même pâleur, il ne les distingua plus l'une de l'autre—unique visage de son amour. Le cadavre de Jane, c'était le fantôme de la morte ancienne, visible là pour lui seul" (The two women had been identified as one alone. So similar in life, all the more so in death, which had lent them a common pallor, he could no longer tell one from the other—single face of his love. Jane's corpse was the ghost of the former dead woman, visible there to him and him alone) (113–14). The water mounts, obliterates and fills the space adjacent and above, engulfing Ophelia (the beloved/Jane), threatening Hugues and even Rodenbach himself with destruction. Guy Michaud alludes to this spatial model when he envisages (also citing Bachelard) the mounting water engulfing Rodenbach himself: "Pour Rodenbach aussi, comme pour Ophélie, l'eau qui semble dormir est en réalité une eau qui monte, qui monte au-devant de lui, pour le prendre un jour et l'emporter dans la mort" (For Rodenbach, like for Ophelia, the seemingly placid water is in reality a water that rises, rises before him, to take him one day and transport him to death).[4]

The other device by which Rodenbach creates this psychological landscape is a powerful synesthetic imagery which (quite literally) gives voice to the city. The bells are especially eloquent, they are the dominant voice of the novel—they sing, they chastise, they console. In the next to last chapter, as the loyal and devout servant, Barbe, makes preparations for the Feast Day of the Holy Blood procession, the sound of the bells fills the air:

> . . . les cloches âgées, les exténuées, les aïeules, béquillant, celles des couvents, des vieilles tours, celles qui sont casanières, valétudinaires, qui restent coîtes toute l'année, mais cheminent et font cortège le jour de la procession du Saint-Sang—toutes semblaient, par-dessus leurs robes de bronze usées, avoir de joyeux surplis blancs, des linges tuyautés en plis d'éventail. Barbe écoutait les sonneries, le gros bourdon de la cathédrale qu'on n'entendait qu'aux grandes fêtes, lent et noir, frappant comme d'une crosse le silence. . . . Et aussi toutes les clochettes des plus proches tourelles—émoi, liesse de robes argentines, qui semblaient dans le ciel s'organiser aussi en cortège . . . (98–99)

> (. . . aged bells, the played out ones, the grandmothers on crutches . . . those valetudinarians which stay quiet all year, but come out to take their places on the day of the Holy Blood procession—all seemed, beneath their worn bronze dresses, to wear bright white surplices, crimped underwear in fan folds. Barbe listened to the ringing, the great cathedral bell heard only on important holidays, slow and black, strik-

ing the silence like a crosier. . . . And also all the small bells from nearby turrets—agitation, merry tinkling of silver dresses, also apparently organizing themselves into procession in the sky . . .)

As they ring, the bells "sèment dans l'air des poussières de sons, la cendre morte des années" (scatter the dead ashes of the years . . . into the air in a dust of sounds) (11); they produce "une fumée de sons" (a smoke of sound) (78); and they seem to be shedding petals of "fleurs de fer" (flowers of iron) (114). The bells are the voice of Hugues's Ophelia, of his dead wife. As he walks alongside the canals he is able to discern "son visage d'Ophélie en allée . . . sa voix dans la chanson grêle et lointaine des carillons" (her Ophelia face floating along . . . her voice in the high-pitched distant song of the carillons) (16). Theirs is a voice which comes to haunt him: "Les cloches persuadaient, d'abord amicales, de bon conseil; mais bientôt inapitoyées, le gourmandant—visibles et sensibles pour ainsi dire autour de lui" (At first friendly, the bells offered good advice; but soon they ceased to commiserate, chiding him—visible and palpable around him so to speak) (84). There is throughout the book an insistent synesthetic imagery, tying visual imagery, sound, touch, and emotion. The organs on Sundays "semblaient draper par-dessus les fidèles des velours noirs et des catafalques de sons" (seemed to drape the assembled faithful with black velvet and catafalques of sound) (29).

> Et le trop-plein des gouttières avait beau dégouliner, le tunnel des ponts suinter des larmes froides, les peupliers du bord de l'eau frémir comme la plainte d'une frêle source inconsolable, Hugues n'entendait plus cette douleur des choses; il ne voyait plus la ville rigide et comme emmaillotée dans les mille bandelettes de ses canaux. (42)

> (That the rain spouts dripped, that the tunnel below the bridge wept cold tears, that the waterside poplars rustled like the lament of a frail and inconsolable spring, all were in vain. For Hugues no longer heard this sorrow of things, nor saw the hard edges of the city as if swaddled in the thousand bandages of its canals.)

In the silence of his rooms Hugues hears the chandelier which "au-dessus de sa tête, dans le silence clos des salons, émiettait de son goupillon de cristal grelottant la bruine d'une petite plainte" (above his head, in the enclosed silence of the rooms, gave out from its aspergillum of shivering crystal a gentle spluttering sigh) (50). The street lamps are wounds that bleed into the darkness (56). Jane's voice is a dark flood which he "drinks" (70). "Les peupliers du bord se plaignirent" (The poplars on the bank were complaining) (91). The swan cries out in a "voix blessée, presque humaine" (wounded voice, almost human) (92).

Parallels are established between music and architecture:

> Saint-Sauveur . . . d'où parfois tombe une musique qui se moire et déferle. . . . Cette musique était vaste, ruisselait des tuyaux sur les dalles; et c'est elle, eût-on dit, qui noyait, effaçait les inscriptions poussiéreuses sur les pierres tumulaires et les plaques de cuivre dont partout la basilique est semée. On pouvait dire vraiment qu'on y marchait dans la mort! (78–79)

> (Saint Sauveur . . . whence now and then tumbles forth music which shimmers and unfurls. . . . This music was vast, ran down pipes onto the flagstones; and that, one would have said, is what drowned and erased the dusty inscriptions on the tombstones and brasses scattered all over the basilica. It could truly be said that there one walked in death!)

Rodenbach's fascination with synesthesia is evident, too, in his descriptions of the microcosmic world of paintings by the great Flemish masters. In the *Shrine of Saint Ursula* by Memling, for instance, Hugues discovers angel musicians: "Ainsi le martyre s'accompagne de musiques peintes" (Thus the martyrdom is accompanied by painted music). The martyr-virgins are like flowers, masses of azaleas; their blood drips pink, like petals; like rubies congealing into "des diadèmes éternels" (eternal diadems). The painting was "like prayer" (80–82).

The line drawing (p. 106)[5] produced by Rodenbach's Belgian compatriot Fernand Khnopff (1858–1921) that served as frontispiece for the 1892 edition of *Bruges-la-Morte* sketches in its shorthand the essential elements of the novel: the juxtaposition of the two main "characters"—*la morte* and the city of Bruges—and all the encompassing "ophélisation." The dead woman (her face surrounded by an aureole of the all-important long tresses) lies on a bier that seems to float on the waters of the canal. The upper portion of the composition is dominated by the three arches of the bridge at the entrance of the Beguinage. This relatively minor drawing, however, only hints at the importance of Bruges to the overriding theme of the inner landscape in Khnopff's oeuvre.

A turning inward is expressed in the artist's ex libris, "Mihi"[6] as well as in his motto inscribed on an art-altar in his self-designed aesthetic temple-home: "On ne a que soi" (One has only oneself).[7]

This does not, however, indicate an elaboration of biographical details but rather, to the contrary, the withdrawal into a private psychological reality. It is a work about art making yet devoid of a self-confessional element. The painter creates a world of reflections—in mirrors, in glistening watery surfaces—in which he himself, however, is not represented. It is an art that is self-referential without being self-representational. The visage of his sister Marguerite or those of other Pre-Raphaelite beauties are his avatars. Bruges is the sacrosanct landscape of his childhood, a landscape of memory and sentiment, a place to which he never returns, neither in reality nor in his art. Khnopff embraces Rodenbach's text itself and the accompanying *similigravure* by Ch. G. Petit after photographs by Lévy and Neurdein in particular (rather than the city in reality) as the models for his many works which depict Bruges.

Khnopff's is an art about looking, about reality and representation, a narcissistic contemplation of the artist's task. And yet his oeuvre is almost devoid of self-portraits just as it eschews the mythological or allegorical reference. Instead he manipulates a vocabulary of neutral forms and opaque or hermetic subjects that communicate his inner aesthetic and psychological world. Expanses of stagnant, mirroring water fill the surfaces of the compositions. Reflection dominates real structure. Khnopff plays with radical spatial configurations—abrupt juxtapositions of near and far or compositions within the composition and "real" space—juxtapositions that cannot be explained or grasped rationally. The manipulation of illusionistic space and flatness tends toward abstraction.[8] Khnopff's hyperintensive attention to his medium—creating velvety charcoal surfaces or brittle and delicate pen lines; the manipulation of anaturalistic and often monochromatic color schemes—endows the works with an obtrusive sensuality, a peculiar ontological authority.[9]

The work of the French symbolist master, Gustave Moreau, departs less radically from a basis in allegory and myth. Nonetheless Moreau evolves an expressive painterly surface of fluid, abstract or nondescriptive forms. In *Orpheus Lamenting at the Tomb of Eurydice*, for instance, personal grief and sadness is invested with mythoheroic proportions derived from Orpheus's tragic loss of Eurydice and with an aura of saintly martyrdom.[10]

It is noteworthy in the context of the importance of synesthetic vocabulary in Rodenbach's work that Moreau describes his painting in terms of sounds or the absence thereof and their emotional

Fernand Khnopff. *Secret-Reflection*. 1902, pastel on paper. Groeningemuseum, Stedelijk Museum voor Schone Kunsten, Bruges.

Fernand Khnopff. *I Lock My Door upon Myself.* 1891, oil on canvas. Neue Pinakothek, Munich.

Gustave Moreau. *Orpheus Lamenting at the Tomb of Eurydice*. 1891–97, oil on canvas. Gustave Moreau Museum, Paris. (photo: Musées Nationaux).

significance. Moreau writes, "La grande voix des êtres et des choses est éteinte . . . le chantre sacré se tait pour toujours" (The great voice of beings and objects is extinguished . . . the sacred singer is quiet for always).[11] Orpheus does not cry out in his anguish but succumbs to his distress in mute sorrow. This is an image of intense physical and emotional suffering turned inward. Sound is squelched by the weight of grief:

> L'âme est seule, elle a perdu tout ce qui était la splendeur, la force et la douceur; elle pleure sur elle-même, dans cet abandon de tout, dans sa solitude inconsolée; elle gémit et sa plainte lourde est le seul bruit humain de cette solitude de mort. . . . Le Silence est partout, la lune apparaît au-dessus de l'édicule. . . . Seules les gouttes de rosée, tombant des fleurs d'eau, font leur bruit régulier et discret, ce bruit plein de mélancolie et de douceur, ce bruit de vie dans ce silence de mort.[12]

> (The soul is alone, having lost all that was its splendor, its force and sweetness, it laments itself, in this complete abandon, in this inconsolable solitude; it laments and its heavy complaint is the only human sound in this deathly solitude. . . . Silence is everywhere, the moon appears above the pavilion. . . . Only the drops of dew, falling from the flowers of water, make their regular and discreet noise, this sound full of melancholy and sweetness, this sound of life amid the silence of death.)

Indeed, the brooding and expressionistic landscape seems to flow with the anguish of the poet. The tree in the background is afire with red; the foreground is covered with fluid patches of saturated colors, as though made molten by the intensity of the poet's passion. The synesthetic ideal, the potency of pure plastic means, the psychological or emotional power of the landscape are the themes of Moreau's work as of the symbolist period generally. Moreau's ideas are entirely consistent, for instance, with those of the critic Gustave Kahn: "Le but essentiel de notre art est d'objectiver le subjectif (l'extériorisation de l'Idée) au lieu de subjectiver l'objectif (la nature vue à travers un tempérament)" (Our art's essential aim is to objectify the subjective [the exteriorization of the idea] instead of subjectifying the objective [nature seen through a temperament]).[13] Moreau emphasizes the role of the artist's imagination in his manipulation of the motif in nature, the importance of an unconscious or psychological reality:

> . . . une chose domine chez moi, l'entraînement et l'ardeur la plus grande vers l'abstraction. L'expression des sentiments humains, des

passions de l'homme m'intéresse, sans doute vivement, mais je suis moins porté à exprimer ces mouvements de l'âme et de l'esprit qu'à rendre pour ainsi dire visibles les éclairs intérieurs qu'on ne sait à quoi rattacher, qui ont quelque chose de divin dans leur apparente insignifiance et qui, traduits par les merveilleux effets de la pure plastique, ouvrent des horizons magiques, je dirai même divins.[14]

(One thing dominates in me, an attraction to and the greatest ardor about abstraction. The expression of human feelings and man's passions interests me a great deal no doubt; but I am less inclined to express these movements of the soul and spirit than to render visible, so to speak, the interior flashes that one cannot compare to anything, but which carry something divine in their apparent meaninglessness and which, translated by the marvelous effects of pure plastic form, open up magic, I would say even divine horizons.)

This concept parallels the advice of Paul Gauguin to his younger colleague Emile Schuffenecker in 1888: "Ne copiez pas trop d'après nature. L'art est une abstraction; tirez-la de la nature en rêvant devant" (Don't copy nature too much. Art is an abstraction; derive this abstraction from nature while dreaming before it).[15]

Moreau's painting was discussed by the theosophist critic and theorist Edouard Schuré, in his elaborate essay *Précurseurs et révoltés,* as an example of "psychological painting," in which the emotional power of form and color in the landscape is "analagous to that of the Wagnerian orchestra":

Ici nous voyons le monde d'en haut, par le côté de l'Esprit . . . Devant tel tableau du maître, nous avons l'intuition d'un monde plus homogène, où les éléments plus dociles et plus fluides revêteraient les formes et les couleurs de nos pensées. Le paysage joue ici un rôle analogue à celui de l'orchestre wagnérien. Par ses nuances et ses harmonies, il module les émotions du drame intérieur et les prolonge en arrière et en avant, dans un prodigieux au-delà du temps et de l'espace. . . . C'est du centre vivant de l'âme qu'il crée son monde, c'est selon les lois de l'âme qu'il le modèle et qu'il l'achève. Son art mérite donc à tous égards le nom de peinture psychique.[16]

(Here we see the world from on high, from the point of view of the Spirit. . . . Before such a painting by the master, we have an intuition of a more homogenous world where more docile and fluid elements assume the forms and colors of our thoughts. Here the landscape plays a role analogous to that of the Wagnerian orchestra. Through its nuances and harmonies, it modulates the emotions of an interior drama and prolongs them back and forth, in a prodigious world outside of time and space. It is from the living center of the soul that he creates his world, it is in accordance with the laws of the soul that he models and completes it. His art merits in all regards the name of psychological painting.)

For Téodor de Wyzewa, cofounder of the *Revue Wagnérienne,* Moreau was "le symphoniste des émotions raffinées" (the symphonist of refined emotions).[17] Wyzewa's praise, not only of Moreau, but of Redon, Bartholomé, Whistler, and Fantin-Latour reveals a concept of painting grounded in Wagner's renewal of the arts: encompassing a synthesis of all the arts (plastic arts, literature, music), an ideal vision of art as the creation of life (not merely the representation of objects but the exploration of the emotional or psychological world, that is, the entire human condition or reality).

The symbolist landscape, swelling and reverberating with emotion, is more than a mere backdrop for human drama, but rather constitutes a symbolist or synthetist abstract equivalent of emotion. This psychological landscape (independent of anecdote or narrative), infused into the constituent colors, lines, and forms themselves, parallels the abstraction inherent in Wagner's revolutionary music, which eschewed the traditional operatic form in favor of the "endless melody," the "melodic knot of motifs," the complex interweaving of symbolic themes, the leitmotifs. The abstract, indefinite emotional forces of Wagner's music that Wyzewa prized, inspired his appreciation of the abstract power of painting: "C'est que les couleurs et les lignes, sous l'influence de l'habitude, sont également revêtues pour les âmes d'une valeur émotionnelle, indépendante des objets même qu'elles représentaient" (The colors and lines, through the influence of habit, assume for the soul an emotional value, independent of the objects themselves which they represented).[18]

It was the "émotionnelle, symphonique" Wagnerian quality of Puvis de Chavannes's works that inspired Wyzewa's praise: "Maître, le poète exemplaire de la peinture moderne" (Master, the exemplary poet of modern painting).[19] The critic Alphonse Germain's investigation of Alphonse Osbert and other students and followers of Puvis similarly emphasized psychological qualities, the pure and abstract power of the forms. Osbert's works were termed psychic landscapes.[20] In his discussion of Alexandre Séon ("un peintre idéaliste-idéiste"), Germain uses the terminology of the prominent theoretician of symbolism, Albert Aurier. Aurier differentiated "Idéisme" or true symbolism comprising an expressive unit of form and subjective meaning and "Idéalisme," meaning the

Alphonse Osbert. *Evening Antique.* **1908, oil on canvas. Musée du Petit Palais, Paris.**

more conventional symbolic structures such as allegory and personification in which form and meaning are parallel but not identical.[21] In the works of Séon and Osbert the conventional subject matter (myths, allegories) is diminished in importance as the artists aspire to a correspondence of exterior form and subjective state of mind. For Germain, Séon's work was also a "Symbolisme des teintes." Profound melancholy, even despair, are communicated through reductive landscapes of almost geometric assemblages of broad areas of undifferentiated color. Séon's suppression of color is consistent with the muted palettes of Whistler, Munch, Puvis,

Hammershoi, Carrière, and Khnopff.[22] Gray, mauve, mysterious, and muted tonalities were idealized. Verlaine proclaimed in 1884: "Rien de plus cher que la chanson grise / Où l'Indécis au Précis se joint . . . / Car nous voulons la Nuance encore / Pas la Couleur, rien que la nuance!" (Nothing dearer than gray song / In which the vague and the precise combine . . . / For we still want nuance / Not color, nothing but nuance!).[23] A foggy environment became the antidote for a crude and intrusive reality.[24]

Odilon Redon's works were frequently approached as psychological landscapes. Wyzewa embraced Redon's dark and mysterious landscapes as examples of "la peinture wagnérienne," potent images of negative emotions.[25] Another influential critic and theorist of symbolism, Charles Morice, seems to identify Redon with an aesthetic ideal that reaches beyond Wagnerism—that is, beyond any narrative, historical, or mythical reference, to suggest a dream world beyond time and place.[26] Redon himself acknowledged his submission to the unconscious. His first set of lithographs, published in 1879, was entitled *Dans le rêve,* and is a clear manifestation of his fascination with the unconscious. Many of the compositions within this set, moreover, reveal new conceptions of "landscape." Redon alters the relationship between primary image and surrounding environment through radical manipulation of scale and perspective. In "Vision", for example, the environment surrounding the floating eyeball is not at all neutral but instead instills the composition with a bizarre tension. The floating eye is in itself grotesque and disturbing. However, it is the manipulation of scale (inspired perhaps by the artist's fascination with microscopic sciences) within the composition that creates the aura of nightmare. The artist achieves this by the juxtaposition of the miniaturized couple scurrying on a checkerboard floor and the columns of vast proportions. Redon's compositional experimentation leads to paintings that defy traditional genre distinctions. His luxurious flower still lifes, for instance, are transformed into compositions that can be described as neither still life nor garden scene but rather as the exteriorization of an interior, psychological realm, thought given form. The title of the circa 1912 oil painting, *The Dream*, makes the thematic and formal innovation explicit. The only explicit subject matter is the figure, depicted in profile, closed eyed and meditative. The floral explosion appears to emanate from this figure's fantasy, from some interior realm.[27] Sometimes the artist's means are incredibly minimal. In *Closed Eyes,* circa 1890, for instance, a thinly brushed environment of muted blue and gold,

Odilon Redon. "Vision" from *Dans le rêve.* 1879, lithograph.
Copyright: British Museum, London.

Odilon Redon. *The Dream*. ca. 1912, oil on canvas. Hahnloser-Jäggli Stiftung, Winterthur.

light directed from an unseen source at the right of the composition, the suggestion of a bath of unmoving water provides a synesthetic or metonymic environmental equivalent for the contemplative state of mind pictured in the meditative figure. Redon's own words, once again, attempt to capture the suggestive quality of his dream landscapes: "Je crois avoir fait un art expressif, suggestif, indéterminé" (I think I have created an expressive, suggestive, indeterminate art).[28] One would in this case, as well, be hard pressed to impose a discussion oriented toward the traditional mode of figure in the landscape. Redon attempts to create an image that is synonymous with quietude, reflection, meditation. One is tempted to suggest a parallel to the rising waters of Rodenbach's Ophélie-Bruges-la-Morte. A threatening sense of death and destruction is, however, entirely absent from Redon's composition. The calm manner in which the figure cedes to the rising tide suggests, instead, Narcissus achieving an oceanic oneness with nature. Redon's landscape is a synonymous equivalent—without recourse to anecdote, description, specificity of cause, situation, or metaphor—of an inner or emotional state.[29]

The Norwegian symbolist, Edvard Munch, very consciously conceived his work in terms of the "dissection of psychic phenomena."[30] The artist's own comments on his famous (and then controversial) painting, *The Cry* (1893), are consistent with this symbolist generation's focus on a psychological reality; an openness to a rich synesthetic vocabulary in art and nature; the conviction that this inner world could be captured in the essential and intrinsic elements of the painting—pure form and color. The Polish writer Stanislaw Przybyszewski, a member of Munch's circle in Berlin from 1892–94, commented on the landscape as an absolute correlative to the inner world:

> Seine Landschaft ist das absolute Correlat zu dem nackten Empfinden; jede Vibration der in höchster Schmerzensextase blossgelegten Nerven setzt sich in eine entsprechende Farbenempfindung um. Jeder Schmerz ein blutroter Fleck; jedes langgedehnte Schmerzgeheul ein Gurt blauer, grüner, gelber Flecke; unausgeglichen, brutal neben einander, wie etwa die kochenden Elemente werdender Welten in wilden Gestaltungsbrünsten. —Er malt so, wie nur eine nackte Individualität sehen kann, deren Augen sich von der Welt der Erscheinungen abgewendet und nach Innen gekehrt haben. Seine Landschaften sind in der Seele geschaut, als Bilder vielleicht einer platonischen Anamnese; seine Gestalten sind musikalisch empfunden, rhythmisch, (. . .) seine Wolken sehen

Odilon Redon. *Closed Eyes*. 1890, oil on canvas. Musée d'Orsay, Paris. (photo: Musées Nationaux).

wie spektroskopisches Farbengemenge aus; die Grenze des Horizontes existiert nicht, die Schiffe scheinen auf dem Himmel zu fahren.[31]

(His landscape is an absolute correlative of bare feelings; each vibration of the nerves, exposed in the highest paint-ecstasy, is translated into the appropriate color sensation. Every pain a blood-red spot; every extended scream of pain, a web of blue, green, and yellow spots; imbalanced, brutally juxtaposed, something like the brewing elements of emerging worlds in wild creative heat. —He paints, as only a naked individuality can see, whose eyes are turned away from the world of events toward his inner world. His landscapes are seen in the soul, as pictures of a platonic anamnesis; his forms are musically invented, rhythmically, . . . his clouds resemble spectroscopic color mixtures; the horizon line does not exist, the ships seem to float in the sky.)

Indeed, Przybyszewski described the emotional force of Munch's paintings as "Seelenlandschaften" (soulscapes).[32]

An examination of *The Starry Night* and related compositions reveals the evolution and refinement of Munch's *Seelenlandschaft*. The man and woman, lovers, who dominated the immediate foreground in a related lithograph dated 1896, are reduced to a rather inexplicable red or fiery bulbous shape in the foreground of the canvas. Specific human references, narrative details are eschewed in favor of a pure landscape in which, and in symbolist fashion, forms and colors pulsate with emotion. Reinhold Heller has thoroughly demonstrated the importance of international decadence, a reaction against naturalism and positivism, and the critical reception of Munch's works as psychologically potent, and specifically as evocations of "states of mind."[33]

The fascination with things psychological seems almost universal during this period. Artists, writers and critics, architects and designers were obsessed with the inner landscape, with the emotional power of color, line, and form. Just as in painting, the landscape was no longer conceived as a neutral backdrop for historical or mythological action, so the house, the architectural interior, the chair, the vase were no longer conceived as emotionally neutral objects or settings. Rodenbach explored the life of the object in "La Vie des choses" in *Le Règne du silence*. His fellow Belgian, Xavier Mellery, produced a related series of drawings entitled "L'Ame des choses," which communicate a force or voice hidden in the everyday object.[34] Perhaps with less theatrical lighting and exaggerated sense of mystery than Mellery, the Danish artist Vilhelm Hammershoi painted interiors, entirely stripped of decorative

Edvard Munch. *The Starry Night.* **1893, oil on canvas. Von der Heydt Museum, Wuppertal. (photo courtesy Antje Zeis-Loi).**

details, the architectural setting reduced to almost abstract assemblages of variously illuminated planes. These works, though related to the grand tradition of Dutch interiors, are quite radically symbolist in the manner in which emotion is expressed through the essential means of form, line, and color and without reliance on anecdote or narrative.[35]

The influential Viennese critic and writer, co-founder of *Ver Sacrum,* Hermann Bahr, defined art as the expression of an inner reality:

Der Künstler nimmt aus der Welt, was ihm als Zeichen seines seelischen Lebens dienen kann, was er als sich selbst empfindet. Das andere eliminiert er. Was nicht sein Symbol ist, lässt er also ohne Leben weg; die Welt lebt nur also, insofern sie seine Seele ist. Sein Verfahren ist, die Welt der Sinner auf das Leben seiner Seele zu reduzieren.[36]

Vilhelm Hammershoi. *Open Doors.* **1905, oil on canvas. The David Collection, Copenhagen. (photo courtesy Ole Woldbye).**

(The artist takes from the world that which can serve him as signs of his interior life, what he discovers as himself. The rest he eliminates. That which is not his symbol, he simply leaves lifeless aside; the world, therefore, only lives insofar as it is his soul. What he does is reduce the world of the senses to the life of his soul.)

Bahr's aesthetic notions reflect his animated interest in contemporary psychological theory and method. Indeed, Bahr's *Zur Ueberwindung des Naturalismus,* which appeared in 1891, included two sections on "Die neue Psychologie," in which new methods in psychology are likened to modern aesthetics. New psychology and the new school of painting aim at the raw truth of feelings, direct sensations—"auf den Nerven"—unfiltered by consciousness or memory, or processes of rational ordering.[37] Bahr also articulated his architectural ideal in psychological terms—it, too, a reflection of the soul, the inner nature. In his ideal interior, every line and space, every swatch of wallpaper, each chair and lamp should reflect the music of the soul.[38]

Bahr's notions about art and architecture bring together several of the central themes of the symbolist aesthetic: a belief in the inherent expressive power of form and color; the ideal of the *Gesamtkunstwerk* eradicating barriers between the arts and, specifically in the realm of the visual arts, between high art and applied art; and this based on a rich synesthetic vocabulary. The Belgian Henry Van de Velde, whose artistic life encompassed the roles of painter, designer, and architect and was, therefore, in itself symbolic of the ideal unity of the arts, similarly propounded the emotional and psychological significance of line and form. Tellingly, it is an architectural metaphor that Van de Velde uses to explain the emotional significance of artistic expression: "Car l'Art de demain sera plus personnel qu'aucun de ceux qui l'ont précédé. En aucun temps l'homme n'a pris autant de souci de se reconnaître et le lieu où il glorifiera le mieux cette individualité c'est dans le foyer que chacun de nous édifiera selon sa volonté, selon son coeur" (The art of tomorrow will be more personal than any that has preceded it. At no other time has man taken so much care to recognize himself, and the place where he will best glorify this individuality is in the home that each of us will design according to our desires, our soul).[39]

For the great master of Art Nouveau glass in France, Emile Gallé, the artistic process was "the execution of personal dreams".[40] Gallé was enthralled by new psychological theories and specifically shared with his compatriot from Nancy, Hippolyte Bernheim, an interest in hypnotism and suggestibility. Like Bahr (and sharing the Viennese critic's enthusiasm for contemporary psychological concepts), Gallé articulated an ideal of the metapsychological reality of the interior: "The painter of the walls that surround me should act as a poet, a magician; he must transfigure wood into bouquets, rugs into prairies, wallcoverings into ether, where, completely captive, I inhale. It is not enough that this music puts me to sleep for an instant . . . the decorative object must console me . . . with nuances that lead me to envision the shape of an alternative world."[41] Gallé's works were at times framed by art critics in psychological terms: "A very special art; its every manifestation provokes dreams and enchantment! The crystal's translucence is charged with reflections where memories of flowerings and flowerings of memories palpitate. For some, this amounts to nothing more than pleasurable refinements and voluptuous eyefuls. Others will find the delights of suggestion, an abandonment to the

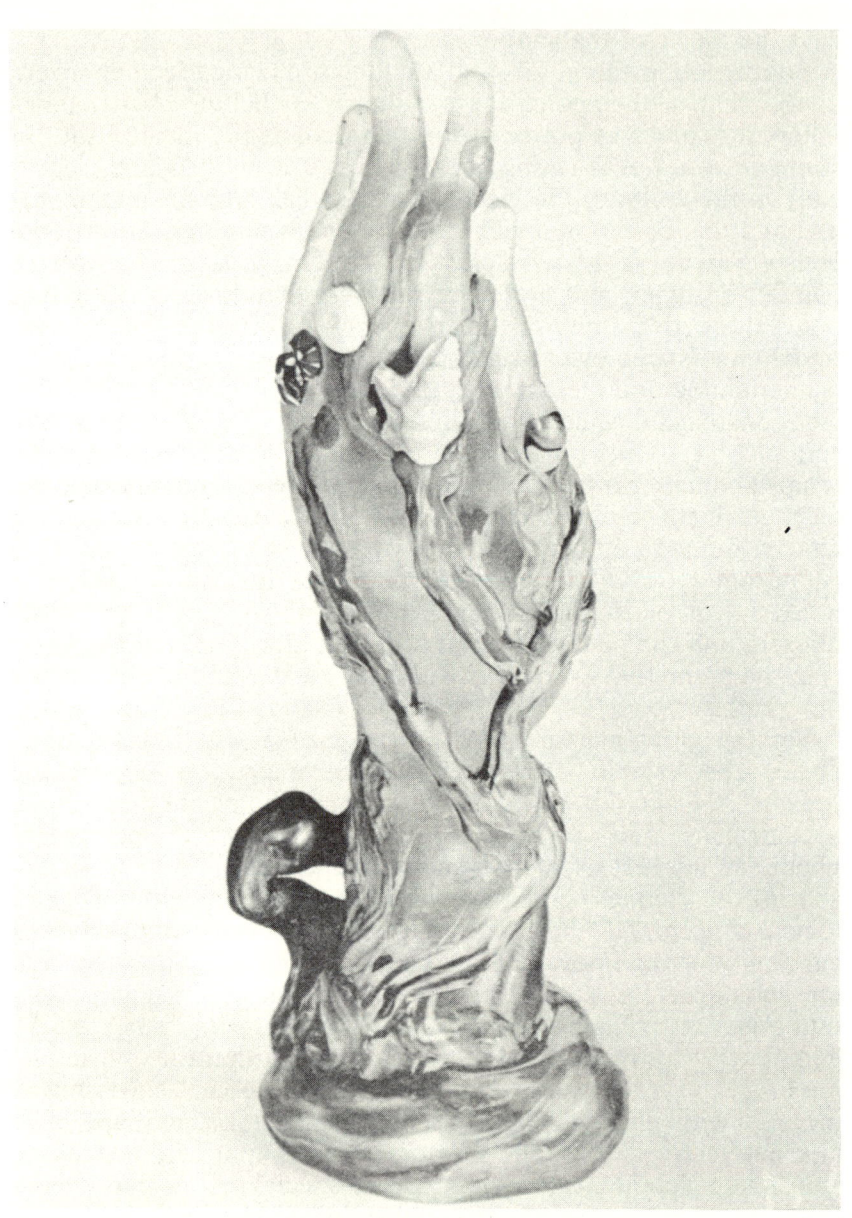

Emile Gallé. Vase, 1900. Musée de l'Ecole de Nancy. (photo: Musées Nationaux).

fluid thread that springs from our interior space."[42] How similar are the statements of Gallé and the contemporary French critics and those of Bahr in his journal in 1889: "Wir wollen überall die Synthese des Aeusserlichen und des Innerlichen, Welt und Ich, der wildesten Kraft (brutal, ungebrochen) und der zartesten, überreiztesten Raffiniertheit" (We want everywhere a synthesis of the exterior and the interior, of the world and the self, of the most savage [brutal, untamed] force and the most tender and hypersenstive refinement).[43] The psychiatrist often shared and reinforced these aesthetic theories. For instance, for Lou Andreas-Salomé, the arabesque form of Art Nouveau or the all-over ornamentation of Jugendstil was surely not mere decoration, but rather a line that breathes with the rhythms of nature as well as manifests the creative and profoundly subjective impulse of the artist-genius.[44] The interaction between the realms of psychology and Art Nouveau or Jugendstil aesthetics has been analyzed in terms of a crisis of identity associated, moreover, with an emerging sense of modernity. This equation of the cult of the individual, an aesthetic of the nerves, was part of an emerging sense of modernity, but was impacted, too, by distinct spirits of nationalism.[45]

The fascination with psychology and specifically the desire to give outer form to an inner landscape of thought and emotion figure significantly in the attempts of the theoreticians and critics, and of the artists themselves during the 1890s, to evolve a nomenclature to describe accurately their movement away from impressionism and naturalism. Mallarmé's metaphysical ideal, of course, was to "clothe the idea in sensible form," never to name but rather to suggest. For many, the rejection of symbol and metaphor, narrative and anecdote, and the release of the unconscious was ideally achieved through capturing musical tones in visual form. For the Wagnerist, Wyzewa, the emotional, symphonic quality was most important. Edouard Schuré, within the framework of his theosophical idealism, wrote of "psychological painting." Alphonse Germain struggled with Aurier's terminology of "Idéalisme" and "Idéisme" but emphasized Osbert's attempt to paint "psychological landscapes"; the Norwegian Aubert emphasized the "neurasthenic" qualities of Munch's art; his compatriot Arne Garborg used the term "Neo-Idealism" but emphasized the importance of the "soulscape";[46] for Hermann Bahr, the champion of a "romanticism of the nerves," the turn away from naturalism involved the desire to explore an interior world, to "model our interior universe";[47] Bahr emphasized a universal and synesthetic artistic language:

"darum handelt es sich: um eine neue Sprache, welche Nervenstände ausdrücken und mitteilen soll, indem sie die an ihnen charakteristischen Farben und Klänge gibt, welche von ihnen unzertrennlich sind" (The concern is with a new language which expresses states of the nerves and communicates them by presenting the colors and tones characteristic to them and inseparable from them).[48] Bahr's confidence in the expressive power of pure line, form, and color—which signify nothing but awaken sentiments through their force alone—heralds the advent of abstraction.[49] Indeed, one cannot ignore the importance of symbolism to the evolution of nonfigurative abstraction in the first decades of the twentieth century—in the works of Kandinsky, Mondrian, and Kupka, for instance. Symbolism, and specifically the notion of the soulscape, also informs Italian futurism. The futurists questioned conventional forms and genres: "Tutto in arte è convenzione, e le verità di ieri sono oggi, per noi, pure menzone. Affermiamo ancora une volta che il ritratto, per essere un'opera d'arte, non può né deve assomigliare al suo modello, e che *il pittore ha in sé i paesaggi che vuol produrre*" (All is conventional in art. Nothing is absolute in painting. What was truth for the painters of yesterday is but a falsehood today. We declare, for instance, that a portrait to be a work of art must not be like the sitter and that the painter carries in himself the landscapes which he would fix upon his canvas).[50] The February 1912 proclamation at the time of the Bernheim Jeune exhibition in Paris makes very evident the importance of the symbolist notions of "state of mind" and "soulscape" to the futurist aesthetic:

> La simultanéité des états d'âme dans l'oeuvre d'art: voilà le but enivrant de notre art. . . . Pour faire vivre le spectateur au centre du tableau, selon l'expression de notre manifeste, il faut que le tableau soit la synthèse de *ce dont on se souvien*t et *de ce que l'on voit*. . . . Le désir d'intensifier l'émotion esthétique fondant en quelque sorte la toile peinte avec l'âme du spectateur, nous a fait déclarer que celui-ci "doit être placé désormais au centre du tableau." . . . Eclairons encore notre idée par une comparaison tirée de l'évolution de la musique. Nous avons non seulement abandonné d'une façon radicale le motif entièrement développé suivant son équilibre fixe et par conséquent artificiel, mais nous coupons brusquement et à plaisir chaque motif par un ou plusieurs autres motifs, dont nous n'offrons jamais le développement entier, mais simplement les notes initiales, centrales ou finales. . . . Comme vous voyez, il y a chez nous non seulement variété, mais chaos et entrechoc de rythmes absolument opposés, que nous ramenons

néanmoins à une harmonie nouvelle. . . . Nous parvenons ainsi à ce que nous appelons *la peinture des états d'âme*.[51]

(The simultaneousness of states of mind in the work of art: that is the intoxicating aim of our art. . . . In order to make the spectator live in the center of the picture, as we express it in our manifesto, the picture must be the synthesis of what one remembers and of what one sees. . . . With the desire to intensify the aesthetic emotions by blending, so to speak, the painted canvas with the soul of the spectator, we have declared that the latter "must in future be placed in the center of the picture." . . . We may further explain our idea by a comparison drawn from the evolution of music. Not only have we radically abandoned the motive fully developed according to its determined and, therefore, artificial equilibrium, but we suddenly and purposely intersect each motive with one or more other motives of which we never give the full development but merely the initial, central, or final notes. As you see, there is with us not merely variety, but chaos and clashing of rhythms, totally opposed to one another, which we nevertheless assemble into a new harmony. We thus arrive at what we call the painting of states of mind.)

This is the context then of Rodenbach's soulscape or psychological landscape in *Bruges-la-Morte*. How does Rodenbach create the radical equation between Bruges and La Morte and Hugues's psychopathic obsession? Silent, omnipresent water provides the stifling, muffling, claustrophobic environment suitable to the turning inward, to the all-encompassing obsession. The mirrorlike symmetry of the book arrests the motion that attends normal narrative development, allowing instead for radical transformation and reversal: place is now within, landscape is soulscape. The symbolist soulscape—in the realm of literature, painting, or the decorative arts and architecture—is a complex notion, a composition of hieroglyphs of emotion by which the artist plumbs his own psychological depths and summons up his inner voice (narcissism) but simultaneously speaks directly (the priestly, cosmogenic function) to the psyche or soul of the viewer, suggesting, evoking, or provoking fantasy and dream.

Considering the perceived permeability of inner world and outer reality, it is hardly surprising that water imagery, fluid and changing in form, mirroring and profound, comes to dominate. We note, for instance, the critic's poetic description of the psychological adventure of Gallé's creations from molten glass: "an abandonment of the fluid thread that springs from our interior space" and Rodenbach's articulation of the city as "un état d'âme . . . [qui] se propage à nous en un fluide qui s'inocule et qu'on incorpore avec la nuance de l'air" (a state of mind . . . [that] spreads to us in a fluid which inoculates and which one incorporates with the nuance of the air) (76).[52] One can as well in this context consider the energetically modeled, seemingly billowing and fluid bronze surface of Auguste Rodin's *Gates of Hell*. The unifying element of this massive, epic sculpture—rather than a literary or narrative program—is the "sea" of bronze. It is, too, a spatially irrational plane, more readily described as a field of rhythmic energy than a surface that bears the complex assemblage of Rodin's Thinker's inner world.[53] In their desire to plumb the unconscious and discover a vocabulary that communicates directly an inner reality, the symbolists move toward a rich and suggestive synonymy, by which image, meaning, and effect are one.

Notes

1. Georges Rodenbach, *Bruges-la-Morte* (Paris: Flammarion, 1978), 75–76 and English trans., Philip Mosley (Paisley, Scotland: Wilfion Books, 1986; Chester Springs, Pa.: Dufour Editions, 1991), 51. All further references to the French text will be in parentheses within the text.

2. Gaston Bachelard, *L'Eau et les rêves: Essai sur l'imagination de la matière* (Paris: José Corti, 1991), 121.

3. See "Ophelia Becomes Medusa: Reversals and Ambiguity in Georges Rodenbach's *Bruges-la-Morte*" in this volume. Professor Lowrie situates this "hinge" in chapters 6 and 7.

4. Guy Michaud, *Message poétique du symbolisme* (Paris: Nizet, 1947), 493. All translations are the author's own unless otherwise noted.

5. Robert L. Delevoy, *Fernand Khnopff*, with catalogue raisonné by Catherine de Croes and Gisele Ollinger Zinque (Brussels: Cosmos Monographies, Editions Lebeer-Hossmann, 1979), cat. no. 200.

6. Ibid., cat. no. 196.

7. Ibid., cat. no. 197.

8. Concerning *I Lock My Door upon Myself*, see L. D. Morrissey, "Isolation of the Imagination: Fernand Khnopff's 'I Lock My Door upon Myself,'" *Arts* (December 1978): 94–97; S. Burns, "A Symbolist Soulscape: Fernand Khnopff's 'I Lock My Door upon Myself,'" *Arts* (January 1981): 80–89; Günter Metken, "In Sich Vergraben—Zu einem Bild von Fernand Khnopff," in *Wunderblock—eine Geschichte der Modernen Seele* (Vienna: Wien Festwochen, 1989), 433–39.

9. See in this regard Reinhold Heller, "The Art Work as Symbol," in *Fernand Khnopff and the Belgian Avant-Garde*, exh. cat. (New York: Barry Friedman, 1983), 10–15. See Dorothy Kosinski, "The Gaze of Fernand Khnopff," *Source* (essays in honor of Gert Schiff), 11, nos. 3–4 (spring–summer 1992), 26–33.

10. See Dorothy Kosinski, *Orpheus in Nineteenth-Century Symbolism* (Ann Arbor, Mich.: UMI Research Press, 1989), 151ff. This lamenting Orpheus is through Moreau's syncretic poetry a saintly martyr, a pagan Saint Sebastian as it were, a hybrid poet-artist in confrontation with cosmic forces of the universe.

Moreau's text parallels God's control of the artist to the bird keeper's cruel taming of the bird, "gouging out their eyes so that they might sing better."

11. *Cahier rouge,* unpublished notebook, Paris, Gustave Moreau Museum, 65.
12. Ibid.
13. Gustave Kahn, "Réponse des symbolistes," *L'Evénement* (28 September 1886).
14. Gustave Moreau, *L'Assembleur de rêves: Ecrits complets,* preface Jean Paladilhe, ed. Pierre-Louis Mathieu (Fontfroide: Bibliothèque Artistique, 1984), 29. Philippe Jullian, *The Symbolists* (Oxford: Phaidon, 1973), 50, attributes the following to Moreau: "What importance does Nature have by Herself? She is nothing more than excuse for the artist to express himself. . . . Art is the never ending search for the expression of internal feelings by means of plastic form."
15. Paul Gauguin, letter to Emile Schuffenecker, Pont Aven, 14 August 1888, *Correspondance de Paul Gauguin (1873–1888),* ed. V. Merlhès (Paris: Fondation Singer-Polignac, 1984), 210.
16. Edouard Schuré, "La Peinture psychique et le symbolisme transcendant," in *Précurseurs et révoltés* (Paris: Perrin, 1920), 340. This chapter was originally published as an article in *Revue de Paris* (1 December 1900): 587–622.
17. Téodor de Wyzewa, "La peinture wagnérienne—le Salon de 1885," *La Revue Wagnérienne* 1 (1885): 154–56.
18. Wyzewa, "Notes sur la peinture wagnérienne et le Salon de 1886," *La Revue Wagnérienne* (8 May 1886) (Geneva: Slatkine Reprints, 1968), 2:106.
19. Ibid., 110–11. In his study of Puvis, Marius Vachon associated three works as "une trilogie de la misère"; see *Puvis de Chavannes* (Paris: Société des Editions Artistique, 1895).
20. See Jullian, *The Symbolists,* 50, concerning Germain's discussion of Osbert's psychic landscapes.
21. G.-Albert Aurier, "Le Symbolisme en peinture—Paul Gauguin," *Mercure de France* 2 (March 1891): 155–65.
22. Alphonse Germain, "Un Peintre idéaliste-idéiste—Symbolisme des teintes—Alexandre Séon," *L'Art et l'Idée* 2 (February 1892): 109–10. In regard to Germain's "Symbolisme des teintes," see Reinhold Heller, "Edvard Munch's 'Night': The Aesthetics of Decadence, and the Content of Biography," *Arts* 53, no. 2 (October 1978): 80–105, esp. 87, concerning the importance of monochromatic compositions in the oeuvres of painters championed by the Norwegian critic, Andreas Aubert (Munch, Whistler, Böcklin, Puvis, Hammershoi) and the Viennese writer and critic, Hermann Bahr (Whistler, Carrière, Burne-Jones, Khnopff, Munch), for instance; and the importance of blue in particular to the decadent, antinaturalistic aesthetic. Heller provides a good résumé of the evolution of theories of subjective and synesthetic significance of color in romanticism through symbolism (Baudelaire, Delacroix, Runge, Goethe, Rimbaud, Seurat, Charles Henry, Schopenhauer).
23. Paul Verlaine, "Art poétique," in *Oeuvres poétiques* (Paris: Garnier, 1969), 261–62.
24. The following statement is attributed to Wyzewa: "Satiated with light too vivid and too crude, we longed for fog." In J. Milner, *Symbolists and Decadents* (London: Studio Vista; New York: Dutton, 1971), 52.
25. Wyzewa, "La Peinture wagnérienne—le Salon de 1885," identifies Redon's landscapes with bitterness, fear, and cruelty. In this regard see Robert L. Delevoy, *Symbolists and Symbolism* (Geneva: Skira, 1982), 47.
26. Charles Morice, *La Littérature de tout à l'heure* (Paris: Perrin, 1889),

358–79. In this regard see Richard Hobbs, *Odilon Redon* (Boston: New York Graphic Society, 1977), 74.

27. See Kosinski, *Orpheus,* 161 and fig. 5.22, concerning the palpable manifestation of the artist's thoughts as part of the complex of themes of muse and creative burden in the sculpture of Auguste Rodin.

28. Odilon Redon, *A soi-même, journal (1867–1915)* (Paris: J. Corti, 1961), 116. In this regard see Hobbs, *Odilon Redon,* 168.

29. See Kosinski, *Orpheus,* 200ff.

30. A manuscript letter by Munch, preserved in the archives of the Munch Museet, Oslo (T2734), is quoted by Pierre-Louis Mathieu, *La Génération symboliste, 1870–1910* (Geneva: Skira, 1990), 23.

31. *Das Werk des Edvard Munch,* ed. Stanislas Przybyszewski (Berlin: S. Fischer Verlag, 1894), 24ff. See in this regard *Edvard Munch* (Essen: Museum Folkwang; Zürich: Kunsthaus; and Oslo: Munch Museum, 1987), cat. no. 30.

32. *Das Werk des Edvard Munch,* 17.

33. Heller, "Edvard Munch's 'Night,'" 80–105; esp. 83 n. 41, about Knut Hamsun in the Norwegian journal *Samtiden.* The critic Andreas Aubert championed not only Munch, but Puvis de Chavannes, Böcklin, Max Klinger, Gabriel Max, and Vilhelm Hammershoi as neurasthenics, proponents of a psychologically oriented art.

34. See Robert Goldwater, *Symbolism* (New York: Harper and Row, 1979), 210–11, and Sarah Faunce, "Seurat and 'the Soul of Things,'" in *Belgian Art, 1880–1914* (New York: Brooklyn Museum, 1980), 41–56, concerning the importance of this notion of expressing an essential and mysterious quality of the inanimate in literature (Verhaeren) and the fine arts in Belgium in the 1880s and 1890s.

35. Hammershoi was in fact linked by contemporary critics to Rodenbach, precisely because of his emotion-or mood-rife compositions. A landscape such as *St. Peter's Church, Copenhagen* (1906, Statens Museum for Kunst, Copenhagen), might well be compared to the claustrophobic and melancholic silence of *Bruges-la-Morte.* (See *Northern Light, Realism and Symbolism in Scandinavian Painting, 1880–1910* [New York: Brooklyn Museum, 1982], 132.) Similarly, the pointillist landscapes of the 1890s by Henry Van de Velde, in their monochromatic coloration, the almost total absence of people and movement, and the clear intention of evoking memories and dreamscapes rather than depicting real scenes from nature also come to mind. See, for example, *Childhood Landscape,* 1891, oil on canvas, Collection Mr. and Mrs. Arthur G. Altschul, New York, no. 28, in *Henry Van de Velde* (Antwerp: Koninklijk Museum voor Schone Kunsten and Otterlo: Rijksmuseum Kröller-Müller, 1988).

36. Hermann Bahr, undated journal entry, *Prophet der Moderne: Tagebücher 1888-1904,* ed. Reinhard Farkas (Vienna: Böhlau Verlag, 1987), 70.

37. Bahr comments: "Die alte Psychologie findet immer nur den letzten Effekt der Gefühle, welchen Ausdruck ihnen am Ende das Bewusstsein formelt und das Gedächtnis behält. Die neue wird ihre ersten Elemente suchen, die Anfänge in den Finsternissen der Seele, bevor sie noch an dem klaren Tag herausschlagen.... Die Psychologie wird aus dem Verstande in die Nerven verlegt.... Darum wird die neue Psychologie, welche die Wahrheit des Gefühles will, das Gefühl auf den Nerven aufsuchen, gerade wie die neue Malerei, welche die Wahrheit der Farbe will, die Farbe in den Augen aufsucht, während alle alte Kunst sich ins Bewusstsein versperrte, das in alles Lüge trägt" [The old psychology still only finds the end effect of feelings, expression formed at the end of consciousness

and retained in memory. The new [psychology] would look for the initial elements of feeling, the beginnings in the dark regions of the soul before they emerge into the clarity of day. . . . Psychology is transferred from the intellect to the nerves. The new psychology, therefore, which seeks the truth about feelings, looks for feelings in the nerves, just as the new painting, which insists on true colors, looks therefore for colors in the eyes, while all older art barricaded itself into consciousness which carries lies into everything]. *Zur Ueberwindung des Naturalismus, Theoretische Schriften 1887–1904,* ed. Gotthart Wunberg (Stuttgart: W. Kohlhammer Verlag, 1968), 57–58. See also in this regard, Harald Leopold-Löwenthal, "Les Minutes de la société de psychanalyse," in *Vienne, 1880–1938, l'apocalypse joyeuse,* ed. Jean Clair (Paris: Editions de Centre Pompidou, 1986), 132.

38. See Carl E. Schorske, "De la scène publique à l'espace privé," in *Vienne, 1880–1935, l'apocalypse joyeuse,* 76, citing Bahr, *Sezession* (Vienna: Wiener Verlag, 1900), 37: "Je devrais donc d'abord dire à un architecte ma beauté intérieure. . . . Il me connaîtrait alors, il pourrait sentir ma nature. C'est elle qu'il devrait exprimer par une ligne: il lui faudrait trouver le geste de ma nature. . . . Au-dessus du porche serait écrit un vers: le vers qui correspond à ma nature, et ce que dirait ce vers en paroles ce serait aussi toutes les couleurs et toutes les lignes, tous les papiers-peints, chaque chaise, chaque lampe étant toujours le même vers. Je retrouverais dans une telle maison mon âme partout comme dans un miroir. . . . Ce serait ma maison. Et là je pourrais vivre pour moi-même, contemplant mon propre visage et prêtant l'oreille à ma propre musique." [I should first explain my interior beauty to an architect. . . . He would know me then, he could feel my nature. It is that which he should express with line: he must find the gesture of my nature. . . . A verse would be inscribed above the entrance: a verse which corresponds to my nature. What this verse would say with words, would be expressed by all the colors and all the lines. Every wall paper and every chair, every lamp, all of these would be the same verse. I would find my soul everywhere in such a house, as in a mirror. . . . That would be my house. And in it I could live for myself, contemplating my own face, hearing my own music].

39. Henry Van de Velde, *Aperçus en vue d'une synthèse d'art* (Brussels: Monnom, 1896), 31.

40. Emile Gallé, *Ecrits pour l'art* (Paris: Laurens, 1908), 350, as quoted by Debora L. Silverman, *Art Nouveau in Fin-de-Siècle France: Politics, Psychology, and Style* (Berkeley: University of California Press, 1989), 237.

41. Gallé, 198, as quoted by Silverman, *Art Nouveau,* 239.

42. Louis de Fourcaud, "Les Arts décoratifs aux Salons de 1894," *Revue des Arts Décoratifs* 15 (1894–95): 2, as quoted by Silverman, *Art Nouveau,* 241.

43. Bahr, *Tagebücher,* 48. In this regard see Jacques Le Rider, *Modernité viennoise et crises de l'identité* (Paris: Presses Universitaires de France, 1990), 64 in particular. Note Le Rider's (pp. 25 and 34) acknowledgment of Bahr's important role as cultural broker between Austria and France, but also his vision of Bahr as a kind of intellectual chameleon self-consciously keeping one step ahead of the next "ism."

44. See in this regard Lou Andreas-Salomé, "Friederich Nietzsche in seinen Werken" (1894), in *L'Amour de narcissisme: Textes psychanalytiques,* trans. Isabelle Hildenbrand, pref. Marie Moscovici (Paris: Gallimard, 1980); and "Narzissimus als Doppelrichtung," *Imago. Zeitschrift für Anwendung der Psychoanalyse auf die Geisteswissenschaften* 7, no. 4 (1921): 361–86. See also Le Rider, *Modernité viennoise,* 90.

45. Note the importance of these themes in Le Rider, *Modernité viennoise,* and Silverman, *Art Nouveau.*

46. Heller, "Edvard Munch's 'Night,'" 81, 83.

47. Bahr, "Die Décadence," in *Studien zur Kritik der Moderne* (Frankfurt am Main: Ruetten and Loening, 1894), 21. In *Zur Ueberwindung des Naturalismus,* Bahr champions Maeterlinck as an exponent of the "romanticism of the nerves": "Wenn sie Recht behielten, dann wäre die Kunst des Maurice Maeterlinck als die Kunst der Neurose die wahre Kunst der Moderne. . . ." (102). [If they are right, then the art of Maurice Maeterlinck, the art of the nerves, would be the true art of the modern. . . .]

48. Bahr, "Maeterlinck," in *Zur Ueberwindung des Naturalismus,* 100. English translation from Heller, "Edvard Munch's 'Night,'" 86.

49. Dieter Bogner, "Une Moderniste optimiste: La Voie abstraite," in *Vienne, 1880–1938, l'apocalypse joyeuse,* 648, cites Bahr, "Impressionismus" (1903): "on peut imaginer un tableau dont le seul effet serait celui produit par ses couleurs qui ne signifient rien, ne dépeignent et ne représentent rien, mais doivent éveiller des sentiments et créer une atmosphère par leur seule force" (from Heinz Kindermann, *Essays von Hermann Bahr* [Vienna: H. Bauer, 1962], 186). [one can imagine a painting which would only have the effect produced through colors which in themselves signify nothing, neither depicting nor representing anything, but which should evoke sentiments and create an atmosphere by their sheer force]

50. "La Pittura Futurista, Manifesto Tecnico," 11 April 1910, as quoted in *Archivi del futurismo,* ed. Maria Drudi Gambillo, Teresa Fiori (Rome: DeLuca Ed., 1958), 65 (emphasis is mine).

51. "Les Exposants au public," as quoted in *Archivi del futurismo,* 104–8. The text goes on to explain how the psychological or inner reality is expressed in pure form, line, and color of the painting, warning that "it is practically impossible to express in words the essential values of painting."

52. For Fourcaud on Gallé, see n. 42. Note Bahr, cited in nn. 36 and 37, concerning the synthesis of inner and outer worlds.

53. Goldwater, *Symbolism,* 166, credits Rodin with the following statement about psychology and his art: "The sculpture of antiquity sought the logic of the human body. I seek its psychology."

Symbolization of Urban Space in *Bruges-la-Morte* and in Andrei Bely's *Petersburg*

Peter I. Barta

RODENBACH'S *Bruges-la-Morte* (1892) and Bely's *Petersburg* (1916) occupy a distinguished position in the tradition of the European novel: named after the city that serves as the protagonist, each stands as prominent representative of the small corpus of symbolist novels. While Bely was undoubtedly familiar with Rodenbach, nothing seems to indicate that *Bruges-la-Morte* overtly informs the consciousness of Bely's novel. Literary influence will not, therefore, serve as the primary point of reference in this study. Prominent Russian symbolist journals such as *Vesy, Zolotoe runo,* and *Russkaya mysl'* reviewed Rodenbach's works but considered him a somewhat marginal figure. Verhaeren, Mallarmé, Baudelaire, Wedekind, Wilde, and Nietzsche clearly had a greater impact on Russian intellectual life than Rodenbach.[1] M. V. Veselovskaya translated some of Rodenbach's prose into Russian. Zinaida Vengerova's study of Rodenbach indicates that translations of *Le Carillonneur* and *L'Art en exil* attracted greater attention in Russia than *Bruges-la-Morte* (Veselovskaya translated it into Russian in 1904 under title *Myortvy Brugge*).[2] Although the superficial similarities between the two cities and the two authors do not in themselves justify a comparison of the two texts, they are significant enough to be mentioned. Each was the son of a well-known scientist. Neither Rodenbach nor Bely were natives of the cities of their novels. Furthermore, they did not live there when they wrote them. Both Rodenbach and Bely wrote dramatic versions of their novels: Bely's historical play in ten scenes, based on *Petersburg,* is entitled *Gibel' senatora* (The death of the senator) and Rodenbach's play *Le Mirage,* based on *Bruges-la-Morte,* served as the source of Paul Schott's libretto for Korngold's opera, *Die tote Stadt.*[3]

Turning to the two cities, we may note that the sea had a decisive role to play in the history of both Bruges and Petersburg. In 1475, it withdrew from the Flemish city; the canals are indeed dead arteries. Petersburg, by contrast, is anything but "dead": it has been flooded by the sea on many occasions in its relatively short existence. The nervousness with which the city anticipates the potentially devastating rise of the sea level is one of the reasons for the feverishness and explosiveness that pervade not just Bely's novel but most literary accounts of the city.

A more promising point of departure for this study lies in specific thematic affinities between the two texts. Rodenbach emphatically suggests in his foreword that Bruges—a city that "appears almost human"[4]—is the main character of the novel. In his prologue, Bely reveals that the ontological status of the "spirit" of the city is the central problem of *Petersburg*. The narrator of the prologue says of the city that "[i]t only appears to exist."[5] Like Rodenbach, Bely postulates that Petersburg has an intellect of its own. By endowing space with symbolism, both writers personify their cities. Through examining these similarities, we can see that Rodenbach and Bely use the city for the purpose of symbolization in two different ways: in Rodenbach's novel the city's "personality" becomes knowable and gains specificity thanks to its approximation to the human protagonist's state of mind. In Bely's novel, however, the city's mysterious and invisible "center" is beyond the reach of the novel's narrative, which probes the characters' lives, shattered as they are by the experience of Petersburg. The two authors' different application of the symbolic potential of the city for the literary exploration of human consciousness throws light on the versatility of this figure in the fin de siècle period.

The patterns of foregrounding the city exhibit some obvious similarities: characters in both novels spend a great deal of time away from their homes, moving about in the city. In a comparative study of *Bruges-la-Morte* and *Petersburg*, Claude De Grève suggests that the two novels resemble each other in portraying fictional journeys about the city amid factual and recognizable architectural ensembles and monuments.[6] Hugues Viane, the protagonist of *Bruges-la-Morte,* goes out for long walks in search of a soothing alternative to his home, in which he feels dejected. Similarly, fear at home and in the streets prompts Bely's protagonists to be on the move. They are searching even though they are unable to identify the object of their desire. Their unhappiness originates in the implied transcendental center, which is beyond their reach. They constantly sense the presence of an ominous entity, but they are denied access behind its veil, the physical city.

Yet the invisible "soul" of the city keeps reminding the citizens of its existence. Mysterious whispers and moans emanate from behind doors. The islands are "crying"; "babbling" issues from the walls and gateways of the streets at night (Bely, 131). The narrator directly addresses the city:

> Petersburg, Petersburg!
> Precipitating out as fog, you have pursued me with cerebral play. Cruel-hearted tormentor! Restless spectre! For years you have attacked me. I have run along the horrible Prospects, to land with a flying leap on this very same gleaming bridge . . . (Bely, 148)

Desire for control and wholeness is the moving force in both novels, even if Rodenbach's theme is more specific: Hugues's only wish is to reunite with his dead wife. Her spirit and the city appear to be in symbolic unity: harmony with Bruges holds out the promise of a reunion with the dead woman. However, as in *Petersburg,* the "spirit" of the city with its promise of fullness surrounds Hugues in its physical signs—the churches, canals, and statues—but it forever eludes him, slipping out of his reach.

The narrator's futile attempt to capture the "center" of the city accounts for mythicizing its architecture and physical environment.[7] Throughout both novels, the same locations are revisited: inasmuch as these do not change even as time passes, they add an atemporal, eternal background to human actions.[8] The city's physical environment contains its history, a symbolic reenactment of which is produced by the events of the plot. Passions are to remain forever frozen and a love of death rather than of life prevails in *Bruges-la-Morte.* The facades of houses resemble the sterns of ships, alluding to the city's loss of the sea in the fifteenth century.[9] Indeed, the bells in the towers, the gables of houses in the shape of crosses, the Beguinage, the Procession of the Holy Blood, the nuns dressed in black—the color of mourning—all allude to loss: the death of Christ, the death of a loved one, the retreat of the sea.

Bely also utilizes the architecture and physical environment of Petersburg for his mythopoesis: of primary significance are buildings, statues, and ornaments reminding the novel's characters, as indeed the reader, of Peter the Great, the tsar responsible for the city's creation. The tapering spires of the Peter-Paul Fortress, the Admiralty, and, most important, Falconet's statue, the Bronze Horseman, lend the city intense mythohistorical significance. Repressed emotions inform the past and the present, inciting rebellion when sons and fathers plot against each other. The novel's cityscape includes the Mikhailovsky Palace, in which Paul I was murdered. His son, Alexander, was involved in planning his assassination. As the time bomb—set by the son, Nikolai Apollonovich, against his father, Apollon Apollonovich Ableukhov—keeps ticking away in Bely's novel, the Winter Palace, the residence of Russia's rulers, "bleeds" (Bely, 147).

The characters of Bely's and Rodenbach's cities end their peregrinations where they started—at home. A final return to the home offers a resolution of the conflict: an event of apocalyptic proportions changes the life of the main characters for good. A shattering blast diffuses the tension built up during the wanderings about Petersburg: the time bomb explodes and brings down the walls of the family home in both a physical and a metaphorical sense. In *Bruges-la-Morte,* Hugues strangles his lover and unites the image of the "pure" wife and her "evil" double within the confines of death. In fact, apocalyptic symbolism frequently typifies literature of the city. Unlike the "nature" that surrounds humanity, societies build cities in which "human destiny is translated into purely human terms."[10] The odds are against Rodenbach's and Bely's citizens: they fail to accomplish their goals and their search is ultimately futile. Nonetheless, they cannot tolerate the restrictions that frustrate them and they finally rebel. They struggle with an almost personified entity, the city. As suggested already, personification is made possible through the symbolization of the city space. In this general process, the narrative account establishes values.[11] The implied author is the narrator in *Bruges-la-Morte;* his vision is omniscient but he is closest to Hugues's inner world. Thus he monitors a city that is either in, or out of, sympathy with Hugues. He is condescending about the city's narrow-minded attitudes: "nothing escapes attention in such a meagre provincial life" (Rodenbach, 25). His evaluation of Hugues's relationship with his lover is biased and one-sided, however. It reflects the city's intolerance, of which he is himself so critical.

Instead of a unified narrator, as in *Bruges-la-Morte,* many narrating voices disguise the implied author in *Petersburg*. Mikhail Bakhtin suggests that this is the only Russian novel that shows Dostoevskian polyphony.[12] The voices of the various storytellers (who are the products of the same "cerebral play" that generates Bely's city and people) range between pathos and complete irony and, as a result of this, the novel lacks a clearly expressed perspective. In a typically modernist manner, these narrating voices fail to create order in the disorder.

The physical world mediated in the narrative is equally chaotic.

Historically in urban novels the domestic environment resembles, even reflects, the human inhabitants. Besides obvious social markers (rich people have spacious, comfortable homes, while the poor live in cramped impoverished places), the houses also show analogies with their owners' psychological attributes. This comforts the occupants. In *Petersburg,* notwithstanding the strong correspondence between dwellings and their occupants, the domestic space fails to shelter and protect; all of the novel's major characters feel uncomfortable and terrified in their own homes.[13] In *Bruges-la-Morte* the narrator focuses on just one character; nevertheless, the same principle prevails as in Bely's novel. Hugues's home is an extension of his soul, yet he feels oppressed and uncomfortable when he is there. Gaston Bachelard argues that the house is the "non-I" protecting the "I" and allowing the human subject to dream in peace.[14] In terms of phenomenology, the home in Rodenbach's and Bely's novels is the exact opposite of a shelter for well-being.

Hugues chose his house on the quai du Rosaire because of its darkness and silence: the place resembles a tomb.[15] As in the Russian novel, the "mood" of Bruges infiltrates the house in which death is cherished: a group of mementos is crowned by a small casket containing the dead woman's hair. Hugues seeks out the atmosphere of death in order to move nearer to his wife: he arranges the dead woman's objects with loving care so as to sense her presence. And yet he feels uncomfortable and deprived at home: he searches for opiates outside, in the city, and finally entangles himself with his wife's look-alike, the dancer Jane Scott, who becomes his lover. He cannot bear the solitude of his house: he walks about the city, along the quiet streets and canals. When it was raining and cold outside, and he was exhausted, he "sat down in an armchair, tried to read; then, within seconds, drowned in solitude, overcome by the silence of those long hallways, he went out again" (Rodenbach, 48).

No pleasantness—however short-lived—awaits the tired and nervous walkers in *Petersburg* either. They leave their homes because it is intolerable to stay there. In Senator Ableukhov's case this seems paradoxical: we learn from the narrator that the house is an extension of him. It is his "brainchild," as Pallas Athene is of Zeus: "Apollon Apollonovich was like Zeus. Thus, scarcely had the Stranger-Pallas been born out of his head when from there another Pallas, exactly like it, came crawling out. This Pallas was the senator's house" (Bely, 21). His social position dictates that he should have a stately home: his house contains large reception rooms, corridors, and a staircase. But Apollon Apollonovich Ableukhov is terrified of open spaces: in his capacity as a high-ranking bureaucrat he wishes to regulate the wide expanses of his country whose uncontrollability he fears. He draws up boundaries and divides space into geometrical patterns. He follows this system in his house: he has his belongings neatly cataloged and filed away. Except in his bedroom and toilet he feels uncomfortable in the house. The outside world penetrates to a lesser extent into these small areas. Downstairs, however, the big windows reveal vistas of the river and the islands. In these parts of the house the white covers over the large pieces of furniture (the Ableukhov house retains the memory of Senator Ableukhov's wife who left her family home and native land for another man: the furniture had been unused since the senator's wife left), the white walls, and the cold mirrors and statuettes remind him of the endless snow-covered plains of Russia where he once nearly froze to death.[16]

In neither novel does the city allow the inhabitants to appropriate isolated spaces, such as the home, which might offer safety and comfort. But the concept of an ominous outside world penetrating both the walls of the home and the self presents itself with greater urgency and is more central in Bely's novel than in Rodenbach's. The experiences in the streets disconcert Bely's characters. The wish to disappear into the city's seeming infinity fosters people's desire to take to the streets: both the myriapod-like crowd and the dense night annul individual differences between the citizens.[17] And yet, as the senator attempts to disappear in the dark islands at night, he feels that not only the citizens but even the walls of the houses in which they live hate him. Danger seems to lurk behind the dark gates and fences. By itself, this is hardly surprising: the year is 1905 and the action takes place during the revolution. However, people's sense of discomfort in the city is rooted in more than merely political and social factors. The city's actual physical environment is threatening: the waters in the canals are green and bacilli-infested, red streetlights blaze ominously in the black mist. Most of the action in the plot is shrouded in darkness or twilight. In daylight, when the fog lifts, the gilded tapering spires reflect the red rays of the sun blinding the eyes. The city's ubiquitous presence denies its citizens any privacy: they feel like prisoners.[18] Their walls are permeable, like a "second skin,"[19] and inside their homes people sense that they are under surveillance.[20] The source of fear presents itself as an invisible, metaphysical force. Nikolai Apollonovich, like his father, the senator, perceives this force: "from time to time, while passing from the outer door to the inner door of the entryway, a certain strange, very strange state came over him, as if everything that was beyond the door was not what it was, but something else. Beyond the door there was nothing" (Bely, 164). The mysterious city penetrates the consciousness, as Nikolai Apollonovich's nightmare illustrates (he sees himself running along a foggy Petersburg prospect).

The fog fills Hugues's soul in *Bruges-la-Morte:* his "thoughts [are] blurred and drowned in grey lethargy" (Rodenbach, 49). However, Hugues came to Bruges and settled in his house out of choice. The spirit of death here had attracted him in his grief: "This is why he had chosen Bruges, that city from which the sea—like a great happiness also—had retreated" (Rodenbach, 29). Individuals in Bely's novel are deprived of their free will. Peter's idea of building a city through which Western "progress" could be introduced to Russia turned into a rigid and inflexible bureaucracy. The bronze statue of Peter haunts the novel's characters who, in turn, are likened to stone sculptures themselves, suggesting the lack of individual freedom and the inability to effect changes.[21] Citizens are not in harmony with Peter's city. Hugues, however, is in union with Bruges, at least initially. As long as he equates it with his dead wife, Bruges approves of him. Unlike in *Petersburg,* the walls offer Hugues their "advice" (Rodenbach, 8). The city comforts Hugues: the bells ring soothingly and the canals seem to reflect the dead woman's face. Even the song of the carillon reminds him of his cherished wife. Roman Catholicism—embodied in the churches, bells, and statues of Madonnas and the saints—holds out the promise of a reunion with his wife in death. The "intangible telegraphy between his soul" and the city (Rodenbach, 28–29)—a harmony ostentatious by its absence in *Petersburg*—is only disrupted by the appearance of the dead wife's double, Jane Scott. The narrative suggests that Jane's similarity to the dead woman is a "false" analogy because it is restricted to mere physical appearance. The "real" analogy is between the soul of Hugues's wife and the city. The narrator repeatedly foregrounds this issue: before he makes Jane's acquaintance, Hugues sees her on stage performing the role of Helena rising from the dead. She fulfills Hugues's dearest wish—the resurrection of his wife she resembles so much—merely in appearance and not in reality. Similarly, later on, she replaces Hugues's wife only in appearance. For Jane's sake, Hugues renounces his passionate love affair with the dead Bruges and, thus, with the spirit of his wife:

> Although it was an extraordinary chance, Hugues abandoned himself henceforth to the intoxication of this resemblance between Jane and

the dead woman, as formerly he had exulted in the resemblance between himself and the city. (Rodenbach, 30)

The personified city now rejects Hugues for his betrayal. It seems that the church towers, the stone Madonnas, and the pious, bored, and malicious citizens of Bruges all frown upon him. They watch him through their small mirrors, the "espions," as he hurries to Jane. He moves about town in fear now. However, the immediate source of his sufferings, unlike in *Petersburg,* rests more with human than with transcendental agencies. The nuns drive Hugues's loyal servant, Barbe, away from him and the priest's sermon causes him mental anguish as he is torn between loyalties to his wife and Bruges, on the one hand, and the human companionship of Jane on the other. The Catholic city interferes to "resolve" the conflict and "save" Hugues: from its viewpoint, Jane stands for witchcraft, falsity, and sin. The final and fatal disagreement between Hugues and Jane results from the city's denial of privacy for the couple: Hugues prevents Jane from watching the colorful religious procession from his window lest people catch sight of her in his house. As Hugues finally strangles her, he imprisons her youth, vitality, and beauty in the city's all-encompassing deadness. Thus, she no longer threatens the dead Bruges. As she lies dead, the sound of bells is heard: "The city was about to return to its solitude" (Rodenbach, 78). "Order" has been restored, albeit at a terrible cost. With the resolution of the conflict, the novel concludes with closure.

By contrast, the modernist text of Bely's novel has an open ending: the Ableukhov parents die and Nikolai Apollonovich roams the countryside, becoming a follower of the antirationalist Ukrainian philosopher Grigory Skovoroda. As the novel concludes, all of the main characters have left the city. Clearly, this marked structural difference in the two works indicates a significant difference in the symbolization of the urban theme.

Bely and Rodenbach follow the philosophical principle—implicit in European symbolist writing—that Vyacheslav Ivanov defines as an ascent from reality to a higher reality, "a realibus ad realiora." Putting it differently, Emile Verhaeren suggests that in symbolist literature the concrete image may expand in meaning to encompass abstract states of mind.[22] Human lives interlace with the world of objects that cover an invisible consciousness. The human characters and the city around them are in the throes of forces that are incomprehensible but which are, nevertheless, endowed with significance by the human minds perceiving this world. The enigmatic conversations between people, the narrator's contemplations, and the ever-present anticipation of doom significantly slow down the movement of the plot.[23]

"Every city is a state of mind," says the narrator of *Bruges-la-Morte* (Rodenbach, 51). While Bely implies the same, it is clear that he sees his city in very different terms from Rodenbach. When the narrator suggests in no uncertain terms that Bruges is a provincial place, readers have to take his word for it, for they find little evidence in the text to confirm or deny this assertion. The city is depicted in a very limited way. For a start, Hugues—a *flaneur* in the classical sense—is a wealthy man who spends all of his time musing. He has no social ties: he is not a man of business. Furthermore, he has no friends or associates in the town.[24] Moreover, the plot deliberately hides nonreligious aspects of the city: events evolve in and around the churches and the Beguinage. The reader catches an image of the rue Flamand—the secular central area of Bruges—only to learn that Jane is shopping there.[25] This activity is supposed to attest to her shallow and materialistic interests. Similarly, the plot includes a visit to the theater which, as opposed to the church, represents falsity: Jane is a member of the visiting troupe of dancers, suggesting to "dead Bruges" that because of her profession she is phoney and insincere.

Rodenbach captures only the "deadness" of the city and his urban motifs typify this one noteworthy aspect. Bely's novel not only depicts Petersburg in many more of its details but also sees it in universal terms as a symbol of the big city. Clearly, the Russian novel is about an actual metropolis of greater complexity than the quiet Flemish city. But Bely is necessarily drawn to a broader image than Rodenbach for the purpose of symbolization. The novel's diverse characters represent a cross-section of the city's society, ranging from the high-ranking aristocratic civil servant to the police double agent, to the middle-class army officer, to the poor working-class inhabitants of ugly, insect-infested flats on Vasilevsky Island. The plot even extends to the outskirts of the city. The burning chimneys and the soot blackening the air that horrify Styopka, the young peasant approaching the capital on foot, would also be seen outside London and Paris. This is not accidental even on the novel's symbolic level: Petersburg, resembling the West, is an alien entity for the ordinary Russian. As the narrator contemplates the illumination of Nevsky Avenue at night, he compares the sight to a burning red spot, like Gehenna.[26] Bely's thoughts about Basel in his essay, "Our Life is Basel," show some similarities with his ideas about Petersburg.[27] They both represent "the city," which symbolizes the ultimate crisis of Western civilization, brought to the edge of the abyss by the "theoretically minded." Of course, the ultimate source of many of Bely's arguments is Nietzsche's ideas in *The Birth of Tragedy*.

The many components that comprise Bely's city create one large and complex symbol: in a Hegelian way, each is part of the whole and is intelligible only when viewed as such. Irreconcilable with each other as they may seem, they in fact fail to form sets of binary opposites. The state bureaucracy and the revolutionary forces, Western "rationalism" and Eastern "chaos," father and son all stand for the same force.[28] Above and beyond the hostilities felt toward one another, they all join in rushing toward an apocalyptic series of events. The mysterious Bronze Horseman (who, together with the tall seaman or the "Dutchman," symbolizes Peter the Great) stands in the dark square: "the metal lips were parted in an enigmatic smile" (Bely, 149). The enigma is hardly surprising; all of the novel's participants look upon him as a mythical father figure while Peter himself, like everyone else connected with the city, is subject to the "cerebral play" radiating from the unmeasurable mathematical point in the "center" of things. A transcendental intelligence binds the consciousness of characters. While father and son are adversaries, they encounter the same vision as they fall asleep: their heads open to a corridor in which a mysterious figure, the "Turanian," approaches.[29] As human characters merge together as parts of the same force, the city itself appears "contaminated": the Russian critic L. K. Dolgopolov describes how the architectural attributes combine in the text to symbolize the city without actually referring to any concrete building. The house of the Ableukhov family and the ministry where the senator works are impossible to locate because each appears in more than one location. Although the house in which the Likhutins live is a typical Petersburg building, it is not to be found in the street where it is supposed to be.[30] Characters proceed toward their destination in a topographically implausible way. The verifiable but contaminated urban details produce a wholly mysterious cityscape. As Volker Klotz suggests, amid the fog and the identical rows of houses, the city ultimately remains indefinable.[31]

The human population of Bely's city is in fact strangely dehumanized. The passersby appear to the narrator to compose a myriapod; the street looks like a crowded sardine can.[32] Walkers seem dissected like insects: legs, limbs, and backs move about in poor visibility. The novel is saturated with shadows. We learn that the streets transform people into shades:

> The shadow of a policeman would pass, emerge black and distinct from the fog and once more melt away. . . . The shadow of a woman. It did not move off into the fog but stood looking up at a window. . . . The black shadow melted away in the fog. (Bely, 82)

A visitor from the transcendental, "fourth-dimensional" layer encircling the physical city explains that no wall can protect against the inhabitants of his realm:

> The tragedy is that we are in an invisible world: the world of shadows. . . . Petersburg is in the fourth dimension, which is not indicated on maps, which is indicated merely by a dot. And this dot is the place where the plane of being is tangential to the surface of the sphere and the immense astral cosmos. A dot which in the twinkling of an eye can produce for us an inhabitant of the fourth dimension from which not even a wall can protect us. (Bely, 207)

The novel intimates that an ominous transcendental entity prevails.[33] The text is intended to be mythopoetic: while the method of narration is fraught with irony and the characters are grotesquely reduced shadows of individuals, the tone of the novel is prophetic.[34]

De Grève suggests that the city in *Petersburg* is a *ville mirage* whereas in *Bruges-la-Morte* we have a *ville personnage*.[35] The use of the symbol of water, found in both texts, clearly illustrates the difference between the two types of symbolization. In both novels, central characters stand on bridges contemplating suicide by drowning in the canal. Analyzing the phenomenological significance of bridges, Pierre Sansot writes in *Poétique de la ville* that they preserve the "emptiness" even in the middle of the city.[36] They extend over the water that reflects the city, but the water hides the invisible mystery behind its mirrorlike surface. In *Bruges-la-Morte* the meaning of the symbol of the canal alludes to Hugues's predicament. It reminds one of the loss of happiness, the withdrawal of the sea, that is; while its clean surface reflects the dead city, beyond its surface death awaits with a promise to Hugues of reunion with his wife. In *Petersburg*, however, water symbolism is so integrated into the overall symbolization of the city and its "cerebral play" that it is meaningful only within the broad context. It alludes to the regulation of the marshland and the forcing of the sea and the river's delta into canals. Thus it symbolizes the violent creation of the city that cost the lives of thousands of its builders. This process took place at Peter's command. No wonder that throughout the text a schooner, presumably Peter's, is seen sailing by. Water is the origin of the city's life but it is unruly: with constant threats of inundations, it portends annihilation of life. It also alludes to the liquid of the womb and to conception in a disharmonious marriage, generating the conflict between the father and the son, between the ruler and the ruled. This conflict—the son's wish to murder the father—is expressed in the image of the sardine can (which hides the time bomb). Sardines come from water and, in the novel's consciousness, they represent devastation in response to the attempt to imprison uncontrollable energies ("nature") within a small canister ("culture").

Rodenbach, by contrast, does not seek to unveil terrible truths about the universe. The details of the actual city fuse with the states of Hugues's soul and motivate his actions.[37] The result is no less devastating than in Bely, but the novel's statement about the world is translated into personal terms rather than into "cosmic" ones as is the case in *Petersburg*. In her fascinating book, *Literaturnyya kharakteristiki* (Literary portraits), Zinaida Vengerova suggests that Rodenbach's symbolism is "unconscious."[38] He does not pursue "abstract truths"; instead, his lyricism arises as he accounts for the impact of the world of objects on the human soul.[39]

Thanks to Rodenbach's and Bely's influential novels, Bruges and Petersburg have become prominent statements about the imprisonment of human consciousness in an urban world it had originally created to protect the values of civilization. The endings of both novels strongly question some basic tenets of civilization itself. In *Petersburg* its brainchild, the city, turns into a monster, which devours its own children. In *Bruges-la-Morte,* the city has become a dead, crystallized idea, which cannot tolerate the warmth of human life. As characters die, go mad, or run away from their home in these two symbolist novels, the city remains unchanging; its colors and sounds mock those whose limitless imagination is forced into an existence greatly limited by space and time.

Notes

1. These authors are prominent in the issues of *Vesy* 1, no. 1 (1904)—6, no. 12 (1909). Rodenbach's name, however, is mentioned only once. Interestingly enough, *Zolotoe runo* and *Russkaya mysl'*—while generally less concerned with foreign literature than *Vesy*—paid more attention to Rodenbach. See A. Vorotnikov, "Zhorzh Rodenbakh. *Misticheskie lilii* (*Musée de béguinages*). Perevod Marii Veselovskoy, Moskva 1906," *Zolotoe runo* no. 2 (1906): 122–23; M. V. Veselovskaya, "Zhorzh Rodenbakh. Kritiko-biograficheskie zametki," *Russkaya mysl'* no. 4 (1911): 46–70.

2. Zinaida Vengerova, "Zhorzh Rodenbakh," in her *Literaturnyya kharakteristiki* (Literary portraits), vol. 2 (St. Petersburg: A. E. Vineke, 1905), 193.

3. See Appendix B for further details of the opera's genesis.
4. Georges Rodenbach, *Bruges-la-Morte,* trans. Philip Mosley (Paisley, Wilfion; Chester Springs, Penn.: Dufour Editions, 1987), 1. All subsequent citations from *Bruges-la-Morte* will be followed by the author's name and the page numbers in parentheses.
5. Andrei Bely, *Petersburg,* trans. Robert A. Maguire and John E. Malmstad (Bloomington: Indiana University Press, 1978), 2. Unless otherwise indicated, all subsequent citations from *Petersburg* will be followed by the author's name and the page numbers in parentheses.
6. Claude De Grève, "Architectures de pierres et architecture de mots: L'Image de la ville d'art dans 'Bruges-la-Morte' de Georges Rodenbach et 'Petersbourg' d'André Biely," in *Art et littérature.* Actes du Congrès de la Société Française de Littérature Générale et Comparée (Aix-en-Provence: Publication Diffusion. Université de Provence, 1988), 203.
7. Donald F. Friedman, "The Symbolist Dead City: A Landscape of Poesis" (Ph.D. diss., New York University, 1985), 185.
8. Walter Koschmal, "Zur mythieschen Modellierung von Raum und Zeit bei Andrei Bielyj und Bruno Schulz," *Wiener Slawistischer Almanach* 20 (1987): 209.
9. De Grève, "Architectures," 208.
10. Diane Wolfe Levy, "City Signs: Towards a Definition of Urban Literature," *Modern Fiction Studies* 24 (1978): 65–66.
11. Burton Pike, *The Image of the City in Modern Literature* (Princeton: Princeton University Press, 1981), x.
12. Roger Keys, "Andrei Bely and the Development of Modern Russian Fiction," *Essays in Poetics* 8 (1983): 45.
13. Volker Klotz, *Die erzahlte Stadt* (Munich: Carl Hauser Verlag, 1969), 26.
14. Gaston Bachelard, *The Poetics of Space* (Boston: Beacon Press, 1969), 4–5.
15. Friedman, "The Symbolist Dead City," 162.
16. Coldness and iciness as attributes of the devil were well known to Bely's readers from Vladimir Solovyov's *Tri razgovora* (Three conversations) and Dante's *Inferno.* For more on Dante's impact on Russian symbolism, see my article, coauthored with Lena Szilard, "Dantov kod russkogo simvolizma," *Studia Slavica* 35 (1989): 61–95.
17. For a study of *Petersburg* as a Nietzschean "misreading" of classical tragedy, see my article, "Nietzschean Masks and the Classical Apollo in Andrei Bely's *Petersburg,*" *Studia Slavica* 37 (1991–92): 393–403.
18. L. K. Dolgopolov, "Obraz goroda v romane Andreya Belogo 'Peterburg,'" *Izvestiya akademii nauk SSSR,* seriya literatury i yazyka, 34 (1975): 4.
19. Klotz, *Die erzahlte Stadt,* 35.
20. Thanks to Pushkin's image in "The Bronze Horseman," many Russians have considered Petersburg as a "window" on the West, forced into its place by the iron determination of Peter I, the monarch who established the city at the beginning of the eighteenth century.
21. E. G. Mel'nikova, M. B. Bezrodny, and V. M. Paperny, "Medny vsadnik v kontekste skul'pturnoy simvoliki romana Andreya Belogo 'Peterburg,'" *Blokovsky sbornik* 6 (1985): 85–86.
22. Friedman, "The Symbolist Dead City," 106.
23. Ibid., 138.
24. Hans Hinterhäuser, "Tote Städte," in his *Fin de Siècle: Gestalten und Mythen* (Munich: Wilhelm Fink Verlag, 1977), 47.
25. De Grève, "Architectures," 204.

26. See Andrei Bely, *Petersburg* (Moscow: Izdatel'stvo Nauka, 1981), 49. In all other references to *Petersburg,* I rely on Robert Maguire and John Malmstad's translation (see n. 5). This translation is based on the 1922 version of the novel, which abridges the 1916 version. The reference to Gehenna appears only in the 1916 version.

27. Robert A. Maguire and John E. Malmstad, "Petersburg," in *Andrei Bely: The Spirit of Symbolism,* ed. John A. Malmstad (Ithaca: Cornell University Press, 1987), 106–8.

28. Keys, "Andrei Bely," 46.

29. V. Piskunov, "Vtoroe prostranstvo romana Andreya Belogo 'Peterburg,'" *Blokovsky sbornik* 6 (1985): 145.

30. Dolgopolov, "Obraz goroda," 52.

31. Klotz, *Die erzahlte Stadt,* 44.

32. The sardine can is a leitmotivic image. The time bomb, which is supposed to destroy Senator Ableukhov, is placed in a sardine can. Since the reader is aware of this, the narrator metaphorically refers to Nevsky Avenue as a sardine can, hinting at the city's all-pervading "explosiveness."

33. Cerebral play implies the theosophical belief according to which consciousness creates form. Maria Carlson has studied the impact of occult theories, specifically theosophy and anthroposophy, on *Petersburg.* In a talk, entitled "*Petersburg* and the Language of Occultism," given at the 1991 convention of the American Association for the Advancement of Slavic Studies in Miami, Florida, she suggested that according to some theosophists the fourth dimension is the same as the "astral plane." On this plane, the thoughts and feelings of people in the physical reality of Bely's city become a visible and living force. Because "astral matter" is so fluid, the novel is filled with fogs and shadows. These are the constantly changing shapes produced by the cerebral activity of the overactive brains of Russians of the real city, the "physical plane," in the revolutionary days of October 1905.

34. Keys, "Andrei Bely," 40.

35. De Grève, "Architectures," 203.

36. Cited by De Grève, 206.

37. Ibid., 202.

38. Vengerova, "Zhorzh Rodenbakh," 174.

39. Ibid., 188.

From Novel to Film: Cinematic Expression and Aesthetic Integrity in Roland Verhavert's *Brugge-die-Stille*

Michèle K. Langford

TRANSPOSITION, translation, interpretation, reading, illustration, visual rendering—all these terms tend to establish, more or less accurately, a relationship between a film and the text that inspired it. However, when considering Roland Verhavert's film *Brugge-die-Stille* (1981), the word that comes to mind and supplants all others is *reflection*. The film, a reflection of Rodenbach's novel *Bruges-la-Morte;* Bruges the city, reflection of the book, itself a reflection of an epoch—mirroring its own image in the water of its canals.

Bruges-la-Morte brought instant recognition to Rodenbach in 1892 when it was published almost simultaneously with a serial version in the newspaper *Le Figaro* and by the publishers Marpon and Flammarion, with a frontispiece by Khnopff.[1] It would be impossible to separate the poet from the novelist in the work of Rodenbach, and before any consideration of the transposition of *Bruges-la-Morte* to Verhavert's film, it is important to determine what constitutes Rodenbach's personal aesthetic.

As is commonly known, Rodenbach belonged to the group organized around the review *La Jeune Belgique* in which a number of Belgian authors sought to assert their own identity in the vast domain of French literature. Claude De Grève has shown very clearly, however, that the movement was devoid of any narrow nationalism. Its slogan "Soyons nous" (Let's be ourselves), proclaimed by Max Waller, should not be interpreted as a nationalist affirmation but rather as the expression of an "individual consciousness." This group of authors rejected any notion of political or philosophical commitment, and by another slogan—"Nous faisons de la littérature et de l'art avant tout" (We create literature and art before anything else)[2]—opposed the polemic taking place at the time between the various literary schools. But Rodenbach goes one step further by denying the existence of literary schools altogether:

> En réalité, il n'y a jamais eu d'école en littérature, c'est même un signe de médiocrité cette incorporation dans les groupes littéraires qui, comme ceux de la politique, se font et se défont, au gré des intérêts et des rancunes. Ce sont les moutons qui marchent en troupeaux, les lions vont seuls.[3]

> (In reality, literary schools never existed; it is in fact a sign of mediocrity this adhesion to literary groups which, like political groups, are made and dissolved, at the whims of personal interest and grudges. Sheep walk in packs, lions go alone.)

While living in Paris Rodenbach is determined to create his own path. In his nostalgia for his country, Flanders becomes the source of his inspiration as well as the expression of a personal aesthetic, which includes romanticism, decadentism, and symbolism—all of them filtered through his own sensitivity. *Bruges-la-Morte* reflects this aesthetic in a particular way. The city embodies the memories of the author with the expression of a romantic attachment to his origins; but most of all, it becomes his own creation.

Two critics, Anne Cauquelin and Michel Zeraffa, define the role of the city in literature as follows: "Pour nous qui habitons dans nos souvenirs et nos coutumes, la ville n'est pas un lieu, elle est rêvée, habitée, déshabitée avant de devenir un désert" (For us, who live in our memories and our customs, the city isn't a place, it is dreamed, inhabited, disinhabited before becoming a desert).[4] Following this perspective, it becomes obvious that Bruges is not a mere location either for Rodenbach or for Hugues Viane, the novel's protagonist. For both, the city represents a choice.

The author has chosen Bruges, rather than Ghent, where he spent his youth, to symbolize the mystical side of Flanders, and to represent the silent and secretive "Flemish soul." Rodenbach insists in his introduction that this novel contains a study of passion and that the city is "comme un personnage essentiel, associé aux états d'âme, qui conseille, dissuade, détermine à agir" (like an essential character, identified with the soul of its people, which advises, deters, or provokes into action).[5] Rodenbach not only plans to give the city a major role in the novel, but an active part as well.

Viane proclaims that he has chosen Bruges because of the sadness the city evokes. The silence of Bruges offers a parallel to the calm and withdrawn life of the widower. One day, however, Viane sees a woman, and he is stunned by her resemblance to the deceased. He attempts to recapture with her the memory of his dead wife. Jane becomes his mistress and, for a while, he is able to maintain the illusion by realizing a fusion between past and present.

But Viane misstates his motivation for choosing Bruges, the dead city: "elle-même mise au tombeau de ses quais de pierre . . . quand avait cessé d'y battre la grande pulsation de la mer" (herself entombed in the stone of her river banks . . . when the great pulsation of the sea stopped beating there) (24). We can see here the sexual allusion. Robert Ziegler remarks accurately that the book shows Viane "devoted to the deathness of his wife, not the memory of his wife as she was while still alive."[6] But Viane does not choose the past over the future for his life, as Ziegler suggests. The real issue, which is never mentioned, is a struggle for control. Each character, including the city, will take a turn in controlling the situation.

Jeannine Paque has noted the lively aspect of Bruges in the novel: "Bien que *Bruges-la-Morte* ne soit pas un roman réaliste, la ville y vit de toutes ses tours, ses cloches, ses rues" (Although *Bruges-la-Morte* isn't a realist novel, the town lives with its towers, its bells, and its streets).[7] How does Rodenbach succeed in producing a "live" reality for the dead city? If we consider *The Trial* by Kafka, we see that the author creates a live reality for the city by concretizing the abstract. In doing so he evokes a city more terrifying than Manhattan. The town's fearful realism is produced by its dehumanization; both Rodenbach and Kafka were aware that, contrary to popular belief, it is dehumanization that fosters urbanization—not the opposite. Man creates his surroundings. Bruges becomes Viane's creation: we see the city with his eyes, and we experience the city as he dreams it—first as a friend, then as a dangerous enemy.

Viane does not evoke any memories of his past life, when the couple visited foreign countries and large cosmopolitan cities. We can speculate that he does not choose to remember his wife in the larger cities. Is it because these larger cities are responsible for the dehumanization, fragmentation, and disincarnation of his wife? Could he possess her as thoroughly alive as he possesses her in death? Bruges offers cohesiveness, it constitutes a frame that Viane creates, just as he creates the memories themselves. The past on which the story is built is practically nonexistent. Although the couple visited Bruges together, Viane does not evoke any precise sites or situations in which his wife was present. Neither a gesture, nor a word is remembered. Rather, Viane surrounds himself with the objects that once belonged to her, including her hair, preciously kept under glass.[8] Barbe the maid (who is chosen for her silence), the streets, the canals, the houses, the churches—everything contributes to Viane's fixation. For Rodenbach these objects prevent the fragmentation of the poetic vision of Bruges, while for Viane it signifies his love for death over life.

It is essential to make a distinction here between fixation and obsession. A true obsession with the dead woman would have prevented Viane from falling prey to the illusion of resemblance. However, it is his need to give consistency to his memories and to maintain—to "fixate"—the image of the dead woman that opens the way for the intrusion of another woman. The two women will subsequently be fused in his mind, creating the confusion between them and ultimately the substitution of one for the other. Rodenbach suggests in fact that the resemblance perhaps exists only in Viane's imagination: "Tandis qu'il cherchait son visage [celui de sa femme] voici que cette femme, brusquement surgie, le lui avait offert, *trop* conforme et *trop* jumeau" (While he searched for his wife's face, this woman had offered it to him but too similar, with too much likeness) (27, my emphasis). It is Jane's similarity to his wife that troubles Viane. Perhaps Viane fears his wife "alive" as much as the possibility of the fusion of the two women.

In the universe that Viane creates, he has total control; each gesture is programmed and repeated. Nothing can ever be modified. He is furious with the maid who changes the daily schedule because of a holiday. Life, symbolized by the city's celebration, must not enter his programmed environment.[9] When Jane enters his world, life enters with her. Vitality is represented by its most powerful aspect: physical attraction, with the suggestion of procreation.

But a third entity manifests itself with a hold on Viane stronger than death and life itself: the city. The bond that unites Viane to Bruges is threatened by Jane's intrusion, and Viane longs to be one with the dead city again: "Oh! Oui! Hugues aurait voulu être ainsi. Rien qu'une tour, au-dessus de la vie! Mais lui ne pouvait pas s'enorgueillir, comme ces clochers de Bruges, d'avoir déjoué les efforts du malin" (Oh! Yes! Hugues would have liked to be like that. Nothing but a tower, above life! But he couldn't pride himself, as could the bell towers of Bruges, on having escaped the efforts of the devil) (72). Viane is aware that he is losing his soul and the myth of Faust is suggested several times.

Viane's life is again fragmented and in a state of total disarray. He betrays the city and the city betrays him. Viane counts on

Bruges to make Jane his own because "toute cité est un état d'âme, et d'y séjourner à peine, cet état d'âme se communique, se propage à nous en un fluide qui s'inocule et qu'on incorpore avec la nuance de l'air" (every city has a soul, and this soul is communicated; it spreads into us as does the inoculation of a fluid, and it is incorporated in the nuances of the air) (73). Wanting her all to himself, Viane convinces Jane to leave the theater where she is a dancer to remain in Bruges; but in reality it is her death that he symbolically wishes for, the better to possess her. For a while, Jane's vitality seems to win; but the city triumphs in the end when Viane kills Jane.[10] He does not kill her, as critics have too readily believed, because she could not maintain the illusion of her likeness to the dead woman, but rather because death will give back the soul of Bruges to the city. In the end, the bells ring again and the streets are once more deserted while Viane repeats calmly "Morte . . . morte . . . Bruges-la-morte" (102). Death triumphs over life just as, indirectly, good triumphs over evil, the latter personified by Jane and her sexual attractiveness.

Ironically, Viane assumes the role of "film maker" before the time: he does the casting, staging, and directing and Jane dies for not staying with the role of the dead woman for which she is chosen.

With *Brugge-die-Stille,* it seems that Verhavert was aware of the relationship between the notion of control and creation in the novel. The issue of control gives the novel the character of a fairy tale. Traditionally women in fairy tales control men and their world. However, as we have seen, Rodenbach's descriptions of Bruges are extremely realistic. Jeannine Paque notes that the novel lends itself to a sociohistorical reading;[11] critics of the period have compared the interest in Bruges aroused by the novel to the attraction Venice exerts on the public today.[12] The challenge for Verhavert was to retain both aspects: making the city appear "real" while making it the film's main character and rendering its magical mood.

Considerations that concern a film's adhesion or lack of fidelity to the book are not always fruitful and often lead to a dead end. Jacques Detemmerman regrets, nevertheless, certain variations in Verhavert's film.[13] It is true that Verhavert adapted the book in a very personal way (which would surely have pleased Rodenbach) but, more important, in doing so he has maintained throughout the film the "soul" of Rodenbach's novel. Far from lacking in dramatic tension, as Detemmerman suggests,[14] the film gains a strong sense of drama from Verhavert's variations—particularly those he brings to the characters.

From a city of stones to a city of words to a city of images, *Bruges-la-Morte* is cinematic par excellence. Not only do the eyes play an essential role, but cinema more than any other medium creates directly and affects our sense of reality. In the film, the unreal takes the place of what is real and imposes itself as reality. Bruges is real, it exists as a Flemish city with a historical and literary past, and with a multitude of suggestions, evocations, and connotations for the viewer. Yet it is another Bruges that Verhavert brings to the screen: Bruges "the quiet one"—the invisible one. In *Brugge-die-Stille,* Verhavert affects our sense of reality on two levels: by creating a city that "lives" and by the evocation of death that characterizes it.

We first see the city as fluid, with the houses lining the streets reflected in the water of the canals. This is in contrast to the behavior of Viane, who walks resolutely with a firm hold on his cane. The city offers the charm of its meandering narrow streets, but as Viane continues walking, repeating his previous itinerary, we witness the character's rigidity. This rigidity will become a fixation with routine and with attention to the details by means of which he sustains his love for Blanche (the name of his wife in the film).

The dialogue, always succinct, adds another dimension to the reality created visually by Viane's actions. Viane is jealous of Maurice, Jane's *maître de ballet,* and pleads with her: "Il faut renoncer à la danse. Je suis malheureux quand vous dansez" (You must give up dancing, I am unhappy when you dance). The viewer becomes aware of another level of reality in direct opposition to the visual evocation. Although he seems distant and remote, Viane is falling hopelessly in love. Both seek something from the other. Viane wants Jane to himself and wants her alive but lifeless. Jane refuses to be "the woman of a dream." What she wants is to *enter* Viane's life or at least his house. A desire that will prove fatal to her in the best tradition of magic realism.

When considering the film maker's subtle play of colors, one finds it evident that the faded tones are dictated by the novel; yet Verhavert gives them a new meaning. For example, without ever becoming vivid, the colors become more lively when Jane is present, whereas the evocation of the deceased wife brings a glow to the picture on the screen. When Viane holds the reliquary containing Blanche's hair, the scene becomes aglow, suggesting both a divine light and a ghostly presence.

The camera's angles themselves constitute a language. Someone is looking and eyes are constantly on the move. Viane's lust for Jane is suggested when he follows her upstairs, and a low-angle shot frames Jane's legs. These eyes are not always, however, those of the characters. At times, the city looks down from the top of its buildings at the people below or it is the "eye of God" looking at the woman in the street. The view of the city is a vertical one, with a multitude of stairs, and the reflection of the houses in the canals adds to the sense of verticality. The city is constantly looking, as the high angle shots oppress the characters in the street, or low angle shots from the canals to the houses above evoke the "espions," the little mirrors fixed to windows in which people spy on the passersby. The spectator finds himself involved in a form of voyeurism, while the feeling of being watched is strongly emphasized, adding to the sense of drama and underlining the presence of someone unseen who will bring about the denouement.

But it is in the treatment of the characters that we find Verhavert's most personal contribution. Certain variations are made for dramatization: the film begins with Blanche's death, whereas in the novel Viane's wife has been dead for five years. But Verhavert uses this opportunity to introduce an element that will be at the core of the film's drama. At the moment of her death, Blanche says to Viane: "Do not forget us" and he answers "Never." This promise seals his fate. With this addition, Verhavert not only suggests that Viane's fault is his failure to love death more than life, but that he is unfaithful and perjured. He is manipulated by both women; first under the spell of Blanche, then Jane, then Blanche again when he becomes her instrument in Jane's death.

When Viane loses control of the situation, he fails to maintain the illusion and, if we follow our parallel, as a "film director" he loses control of the set, casting, costumes, and makeup; it is most evident in the dress sequence when Jane appears wearing Blanche's dress, provoking Viane's fury.

With this sequence in particular, Verhavert enters into a dialogue with other film makers concerning the film's relation to life, art, and death. In *La Chambre verte* (1978)—considered by critics to be François Truffaut's most philosophical film—Truffaut questions whether the film medium can represent anything lifelike.[15] With death as a starting point, life is most strongly evoked by an obsession for preserving memory. But as Julien Davenne (the bereaved husband in Truffaut's film) finds out, neither photographs of the deceased nor the statue of Julie (the dead wife) can bring the memory to life.

Brugge-die-Stille and *La Chambre verte* are both films about film making. For Truffaut, the green room and the small chapel that Davenne later restores to house the portraits of all his deceased friends represent the space that as a "director" he brings to life. In *L'Histoire d'Adèle H* (1975) Truffaut also portrays passion; however, the title suggests that Hugo's daughter, with her obsessive love, is the leading character of the film. In contrast, it is the room that gives its name to *La Chambre verte*. Bruges, Verhavert's main character, is also an empty space of which, as film maker, he becomes the architect.

Both film makers choose death to represent the primary material for their craft. In its permanence death guarantees art's immortality, and the cult of the dead maintains the memory. Life, however, intrudes and imposes itself, life not represented by sexuality as in Rodenbach's book, but by a delicate femininity—a femininity that evokes another dead woman: Viane's mother who died when he was born.

Although Verhavert is not present in the film (Truffaut played Davenne in *La Chambre verte*), we hear the film maker through Viane's character. In another sequence, shortly after meeting Jane, Viane is conversing with her: "Bruges est un rêve—un décor—vous le pensez aussi?—Bruges est morte—un peu de vin?" (Bruges is a dream—a decor—you think so too?—Bruges is dead—a little more wine?). The couple remains in the frame, but we do not hear their conversation anymore. As Jane speaks, we see her lips moving, yet Viane does not seem to be listening. His last words echo therefore in the viewer's ear, and our interest remains with the city—a "decor," as Viane suggested. The characters and the action are subordinate to the city, which becomes the subject of this sequence. Indeed, dialogues like this one between the two main characters are one of the elements that makes *Brugge-die-Stille* a "film about film." The emphasis is on filming, and it underlines the importance of the film maker.

The question of whether Viane continues to love his wife through Jane is never clearly posed. In the dress sequence, we see Viane's confusion. Does he think he is seeing his dead wife? In *La Chambre verte,* Truffaut maintains the same ambiguity when Davenne orders the destruction of the wax model of his dead wife because he "cannot bear her look—the way her eyes stare blankly into space."[16]

Rodenbach in *Bruges-la-Morte* and Truffaut in *La Chambre verte* both suggest that it is the dissemblance between the work of the artist and the model that brings about the anger of the bereaved husbands; in Verhavert's film, however, it is Jane's resemblance to the deceased that infuriates Viane. Jane's apparition functions as a "live" photograph of his wife. Roland Barthes explains in *Camera*

Lucida how he realized, when he found a photograph of his dead mother, that we "interrogate the evidence of Photography, not from the viewpoint of pleasure, but in relation to what we romantically call Love in Death."[17]

In the dress sequence, Jane's apparition interrupted the narrative of Viane's fiction on which he had built his life. In his fury, Viane drags the dress through the streets of Bruges and throws it into the canal. The dress does not float as we would expect, but sinks slowly in the stagnant water reflecting the houses lining the canal. Death is strongly suggested here, with an allusion to Ophelia, insanity, and suicide; but for the first time, we have the image of Bruges as dead*ly* city, with the first evocation of murder. Symbolically, isn't it Blanche that Viane attempted to kill?

Both Jane in *Brugge-die-Stille* and Cecilia, Davenne's young companion in *La Chambre verte*, are represented as sensitive and loving women, whereas Jane in Rodenbach's novel is vulgar—a sort of *demi-mondaine*, who in many ways resembles Odette of Proust's *Du côté de chez Swann*. She is without principles and deceives Viane as soon as she is certain of her power over him. When Viane requests that she put on Blanche's dress, she laughs, making fun of the dress for being out of style. In the film, on the contrary, Jane handles it with respect. When she appears, she says simply: "Do you find me pretty?" She is then stunned by Viane's violent reaction. Why did Verhavert choose to make Jane the victim rather than the cause of Viane's fury? One reason is that Verhavert took literally Rodenbach's intention, announced in his introduction, to make *Bruges-la-Morte* a study of passion.

Each character in the film, including Jane, is a victim of his or her passion—a passion that will lead to the ultimate destruction of the character with a Racinian inexorability. Viane's passion for Jane will lead him to forget Blanche, to renege on the promise made to his dying wife never to forget her. Obsessed with Jane, he forgets to buy the flowers, as he had done regularly, to set in front of the deceased's photograph. Even Rosalie, the maid (Barbe in the novel), is consumed by her passion: religion, for which she sacrifices the present; as for Jane, her life belongs to her art: dance.

In the book, Jane's life in the theater signifies that she is a "loose" woman: "Les danseuses ne passent guère pour être puritaines" (Dancers are rarely considered puritans) (37), comments the narrator to explain Viane's cavalier attitude when he accosts an unknown woman in the street. In the film, however, Jane is characterized by her art, and dance is her *raison de vivre* throughout the film. When she is in the house of Viane's dead parents (death functions as a leitmotif), she says: "Là, je pourrais danser, la danse est ma passion" (Here I could dance, to dance is my passion). Whereas Jane, in the novel, symbolizes life by her sexuality, life is represented in the film by movement. Jane dances and Viane looks at her, but he is almost always immobile. The film's title, *Brugge-die-Stille,* therefore acquires its full meaning.

Finally, the most passionate of all characters is the city. In the book, Rodenbach dramatizes the participation of the city in the action: the city triumphs when Viane kills Jane with a braid of his wife's hair, so preciously preserved. Death, as Viane predicted when he was consumed by his desire, takes its revenge on life—a life that had temporarily brought chaos to Bruges.

The city imposes itself also at the end of *Brugge-die-Stille.* Verhavert utilizes cinematic symbolism to represent Bruges's passion for death: the city is last to participate in the action and the film maker brings into play the association between the dead woman and the dead city. But it is through Blanche that the city will act. Blanche, whose presence in Bruges is suggested throughout the film, lures her rival into the house, as into a trap (Jane seems to enter the garden as if under hypnosis). In the house, Jane moves from room to room as if guided to the spot where the murder will take place. The city in the film acts as a medium, but it is Blanche (never seen) who kills her rival with her own hair. The dramatic tension in the film is a result of the rivalry between the dead woman and the living one. Following the cinematic symbolism established by Verhavert, the film ends on a still frame as all movement ceases.

The novel embodies Rodenbach's aesthetic, in accordance with a very particular symbolization. Paul Gorceix describes it as follows: "Chez Rodenbach, la symbolisation s'élabore à travers les connotations diffusées par le contexte, à partir d'une syntaxe strictement maîtrisée et par la connivence qui s'instaure entre les sujets et les choses" (For Rodenbach, symbolization is realized through the connotations suggested by the context, with a totally controlled syntax and by the relationship that takes place between subjects and things).[18]

The city, as symbol, presents similarities with the author's life. Bruges is subject to foreign influences (Jane is French), so we see here a parallel with the author's relation to French literature, as he too is subject to the influences of the literary climate of Paris. Furthermore, the city is subject to a temporary alienation when it loses briefly its identity as the dead city, a sense of alienation shared by Rodenbach, an expatriate in Paris. But the city affirms its own identity, triumphantly, not as a Flemish city (although it is profoundly anchored in the Flemish soul) but as a unique city, comparable with no other. It incorporates, filters all the foreign influences as only a city is capable of doing, and then, in turn, intervenes in the life of its inhabitants, forming their dreams and identifying with their states of mind. More directly, the city becomes author/creator and even film director (by anticipation) when it becomes the one who (returning to Rodenbach's intoduction) "advises, deters, or provokes into action." When he brings the book to the screen, Verhavert accomplishes a number of things: he not only mirrors the "soul" of the book, its author, and the city, but he infuses into the film a number of considerations about life, art, and death that place him in the tradition both literary and cinematic of the most ambitious scope.

Notes

A different version of this essay appeared in French in *La Communication cinématographique: Reflets du livre belge,* ed. Jean-Paul Nola and Josette Gousseau (Paris: Didier-Erudition, 1993), 215–24.

1. Claude De Grève, *Georges Rodenbach* (Brussels: Editions Labor, 1987), 11.
2. This translation and all other translations in the text are my own.
3. Cited by De Grève, *Rodenbach,* 13.
4. Anne Cauquelin and Michel Zeraffa, *La Ville n'est pas un lieu* (Paris: Union Générale d'Editions, 1977), 10.
5. Georges Rodenbach, *Bruges-la-Morte* (Brussels: Editions Jacques Antoine, 1977), 9. All further references to this work appear in the text.
6. Robert Ziegler, "Resurrected Time in Rodenbach's *Bruges-la-Morte,*" *Studi Francesi* 97 (1989): 97–102.
7. Jeannine Paque, *Le Symbolisme belge* (Brussels: Editions Labor, 1989), 63–64.
8. Paul Gorceix in *Le Symbolisme en Belgique* (Heidelberg: Carl Winter, 1982) has shown the importance of the hair in Rodenbach's work, reminiscent of the Baudelairean theme.
9. Paul Gorceix notes that the Procession du Saint-Sang is a high point of the religious spring celebrations.
10. Ginette Michaux follows very convincingly the dissociation in the novel between Bruges-the-dead-city and Bruges-the-live-city, in "La Logique du meurtre dans *Bruges-la-Morte* de Georges Rodenbach," *Les Lettres Romanes* 40, nos. 3–4 (1986): 227–33.
11. Paque, *Symbolisme belge,* 63–64.
12. "Nous sommes invités à une véritable visite touristique (We are invited to a real tourist visit): le quai du Rosaire, le quai Vert, le quai du Miroir, le Pont du Moulin, la Grand' Place, l'immense Tour des Halles, la rue Flamande . . ." Ibid., 63.
13. Jacques Detemmerman, "De *Bruges-la-Morte* à *Brugge-die-Stille* ou les avatars scéniques et cinématographiques d'un thème," in *Théatre de toujours*

d'Aristote à Kalisky (Hommages à Paul Delsemme), ed. Gilbert Debusscher and Alain Van Crugten (Brussels: Editions de l'Université Libre de Bruxelles, 1983), 171.

14. "Ces quelques faiblesses n'empêchent pas *Brugge-die-Stille* d'être une oeuvre attachante. La sobriété et la justesse des dialogues, l'absolue beauté de la photographie rendent fort bien une partie du roman. Quant à l'interprétation, elle est d'un excellent niveau. Ces qualités ne réussissent malheureusement pas à faire oublier le manque de tension dramatique du film" (Those few weaknesses don't prevent *Brugge-die-Stille* from being an engaging work. The moderation and aptness of the dialogues, the sheer beauty of the photography convey part of the novel very well. These qualities unfortunately fail to make us forget the film's lack of dramatic tension). Detemmerman, "De *Bruges-la-Morte*," 181.

15. Inez Hedges, "Truffaut and Cocteau—Representations of Orpheus," in *Breaking the Frame* (Bloomington: Indiana University Press, 1991), 52.

16. Ibid., 53.

17. Cited by Hedges, 57.

18. Paul Gorceix, "Symbolisation, suggestion et ambigüité—Georges Rodenbach, Max Elskamp, Maurice Maeterlinck," *Les Lettres Romanes* 40, nos. 3–4 (1986): 216.

Appendix A: Some Further Links between Rodenbach's Work and the Cinema
Philip Mosley

IN her essay in this collection, Michèle Langford discusses the Belgian director Roland Verhavert's film version, *Brugge-die-Stille*, of Rodenbach's *Bruges-la-Morte*. In the course of research on Rodenbach for his essay, Peter Barta came upon a single reference to a 1915 Russian film based on *Bruges-la-Morte* entitled *Gryozy*, directed by Khanzhonkov and with a script by M. Basov and V. Turkin. In the course of my own research, I came across references to two films—*Nocturno* (1971), directed by Hajo Gies and *Bruges-la-Morte* (1977), directed by Ronald Chase—about which I have no further information. I also came across three previous plans to make film versions of the novel. The Rodenbach archive in Brussels contains a contract signed in 1919 by Anna Rodenbach, the writer's widow, and Eugene Gugenheim. Then in the 1940s MGM, the Hollywood film studio, bought the film rights to the novel as a vehicle for their leading dramatic actress of the time, Greer Garson. Furthermore, in his book on Rodenbach, José Mirval speaks of a project by the French director, Pierre Chenal, whose career dated from the 1930s, to make a version starring Marlene Dietrich. However, I have found no evidence that any of these plans ever materialized.

In 1980 the French director Alain Dhenaut made a television version of *Bruges-la-Morte*, with a screenplay by Pierre Dumayet, for the FR3 channel in Lille. First screened on 15 November 1980, the film was shown again in 1984. Dhenaut tackled the problem of the novel's interiority by means of various special effects such as the use of slide transparencies. Moreover he found it difficult to shoot the film in an authentic locale, since he was working with an extremely modest budget by cinematic standards. Nonetheless he managed to shoot the exterior scenes in Bruges but the interiors were shot in Paris on studio sets.

Aria (1987), produced by Don Boyd, is a compendium of ten

operatic excerpts interpreted for the screen by ten different directors, including Jean-Luc Godard, Nicolas Roeg, Robert Altman, Ken Russell, and Derek Jarman. The contribution by the Australian director, Bruce Beresford, takes as its subject the aria "Spirits of the Dead Cities" from act 1 of Erich Wolfgang Korngold's *Die tote Stadt*. In Beresford's scene, shot on location in Bruges, the hero Paul remembers a tender moment alone with his wife in their elegant house by the canal.

There are also thematic connections between *Bruges-la-Morte* and other films with similar subject matter. These connections manifest themselves both in Pygmalion-like idealizations of figments of an individual's imagination and in lovelorn or necrophilic fantasies of lonely men haunted by the past and its memories. For instance, Alfred Hitchcock's *Vertigo* (1958, based on the French novel *D'entre les morts* by Pierre Boileau and Thomas Narcejac) recounts the story of a man obsessed by a conviction that the woman he loved, and whom he believed to have seen fall to her death, has miraculously returned to life in the form of another. In identifying similarly obsessive behavior by the male protagonists of other Hitchcock films (notably *Rear Window, Psycho,* and *Marnie*), we should note here the evolution of psychoanalytical film theory in the work of Laura Mulvey and others, especially regarding Freud's theory of scopophilia and the fetishism of the male gaze.

Michèle Langford also refers to François Truffaut's *La Chambre verte* (1978), based on themes from short stories by Henry James, in particular "The Altar of the Dead." Truffaut's film concerns Julien Davenne, a man traumatized by the slaughter of World War One who, in order to replace the fire-gutted "green room" in his house, a room that had contained a shrine to his beloved wife, restores an abandoned chapel in a cemetery. Thus he creates another "green room," rededicating it this time both to his wife and to all the friends he lost in the war. In a further echo of Hugues Viane's experiences, Davenne becomes attached to an attractive young woman but in the end she too fails to break his obsession with the past and the departed.

The Dutch-born Australian director, Paul Cox, seems almost to specialize in this kind of solitary hero, though he imbues his films with a wry sense of humor to offset their pervasive sadness and bizarre eroticism. In *Lonely Hearts* (1981), an unmarried piano-tuner approaching fifty enters into a relationship, after his mother's death, with an equally vulnerable younger woman he meets through an agency. In *Man of Flowers* (1983) he introduces an art collector, haunted by the memory of his dead mother, who pays a young model to pose naked for his platonic pleasure once a week. In *The Golden Braid* (1990, based on Maupassant's short story, "La Chevelure") Cox tells of another collector, this time of antiques, who falls madly in love with a braid of hair which he discovers in a chest of drawers.

Appendix B: From Rodenbach to Korngold: The Intertextual Genesis of *Die tote Stadt*
Philip Mosley

RODENBACH wrote three plays: a one-act collaborative prose sketch, *La Petite Veuve* (1884); a one-act verse play, *Le Voile* (1897), first produced at the Comédie-Française in Paris on 21 May 1894, and the first Belgian play to be performed there; and *Le Mirage* (1901), a four-act play, first published in the 1 April 1900 issue of *Revue de Paris,* then in book form in 1901. *Le Mirage* had also been accepted by the Comédie-Française in Rodenbach's lifetime but was never produced there. It was instead produced at least once (though without much success according to Rodenbach's biographer, Pierre Maes) in German at the Deutsches Theater, Berlin, on 15 [one source says 12] September 1903, as *Die stille Stadt,* from a 1902 translation by the Viennese playwright and poet Siegfried Trebitsch (also the translator of George Bernard Shaw's plays), and renamed *Das Trugbild* on its republication along with his translation of *Le Voile* (*Der Schleier*), in 1913.

Adapted from *Bruges-la-Morte,* the plot of *Le Mirage* involves the characters Hughes, Joris Borluut (the name of the hero of *Le Carillonneur* but a painter here, closer in model to Jean Rembrandt in *L'Art en exil*), Jane, Barbe, Sister Rosalie, and Hughes's wife, Geneviève, who appears as a ghost in the second scene of act 3, set by a bridge on the bank of a canal. At the end of this version of the story, Barbe discovers Hughes on his knees casting cut flowers on Jane's corpse and runs for help, while a distracted Hughes blames Jane's murder on the tress of hair.

Rodenbach's widow, Anna, acquainted Trebitsch with *Le Mirage*. Considering this to be "like a sacred trust," Trebitsch rendered it into German, making few changes to Rodenbach's text, the most significant being the use only of Genoveva's (several names were similarly Germanized) voice to evoke the reappearance of Hughes's wife. Though Trebitsch maintains that his play was "rated highly by Otto Brahm, the former director of the Berlin

Lessing Theater, and brilliantly staged," according to Maes the production enjoyed little success with the public. Trebitsch subsequently "met the young master Erich Wolfgang Korngold in search of a scenario or, even better, a mood or operatic background which could be dramatically elaborated. I urged him to take up the *Trugbild* . . ." Korngold (1897–1957), widely touted as a "new Mozart," already had two one-act operas, *Violanta* and *Der Ring des Polykrates* (both premièred together in Munich in 1916) to his credit, as well as several orchestral and chamber works. Excited by the potential of the story, Korngold began in 1916 to compose the music for the three-act opera, which he named *Die tote Stadt*. Owing to a period of military service and other musical commitments, he was unable to complete the score until August 1920, whereupon several opera houses immediately began to negotiate for it.

Dr. Julius Korngold, the young composer's father, who had succeeded Eduard Hanslick as music critic of the influential Vienna paper *Neue Freie Presse,* offered Trebitsch's play to Hans Müller, a Viennese playwright who had written the libretto to *Violanta*. Müller's treatment proved unsatisfactory to Erich Korngold who, when Müller withdrew from the project for reasons of his own, decided to collaborate with his father on their own libretto under the pen name "Paul Schott." This name (combining the forename of the hero of the opera and the surname of its publisher in Mainz) was a necessary measure to prevent accusations against Julius Korngold of favoritism toward his son.

Die tote Stadt was premiered simultaneously in Hamburg (under Egon Pollak) and Cologne (under Otto Klemperer) on 4 December 1920. It opened in Vienna in January 1921 and in Berlin in 1924, besides being performed in some eighty other opera houses throughout Europe. "A happy coincidence," wrote Trebitsch, made it possible for Rodenbach's son Constantin to be in Vienna at the time of the opera's première there, "and to attend the performance and the revival of his father's fame, for the musical feat of the young master will erect a permanent memorial to the dead poet." It was produced at the Metropolitan Opera in New York in its 1921–22 season in an English version by R. H. Elkin, the first German opera to be performed in the United States after World War One. As Korngold was Jewish and the subject was unashamedly "decadent," Hitler had the opera removed from the authorized repertoire in the 1930s. In 1934, at Max Reinhardt's instigation, Korngold left for Hollywood where he forged a successful career as a composer of film music.

After World War Two, in the 1950s and 1960s, *Die tote Stadt* reappeared on opera stages in Munich, Ghent, Antwerp, Vienna, and other European cities though, in the antiromanticist mood of the time, it was slow to regain critical favor. The identity of "Paul Schott," however, was not revealed by the Korngold family until the successful revival of the opera in New York in 1975. It was recorded under the conductor Erich Leinsdorf in 1976, and was revived in 1983 by the Deutsche Oper Berlin in a controversial production by Götz Friedrich. The company has since established the work in its permanent repertoire, taking it on tour to such cities as Vienna, Los Angeles, and San Francisco.

The characterization and plot of *Die tote Stadt* differs from that of *Das Trugbild* in several important ways. Hughes becomes Paul; Jane becomes Marietta, while Paul's wife is called Marie, thus permitting a Marie/Marietta dual role, which challenged such celebrated sopranos as Maria Jeritza and Lotte Lehmann. Barbe becomes Brigitta and an additional character, Frank, is introduced as Paul's friend. The opera introduces further additional characters in the persons of the theatrical troupe in which Marietta is the principal dancer. As in *Bruges-la-Morte,* Paul murders Marietta with a tress of Marie's hair, but it occurs at the climax of a dream sequence with fashionable Freudian overtones that occupies two-thirds of the entire action. Furthermore Marie appears as a ghost in one scene apparently borrowed from the plot of *Le Mirage/Das Trugbild.* That the murder happens in a dream, from which Paul awakens with the realization that he must leave both house and city of death to start his life afresh, emphasizes Korngold's own optimistic outlook. Although Bruges remains a powerful atmospheric presence throughout the opera, the human drama of the individual characters and their willingness to try to resolve their problems succeed in outweighing the fatalistic and morbid emphases of Rodenbach's original text. Yet the ending of the 1983 Deutsche Oper revival of *Die tote Stadt* reverts to the desperate mood at the end of *Bruges-la-Morte.* As the curtain falls, Paul, pistol in hand, appears to be contemplating suicide rather than, as Korngold described it, departing cheerful and unscathed in the company of Frank.

In the 1983 revival the set design (by Andreas Reinhardt) for act 2 is a replica of *Une Ville abandonnée,* the 1904 drawing of the Hans Memling Square in Bruges by the Belgian symbolist artist Fernand Khnopff (see Dorothy Kosinski's essay in this collection for additional comment on Khnopff). Reinhardt's design even reproduces the empty plinth of a statue (which supports the glass case containing the tress in acts 1 and 3) and the encroaching sea (real water on stage). In addition the portrait of Marie, which hangs on the back wall of Paul's chamber in acts 1 and 3, and from which Marie emerges as Paul's dream begins, is Khnopff's portrait (but in reverse image, with the subject holding a lute) of his sister Marguerite, about whom he was as obsessive (painting her portrait many times) as Hugues/Hughes/Paul is about his dead wife.

During act 2, when the dancing troupe enters, Korngold quotes a passage from the score of Giacomo Meyerbeer's opera *Robert le Diable* (1831), in particular the Resurrection music from the graveyard scene, which Marietta and her partners rehearse as a travesty of the original, in mockery of Paul and his morbid obsession. *Robert le Diable* is also the opera in which Jane performs as a dancer in *Bruges-la-Morte,* when Hugues pursues her into a theater and happens to see her on stage in the nonsinging role of the Abbess. This opera has at least two themes in common with *Bruges-la-Morte:* satanism and fetishism. In the second scene of act 3, amid the ruins of St. Rosalie's Convent, the dead nuns who had turned to heathenism arise from their graves and, with their Abbess, surround Robert, duke of Normandy. Robert "sees" his mother come down from her tomb, just as Hugues "sees" his wife in Jane's portrayal of this action, and as Paul in *Die tote Stadt* "sees," in his dream, the dead Marie emerge from her sepulcher. The nuns dance around Robert (as Marietta dances round Paul, tormenting him with the tress of Marie's hair) until, dazed by their gyrations, he seizes a magic cypress bough (as Hugues and Paul seize the tress) and thus is able to escape from their evil spell (as both Hugues and Paul "escape" the spells cast on them by strangling Jane and Marietta with the tress).

Three undated letters to Anna Rodenbach in the Rodenbach archive in Brussels concern the possibility of a musical version of *Le Mirage* by Georges Montorgueil and Marcel-Samuel Rousseau, but I have found no indications of its completion or production. A three-act musical version of *Le Carillonneur* with lyrics by Jean Richepin and music by Xavier Leroux was first produced at the Opéra-Comique on 3 March 1913, while the Belgian composer, Auguste Dupont, set Rodenbach's poem, "Chant d'automne," to music. Yet in the end, whether one opts for the view of Korngold as a successor to Richard Strauss and Giovanni Puccini, or whether one prefers the comparison with Gustav Mahler, *Die tote Stadt* appears to have reestablished itself in the major operatic repertoire and remains the outstanding musical testament to Rodenbach's work.

References

Carroll, Brendan G. *Erich Wolfgang Korngold: His Life and Works.* Paisley, Scotland: Wilfion Books, 1984.

Palmer, Christopher. "Korngold and *Die tote Stadt.*" Liner notes to 1976 RCA release of opera recording, with English libretto by Ruth and Thomas Martin.

Trebitsch, Siegfried. "Georges Rodenbach." Trans. Ernst Pories. Unpublished manuscript in collection of the Erich Wolfgang Korngold Society, Paisley, Scotland.

Bibliography

The most useful bibliography remains the one compiled by Pierre Maes in his biography of Rodenbach (1952 edition).

CHRONOLOGY OF WORKS BY GEORGES RODENBACH (1855–98)

Le Foyer et les champs. A collection of poems. Paris/Brussels: V. Palmé and G. Lebrocquy, 1877.
Les Tristesses. A collection of poems. Paris: A. Lemerre, 1879.
La Belgique. A historical poem. Brussels: Office de Publicité, 1880.
La Mer élégante. A collection of poems. Paris: A. Lemerre, 1881.
L'Hiver mondain. A collection of poems. Brussels: H. Kistemaeckers, 1884.
Vers d'amour. A collection of poems. Brussels: La Jeune Belgique, 1884. These poems first appeared in the review *La Jeune Belgique,* July-August 1884.
La Petite Veuve, with Max Waller. A one-act prose sketch. Brussels: J. Fink, 1884.
La Jeunesse blanche. A collection of poems. Paris: A. Lemerre, 1886.
La Vie morte. A novel. This early version of *L'Art en exil* appeared in sixteen instalments in *L'Indépendance Belge,* 1–25 June 1886.
Le Livre de Jésus. A collection of poems, unfinished. Published in part in *Oeuvres,* vol. 1, 1923.
"L'Amour en exil." A short story. Paris: *Revue de Paris et de St.-Pétersbourg,* 1888. Offprint from the review, 15 May 1888.
Du silence. A collection of poems. Paris: A. Lemerre, 1888.
L'Art en exil. A novel. Paris: A. Quantin, 1889.
Le Règne du silence. A collection of poems, incorporating reprint of *Du silence.* Paris: Charpentier, 1891.
Bruges-la-Morte. A novel. Paris: Marpon and Flammarion, 1892.
Le Voyage dans les yeux. A collection of poems. Paris: P. Ollendorff, 1893.
Le Voile. A one-act verse play. Paris: P. Ollendorff, 1894.
Musée de béguines. Still lives and short stories. Paris: Bibliothèque Charpentier, 1894.
La Vocation. A novel. Paris: P. Ollendorff, 1895.
"Les Tombeaux." A short story. Paris: Chamerot and Renouard, 1895.
"Les Vierges." A short story. Paris: Chamerot and Renouard, 1896.
Les Vies encloses. A collection of poems, incorporating reprint of *Le Voyage dans les yeux.* Paris: E. Fasquelle, 1896.

Le Carillonneur. A novel. Paris: E. Fasquelle, 1897.

"L'Arbre." A short story. Paris: P. Ollendorff, 1898.

Le Miroir du ciel natal. A collection of free-verse poems. Paris: E. Fasquelle, 1898.

Posthumous Publications of Works by Rodenbach

L'Elite. A series of essays on writers, orators, painters, and sculptors. Paris: E. Fasquelle, 1899.

Le Mirage. A four-act play adapted by Rodenbach from *Bruges-la-Morte*. Paris: P. Ollendorff, 1901. First published in the April 1900 issue of *Revue de Paris*.

Le Rouet des brumes. A collection of stories. Paris: P. Ollendorff, 1901.

Oeuvres, vol. 1. Paris: Mercure de France, 1923.

Evocations. A selection of articles from newspapers and magazines between 1883 and 1898. Brussels: La Renaissance du Livre, 1924.

Oeuvres, vol. 2. Paris: Mercure de France, 1925. These *Oeuvres* reappeared in a two-volume edition. Geneva: Slatkine Reprints, 1978.

Chronology of Known Editions and Translations of *Bruges-la-Morte*

Bruges-la-Morte. Paris: Marpon and Flammarion, 1892.

Bruges-la-Morte. Paris: Flammarion, 1896.

Bruges-la-Morte. Paris: Carteret, 1900.

Bruges-la-Morte. Trans. Thomas Duncan. London: Swan, Sonnenschein, 1903.

Das tote Brügge. Trans. Friedrich von Oppeln-Bronikowski. Leipzig: Reclam, 1903.

Bruges-la-Morte. Paris: Flammarion, 1904.

Det döda Brügge. Trans. Agnes Palmgren (von Kraemer). Helsinki: Helios, 1904.

Myortvy Brugge. Trans. Marii Veselovskaja. Moscow: Kusnerev, 1904.

Bruges-la-Morte. Paris: Flammarion, 1908.

Bruges-la-Morte. Paris: Flammarion, 1910.

Das tote Brügge. Leipzig: Reclam, 1910.

Das tote Brügge. Leipzig: Reclam, 1911.

Das tote Brügge. Leipzig: Reclam, 1913.

Bruges-la-Morte. Paris: Flammarion, 1914.

Das tote Brügge. Leipzig: Reclam, 1918.

La Ciudad de las aguas muertas. Trans. R. Causinos-Assens. Madrid: America, 1927.

Bruges-la-Morte. Paris: Javal and Bourdeaux, 1930.

*Bruges-la-Morte.*Paris: Flammarion, 1937.

*Bruges-la-Morte.*Paris: Flammarion, 1941.

*Bruges-la-Morte.*Paris: Flammarion, 1947.

Brujas, la muerta. Trans. Espasa-Calpe. Buenos Aires: [publisher unknown], 1948.

Bruges la morta. Trans. Piero Bianconi. Milan: Rizzoli, 1955.

Bruges, a morta. Trans. Juracy Daisy Marchese. São Paolo: Clube do livro, 1960.

Das tote Brügge. Stuttgart: Reclam, 1966.

Bruges-la-Morte. Brussels: Editions Jacques Antoine, 1977.

Bruges-la-Morte. Paris: Flammarion, 1978.

Brugge-de-dode. Trans. Marjolijn Jacobs and Jolijn Tevel. Antwerp: Scriptoria, 1978.

Bruges, a doua moarte. Trans. Fanus Neagu and Florica Dulceanu. Bucharest: Univers, 1980.

Bruges-la-Morte. Trans. Philip Mosley. Paisley, Scotland: Wilfion, 1986.

Bruges-la-Morte. Ed. Christian Berg. Brussels: Editions Labor, 1986.

Bruges-la-Morte. Trans. Philip Mosley. Paisley: Wilfion; Chester Springs, Penn.: Dufour Editions, 1987.

Bruges-la-Morte. (Japanese translation). [N.p.]: Hanyakubota, 1988.

Bruges-la-Morte. (Comic strip version by Erwin Cels). Antwerp: Himalaya/Loempia, 1991.

Bruges-la-Morte. (Revision by Terry Hale of Thomas Duncan's 1903 translation). London: Atlas Press, 1993.

CHRONOLOGY OF KNOWN TRANSLATIONS OF OTHER WORKS BY RODENBACH

Le Carillonneur (Zvonar). Trans. A. Mire. Moscow: "Polza," 1897.

Le Rouet des brumes (Prjalka tumanor). Trans. Marii Veselovskaja. Moscow: A. V. Vasilieva, 1901.

Le Mirage (Die stille Stadt) and *Le Voile (Der Schleier).* Trans. Siegfried Trebitsch. Vienna: Wiener Verlag, 1902.

Le Règne du silence (Carstvo molcanija). Trans. I. Golovatchevski. Moscow: Vasiliev, 1903.

Le Carillonneur (Klockspelaren). Trans. Agnes von Kraemer. Helsinki: Helios, 1905.

Le Rouet des brumes (Im Zwielicht). Trans. Friedrich von Oppeln-Bronikowski. Dresden: Reissner, 1905; rpt., Weimar: Gustav Kiepenheuer, 1913.

Musée des béguines (Misticeskija lilii). Trans. Marii Veselovskaja. Moscow: Kusnerev, 1906.

Le Carillonneur (Armonie di Campane). Trans. A. Manzano-Querci. Milan: Remo Sandron, 1910.

L'Arbre/La Vocation (Die Eiche am Freuzweg/Die Berufing). Trans. Friedrich von Oppeln-Bronikowski. Leipzig: Reclam, 1912.

Die dramatischen Werke. Complete drama. Trans. Siegfried Trebitsch. Munich: Georg Müller, 1913.

Agonies de villes (Agonii gorodov) (original 1889 article collected in *Evocations*), plus *L'Arbre/La Vocation* (Russian titles unknown). Trans. Marii Veselovskaja. Moscow: "Mokovskoe Izdatelstvo," 1917.

Le Carillonneur (*Klockspelaren*). Trans. Agnes von Kraemer. Stockholm: Albert Bonniers, 1918.

L'Art en exil (*In Esilio*). [Trans. unknown]. Milan: Facchi, 1919.

Le Mirage (*Bruges la morta*). Trans. Eucardio Momigliano. Milan: Facchi, 1920.

Le Carillonneur (*El Carillonero*). Trans. Andrès Guilmain. Madrid: Estrella, 1920.

Musée de béguines (*Museo de beguinas*). Trans. Andrès Guilmain. Madrid: Estrella, 1920.

La Vocation (*En Destierro*). Trans. Andrès Guilmain. [N.p.]: Diario de la Marina, 1924.

L'Art en exil (Romanian title unknown). Trans. I. Perieteanu. [N.p.], 1926.

"Le Chasseur des villes" ("The City Hunter," originally in *Le Rouet des brumes*). Trans. Jacques Le Clercq. In *Great Stories of All Nations*. New York: Brentano's, 1927.

Le Règne du silence/*Les Vies encloses* (*Visioni di Fiandra: Il regno del silenzio*/*Le Vite rinchiuse*). Trans. Luisa Caico. Rome: C. Voghera, 1931.

Le Carillonneur (*De Bronzen Stem*). Trans. Jean H. P. Jacobs. Maastricht: Leiter-Nypels, 1956.

"L'Ami des miroirs" (originally in *Le Rouet des brumes*). Trans. Shigetaro Mori, in *Chefs d'oeuvre de la littérature fantastique française*, vol. 3. Tokyo: Hakusuî-Sha, 1983.

"L'Eau des anciens canaux" (poem) ("Watter o the auld canals"). Trans. Tom Hubbard, in *European Poetry in Scotland: An Anthology of Translations*. Edinburgh: Edinburgh University Press, 1989.

A selection of fourteen poems taken from *Le Règne du silence*, *Les Vies encloses*, and *Le Miroir du ciel natal*. Trans. Donald Flanell Friedman, in *An Anthology of Belgian Symbolist Poets*. New York: Garland, 1992.

SELECTED CRITICAL STUDIES OF RODENBACH

Berg, Christian. "Bruges, La Morte." *Cahiers du C.E.R.C.L.E.F.* (Université de Paris XII) no. 3 (autumn 1985): 13–40.

———. "Lecture." In *Bruges-la-Morte*. Brussels: Editions Labor, 1986.

———. "Le Lorgnon de Schopenhauer: Les Symbolistes belges et les impostures du réel" [on Rodenbach and Maeterlinck]. *Cahiers de l'Association Internationale des Etudes Françaises* no. 34 (May 1982): 119–35.

Bertrand, Jean-Pierre. "Une Chevelure d'un jaune fluide et textuel: *Bruges-la-Morte* de Georges Rodenbach." *Correspondance* (Spain) no. 3 (October 1993): 23–30.

Bodson-Thomas, Anny. *L'Esthétique de Georges Rodenbach*. Liège: H. Vaillant-Carmanne, 1942.

De Grève, Claude. *Georges Rodenbach*. Brussels: Editions Labor, 1987.

Detemmerman, Jacques. "*Bruges-la-Morte* à la scène et à l'écran." *Revue de l'Institut de Sociologie* (Université Libre de Bruxelles) 3–4 (1985): 275–80. Special issue on "Ombres et lumières: Etudes du cinéma belge." Actes du colloque de février 1984, ed. Adolphe Nysenholc. [Shorter version of 1983 article].

———. "De *Bruges-la-Morte* à *Brugge-die-Stille* ou les avatars scéniques et cinématographiques d'un thème." In *Théâtre de toujours d'Aristote à Kalisky* (Hommages à Paul Delsemme). Brussels: Editions de l'Université Libre de Bruxelles, 1983.

Favre, Yves-Alain. "L'Univers poétique de Rodenbach." *La Licorne* (Poitiers) no. 12 (1986): 63–73. Special issue on "Aspects de la littérature française de Belgique."

Friedman, Donald Flanell. *The Symbolist Dead City: A Landscape of Poesis.* New York: Garland, 1990. [Based on Ph.D. diss., New York University, 1985.]

Gershuny, Walter. "La Spiritualité et la ville: La Flandre mystique de Georges Rodenbach." *Studia Neophilologica* 55 (1983): 187–92.

Gorceix, Paul. "*Bruges-la-Morte:* Un Roman symboliste." *L'Information Littéraire* (November-December 1985): 205–10.

———. "Le Mythe de la clôture et ses images dans le lyrisme de Georges Rodenbach et de Maurice Maeterlinck." In *Studia Belgica: Aufsätze zur Literatur- und Kulturgeschichte Belgiens,* ed. Hans-Joachim Lope. Frankfurt: Peter Lang, 1980.

———. *Réalités flamandes et symbolisme fantastique: "Bruges-la-Morte" et "Le Carillonneur" de Georges Rodenbach.* Paris: Minard, 1992.

———. "Symbolisation, suggestion et ambiguïté: Georges Rodenbach, Max Elskamp, Maurice Maeterlinck." *Les Lettres Romanes* 40, nos. 3–4 (1986): 211–26.

———. *Le Symbolisme en Belgique.* Heidelberg: Carl Winter, 1982.

Joret, P. "Au delà d'un masque: Une Lecture isotopique d'un poème de Georges Rodenbach." *Linguistica Antverpiensia* 18–19 (1984–85): 59–73.

Juin, Hubert. "Lecture de Georges Rodenbach." in *Ecrivains de l'avant-siècle.* Paris: Seghers, 1972.

Laude, Patrick. *Rodenbach: Les Décors de silence.* Brussels: Editions Labor, 1990.

Lowrie, Joyce O. "Mirror, Mirror, on the Wall . . .: Effacement in Georges Rodenbach's 'L'Ami des miroirs.'" *Modern Language Studies* 19, no. 3 (1989): 63–71.

Maes, Pierre. *Georges Rodenbach, 1855-1898.* Paris, 1926; rpt. Gembloux: Duculot, 1952.

Michaux, Ginette. "La Logique du meurtre dans *Bruges-la-Morte* de Georges Rodenbach." *Les Lettres Romanes* 40, nos. 3–4 (1986): 227–33.

Mirval, José. *Le Poète du silence: Georges Rodenbach.* Brussels: Editions "Conférences et Théâtres," 1940.

Paque, Jeannine. "Mémoire de *Bruges-la-Morte.*" In *La Communication cinématographique: Reflets du livre belge,* eds. Jean-Paul de Nola and Josette Gousseau. Paris: Didier-Erudition, 1993.

Pelckmans, P. "La Folie spéculaire: Une Lecture de *L'Ami des miroirs* de Georges Rodenbach." *Cahiers Internationaux de Symbolisme* nos. 42–44 (1981): 163–75.

———. "Les Jeux du temps et de la mort: L'Episode de la mort de Van Hulle dans *Le Carillonneur* de Georges Rodenbach." *Revue des Sciences Humaines* 42, no. 165 (1977): 131–45.

Ruchon, François. *L'Amitié de Stéphane Mallarmé et de Georges Rodenbach* [correspondence]. Geneva: Pierre Cailler, 1949.

Ullrich, Francesca Bianca Crucitti. *Studi su "Bruges-la-Morte" di Georges Rodenbach.* Verona: Università di Verona, 1992.

Vanwelkenhuyzen, Gustave. *Emile Verhaeren et Georges Rodenbach.* Brussels: Palais des Académies, 1956.

Ziegler, Robert. "*Bruges-la-Morte,* une création collective." *Nord* no. 21 (1993): 47–57. [Issue devoted largely to dossier on Rodenbach].

———. "Resurrected Time in Rodenbach's *Bruges-la-Morte.*" *Studi Francesi* 97 (1989): 97–102.

Index

Ackermann, Louise, 31
Aestheticism, 11, 20, 25
Altman, Robert, 188
Andreas-Salomé, Lou, 153
L'Art Moderne, 18
Art Nouveau, 11, 35, 151, 153
Aubert, Andreas, 153
Aurier, Albert, 141–42, 153

Bachelard, Gaston, 38, 65, 69, 70, 87, 132, 165; "ophelization," 36, 48, 69, 131, 134
Bahr, Hermann, 149–51, 153–54; *Zur Ueberwindung des Naturalismus,* 150
Bakhtin, Mikhail, 164
Balakian, Anna, 11
Banville, Théodore de, 17, 20
Barre, André, 119
Barrès, Maurice, 83
Barta, Peter I., 13, 187
Bartholomé, Paul Albert, 141
Barthes, Roland, 56, 125, 126; *Camera Lucida,* 182–83
Basov, M., 187
Bataille, Georges, 96
Baudelaire, Charles, 23, 91, 97, 119, 161; *Les Fleurs du mal,* 24
Beardsley, Aubrey, 46
Beguinage, 31, 32, 34, 35, 84, 104–5, 107, 163; Sainte Elisabeth, 105, 107
Beguines, 35, 105
Belgian literature in French, 12, 18–20, 99–100
Bely, Andrei, 13; *Gibel' senatora,* 161; "Our Life is Basel," 169; *Petersburg* (see *Petersburg*)
Beresford, Bruce, 188
Berg, Christian, 23, 37, 114
Bernheim, Hippolyte, 151
Birkett, Jennifer, 11
Bloy, Léon: *La Femme pauvre,* 31

Bodson-Thomas, Anny, 64
Boileau, Pierre: *D'entre les morts,* 188
Bosch, Jerome, 104
Bosquet, Alain, 23
Bosquet de Thoran, 97
Bourget, Paul, 83
Boyd, Don: *Aria,* 187–88
Brahm, Otto, 190
Bruges-la-Morte: bells, 35, 132–33; chiastic rhetoric, 41, 54–56; eroticism, 26–27, 33, 42; fetishism, 33, 45, 52–54, 193; film versions, 12, 175, 179–85, 187–88; hair, 35, 42, 45, 52, 54, 58; images of Bruges, 20–21, 27–29, 34, 131, 176–79; linguistic strategies, 44–46, 49–51; mirrors and water, 36–38, 41–43, 55, 56–57, 60, 131–32, 134, 155, 171; *mise en abyme,* 42, 56–60; narrative structure, 43–46, 164, 168; Ophelia, 35, 36, 42, 48, 110, 131–32, 133, 146, 183; Ophelia/Medusa ambiguity, 41, 43–44, 46–48, 50–51, 53–56, 58, 60; psychoanalytical interpretations, 37–38; publications of, 19, 20–21; silence as theme, 31–32; symbolist techniques, 30, 35–36, 131–34; symbolization of urban space, 162–63, 165–67, 169, 171–72
Burne-Jones, Edward, 46
Butor, Michel, 125

Carillonneur, Le, 23, 26, 29, 190; art and mysticism, 66, 68, 70, 87, 90–91; bells, 70–72, 92–96; critical reception of, 83, 161; eroticism, 67, 71–72, 73–74, 85–86, 93–96; euphemization of death, 64–65, 75–78; images of Bruges, 66–67, 73, 76–77, 84; metaphoric system, 86–87, 91–92, 96–97; musical version of, 193; spatiality, 68–70, 87–90; temporal aesthetics, 63–74

Caro, Elme, 31
Carrière, Eugène, 143
Cauquelin, Anne, 176
Chase, Ronald: *Bruges-la-Morte* (film), 187
Chenal, Pierre, 187
Compère, Gaston, 22
Coppée, François, 17, 20
Cox, Paul: *Lonely Hearts,* 188; *Man of Flowers,* 188; *The Golden Braid,* 189

Dakyns, Janine, 26
Dällenbach, Lucien, 56
D'Annunzio, Gabriele, 36
Dante, 73, 104
Daudet, Alphonse, 20
Daxhelet, Arthur, 27
Dead city, the, 11, 20, 28, 37, 100–104, 107, 110–11; Bruges as, 11, 27, 28, 66, 83, 101, 104, 107, 109–10
Debussy, Claude: "La Cathédrale engloutie," 37
Decadence, 11, 24–25, 30, 63–64, 79, 116, 126, 148, 176. See also Fin de siècle, the nineteenth century
Décaudin, Michel, 29
De Grève, Claude, 162, 171, 175
Deguy, Michel, 124–25
Denis, Maurice: *Lutte de Jacob avec l'ange,* 47; *Saintes femmes au tombeau,* 47
Detemmerman, Jacques, 179
Dhenaut, Alain: *Bruges-la-Morte* (telefilm), 187
Dijkstra, Bram, 12
Dolgopolov, L. K., 170
Dowson, Ernest, 28
Dujardin, Edouard, 23, 24
Dupont, Auguste, 193
Durand, Gilbert: *Les Structures anthropologiques de l'imaginaire,* 64, 65, 68, 71, 72

Eekhoud, Georges, 29
Elkin, R. H., 191
Elskamp, Max, 18
Eyck, Jan van, 28, 73, 105; *L'Agneau mystique,* 84

Falconet, Etienne-Maurice, 163
Fantin-Latour, Henri, 141

Figaro, Le, 19, 20, 175
Fin de siècle, the nineteenth century, 11–12, 30, 36, 41, 63–64, 99–101, 162. See also Decadence
Flaubert, Gustave, 36
Forestier, Louis, 22
Foucault, Michel, 50
Francophonie, 12
Freud, Sigmund, 24, 52, 188, 192
Freudian psychoanalysis, 126
Friedman, Donald Flanell, 12
Friedrich, Caspar David, 107
Friedrich, Götz, 192

Gallé, Emile, 151–53, 155; Vase, 152 (illus.)
Garborg, Arne, 153
Gauguin, Paul, 140
Gautier, Théophile, 24
Genette, Gérard, 37
Germain, Alphonse, 141, 142, 153
Gies, Hajo: *Nocturno* (film), 187
Gilman, Richard, 24
Giraud, Albert, 19
Godard, Jean-Luc, 188
Goncourt, Edmond de, 20; and Jules de, 83
Gorceix, Paul, 12, 26, 184
Gourmont, Rémy de, 23, 114

Hammershoi, Vilhelm, 131, 143, 148; *Open Doors,* 150 (illus.)
Hanslick, Eduard, 191
Hartmann, Eduard von, 86
Hegelianism, 125, 170
Hellens, Franz, 13, 103–4, 111; *En ville morte,* 103
Heller, Reinhold, 148
Hinterhäuser, Hans, 11
Hitchcock, Alfred: *Vertigo,* 188; *Rear Window,* 188; *Psycho,* 188; *Marnie,* 188
Homer: *Iliad, Odyssey,* 55
Hönnighausen, Lothar, 11
Hospital of Saint John (Memling Museum), 58–59
Hugo, Victor, 17
Huret, Jules, 100
Hutcheon, Linda, 46
Huysmans, Joris-Karl, 24, 27, 34, 36, 43, 63–64, 67; *A rebours,* 31; *Làbas,* 31

Impressionism, 153
L'Indépendance Belge, 18
Ivanov, Vyacheslav, 168

James, Henry: "The Altar of the Dead," 188
Jarman, Derek, 188
Jeritza, Maria, 192
Jeune Belgique, La, 12, 18, 19, 113, 175
Jeune France, La, 17
John the Baptist, 47, 51, 53, 55, 59
John the Evangelist, 59
Johnson, Lionel, 31
Joret, P., 43
Journal de Bruxelles, 19
Joyce, James, 24
Jugendstil, 153
Juin, Hubert, 22, 31, 83

Kafka, Franz: *The Trial,* 177
Kahn, Gustave, 139
Kandinsky, Wassily, 154
Keats, John: "La Belle Dame sans Merci," 36
Khanzhonkov, Alexander: *Gryozy,* 187
Khnopff, Fernand, 20, 47, 51, 131, 134–35, 143, 175, 192–93; *L'Art ou les caresses,* 47; *The Blood of the Medusa,* 47; frontispiece for *Bruges-la-Morte,* 105, 106 (illus.), 134; *L'Entrée du béguinage,* 107, 108 (illus.); *I Lock My Door upon Myself,* 137 (illus.); *Secret-Reflection,* 136 (illus.); *Une Ville abandonnée,* 192
Klotz, Volker, 170
Koppen, Erwin, 11
Korngold, Erich Wolfgang, 191–193; *Der Ring des Polykrates,* 191; *Die tote Stadt,* 13, 29, 161, 188, 190–94; *Violanta,* 191
Korngold, Julius, 191
Kosinski, Dorothy M., 13, 192
Koskenniemi, V. A.: "The Living Bruges," 29
Krafft-Ebbing, R. von, 52
Kristeva, Julia, 126
Kupka, Frantisek, 154

Lacan, Jacques, 37
Laforgue, Jules, 11, 36; *Moralités légendaires,* 30; *Entretiens politiques et littéraires,* 114

Lalo, Edouard: *Le Roi d'Ys,* 37
Lambersy, Werner, 83
Langford, Michèle K., 187, 188
Laude, Patrick, 13, 23
Lehmann, Lotte, 192
Leinsdorf, Erich, 191
Lemonnier, Camille, 12, 111; *La Chanson du carillon,* 107–10; *Un Mâle,* 19.
Lerberghe, Charles van, 18
Leroux, Xavier, 193
Le Sidaner, Henri, 28
Lévy-Dhurmer, Lucien: *Portrait of Georges Rodenbach,* 129, 130 (illus.); *Eve,* 52
Lobelle-Caluwe, Hilde, 59
Longfellow, Henry, 28
Lorrain, Jean, 63; *Songeuse,* 53
Lowrie, Joyce O., 12

Maes, Pierre, 18, 190, 191
Maeterlinck, Maurice, 12, 13, 18, 34, 35, 36, 47, 91, 113–23, 126; "Ame," 114, 118, 121; "Ame de serre," 120; "Aquarium," 116; "Cloche à plongeur," 116, 120, 121; *Pelléas et Mélisande,* 20, 113; "Serre chaude," 115; *Serres chaudes,* 97, 113, 116, 117, 119, 122, 126
Magic realism, 180
Mahler, Gustav, 193
Mallarmé, Stéphane, 11, 20, 23, 38, 49, 52, 83, 86, 100, 124, 126, 153, 161; "Hérodiade," 52
Marx, Jacques, 24
Mauclair, Camille, 23; *L'Ennemie des rêves,* 29
Maupassant, Guy de, 24; "La Chevelure," 35, 189
Mellery, Xavier, 31; "L'Ame des choses," 148
Memling, Hans, 28, 58–59, 72, 73, 84, 105, 109; *Reliquary Shrine of Saint Ursula,* 58–59, 107, 134
Mermall, Thomas, 55
Metzidakis, Stamos, 46
Meyerbeer, Giacomo: *Robert le Diable,* 57, 193
Michaud, Guy, 132
Millais, John Everett, 48
Miller, Henry, 28
Minne, George, 29

Mirval, José, 187
Mockel, Albert, 19
Modernism, 154, 164, 168
Mondrian, Piet, 154
Moréas, Jean, 126
Moreau, Gustave, 41, 131, 135, 139–41; *Dalilah*, 47; *Orpheus Lamenting at the Tomb of Eurydice*, 135, 138 (illus.); *Salomé*, 47; *The Sphinx*, 47
Morice, Charles, 126, 143
Mosley, Philip, 52
Müller, Hans, 191
Mulvey, Laura, 188
Munch, Edvard, 131, 142, 146, 148, 153; *The Cry*, 146, 148; *The Starry Night*, 148, 149 (illus.)
Musset, Alfred de, 23

Nalbatian, Suzanne, 116
Nänny, Max, 55
Narcejac, Thomas: *D'entre les morts*, 188
Naturalism, 23, 24, 25, 30, 148, 153
Nerval, Gérard de, 91, 97
Neue Freie Presse, 191
Nietzsche, Friedrich, 161; *The Birth of Tragedy*, 170
Novalis (Friedrich von Hardenberg), 96, 97; *Die Lehrlinge zu Sais*, 91; *Heinrich von Ofterdingen*, 91

Orpheus, 47, 51, 53, 105, 135, 139
Osbert, Alphonse, 141, 142, 153; *Evening Antique*, 142 (illus.)
Ovid, 54; *Metamorphoses*, 51

Paglia, Camille, 12
Paix, La, 17
Palacio, Jean de, 24
Paque, Jeannine, 26, 177, 179
Parnasse de la Jeune Belgique, Le, 113
Parnassianism, 18
Paz, Octavio, 125
Péladan, Joséphin ("Sâr"): *Le Vice suprême*, 31
Pelckmans, Paul, 75, 79
Petersburg (Bely): narrative structure, 164, 168; symbolization of urban space, 162–63, 165–67, 169–72
Petit, Ch. G., 135
Picard, Edmond, 18, 19

Pierrot, Jean, 11, 36, 63
Pirmez, Octave, 19
Pléiade, La, 113
Plume, La, 17
Poe, Edgar Allan, 36; "The City in the Sea," 37; "Ligeia," 38; "The Man of the Crowd," 38; "William Wilson," 38
Poetics of closure and interiority: in Maeterlinck, 113–15, 118–22, 126; in Rodenbach, 113–15, 119, 123–24, 126
Point, Armand: *Princess and the Unicorn*, 47; *The Siren*, 47
Porter, Laurence, 11
Positivism, 26, 148
Pre-Raphaelites, 35, 46, 52, 135
Proust, Marcel, 31; *Du côté de chez Swann*, 183
Przybyszewski, Stanislaw, 146, 148
Puccini, Giovanni, 193
Puvis de Chavannes, Pierre, 141, 142
Pym, Anthony, 52–53

Raitt, A. W., 23
Redon, Odilon, 131, 141, 143, 146; *Closed Eyes*, 143, 147 (illus.); *Dans le rêve*, 143; *The Dream*, 143, 145 (illus.); "Vision," 143, 144 (illus.)
Régnier, Henri de, 23, 31
Reinhardt, Andreas, 192
Reinhardt, Max, 191
Revue Bleue, 21
Revue de Paris, 190
Revue Wagnérienne, 141
Richepin, Jean, 193
Ridge, George Ross, 30
Riffaterre, Michael, 116–17, 121, 122
Rilke, Rainer Maria, 28
Rimbaud, Arthur, 97
Rodenbach, Albrecht, 17
Rodenbach, Anna, 19, 187, 190, 193
Rodenbach, Constantin (son), 36, 191
Rodenbach, Georges: early career, 17–19; last years, 21; reception of, 22–23; settlement in Paris, 19–20. Works: "Agonies de villes," 120; "L'Ami des miroirs," 38; "L'Amour en exil," 20; "Aquarium mental," 119, 120, 123; *L'Art en exil*, 18, 20, 26, 27, 102, 105, 161, 190; *Bruges-la-Morte* (see *Bruges-la-Morte*); *Le Carillonneur* (see *Le Carillonneur*); "Chant d'automne," 193; "Le Cof-

fret," 18, 35; *Du silence,* 20; *Evocations,* 25, 28, 29, 32, 34, 35; "Fidelity," 17; *Le Foyer et les champs,* 17; *L'Hiver mondain,* 18; *La Jeunesse blanche,* 18, 20; *La Mer élégante,* 18; *Le Mirage,* 161, 190, 192, 193; "Parisian Letters," 17, 19; *La Petite Veuve,* 18, 190; "La Poésie nouvelle," 21; *Le Règne du silence,* 20, 36, 38, 115, 148; *Le Rouet des brumes,* 21; *Les Tristesses,* 17, 18; "La Vie des chambres," 115; "La Vie des choses," 148; *La Vie morte,* 18, 20; *Les Vies encloses,* 113, 123–25; *La Vocation,* 27, 28; *Le Voile,* 190
Rodin, Auguste, 97; *Gates of Hell,* 156
Roeg, Nicolas, 188
Rollinat, Maurice, 23
Romanticism, 176
Rops, Félicien: *Pornocrates,* 47; *The Sacrifice,* 47
Rossetti, Dante Gabriel, 28, 46; *La Ghirlandata,* 52; *Lilith,* 52; *Venus Verticordia,* 52
Russell, Ken, 188
Russkaya mysl', 161
Ruysbroeck, Jan van, 122; *L'Ornement des noces spirituelles,* 122, 126

Samain, Albert, 47
Sansot, Pierre: *Poétique de la ville,* 171
Schopenhauer, Arthur, 86; philosophy of, 31, 84, 100
Schott, Paul (pseud. of Erich Wolfgang and Julius Korngold), 161, 191, 192
Schuffenecker, Emile, 140
Schuré, Edouard, 153; *Précurseurs et révoltés,* 140
Schwob, Marcel: "Les Milésiennes," 63–64
Séon, Alexandre, 141–42
Shelley, Percy Bysshe, 41
Showalter, Elaine, 12
Strauss, Richard, 193
Stuck, Franz von: "Sin," 47
Surrealism, 53, 126
Symbolism, 11, 22, 23–24, 25, 29, 41, 46–47, 52, 53, 99, 114, 154, 156, 168, 176; aesthetics of, 22, 30, 42, 101, 103, 111, 129, 149, 151; Belgian, 99–101
Symbolist novel, 24, 161, 172

Symbolist psychological landscape, 129, 148–51, 153–55; in Gallé, 151; and Italian futurism, 154; in Khnopff, 134–35; in Moreau, 135, 139–41; in Munch, 146, 148; in Osbert, 141–42; in Redon, 143, 146; in Séon, 141–42
Synesthesia, 30, 131, 132–134, 135, 139, 146, 151, 153

Taine, Hippolyte, 26, 86
Thornton, R. K. R., 11
Todorov, Tzvetan, 49
Trebitsch, Siegfried, 190–91; *Der Schleier,* 190; *Das Trugbild* (*Die stille Stadt*), 190–91, 192
Truffaut, François: *La Chambre verte,* 181–83, 188; *L'Histoire d'Adèle H,* 182
Turkin, V., 187
Turner, Joseph Mallord William, 28

Urbain, Anna-Maria, 19. See also Anna Rodenbach

Van Buuren, Maarten, 24
Van de Velde, Henry, 131, 151
Vengerova, Zinaida, 161; *Literaturnyya kharakteristiki,* 172
Ver Sacrum, 149
Verhaeren, Emile, 12, 17, 18, 19, 20, 29, 31, 34, 36, 47, 100, 161, 168
Verhavert, Roland: *Brugge-die-Stille,* 175, 179–85, 187
Verlaine, Paul, 11, 143
Verne, Jules, 36
Veselovskaya, Marii, 161
Vesy, 161
Villiers de l'Isle-Adam, 20, 23, 24, 91; *Contes cruels,* 21; *L'Eve future,* 33; "Véra," 21

Wagner, Richard, 141
Wagnerian art, 22, 140, 143, 151, 153
Waller, Max, 18, 19, 175
La Wallonie, 19
Wedekind, Frank, 161
Weisgerber, Jean, 25
Wilde, Oscar, 161
Whistler, James Abbott McNeill, 141, 142
Wordsworth, William, 28

Wouters, Liliane, 23
Wyzewa, Téodor de, 141, 143, 153

"Young Belgium" literary movement. See *La Jeune Belgique*

Zeraffa, Michel, 176
Ziegler, Robert, 12, 177
Zola, Emile, 30
Zolotoe runo, 161
Zweig, Stefan, 28

OHIO UNIVERSITY LIBRARY
Please return this book as soon as you have finished with it. In order to avoid a fine it must be returned by the latest date stamped below. All books are subject to recall after two weeks or immediately if needed for reserve.

JUN 1 3 2000

MAY 2 8 200

JUN 1 1 1996